Engaged Learning with Emerging Technologies

Edited by

DAVID HUNG

Nanyang Technological University,
Singapore

and

MYINT SWE KHINE

Nanyang Technological University,
Singapore

 Springer

A C.I.P. Catalogue record for this book is available from the Library of Congress.

ISBN-10 1-4020-3668-X (HB)
ISBN-13 978-1-4020-3668-2 (HB)
ISBN-10 1-4020-3669-8 (e-book)
ISBN-13 978-1-4020-3669-9 (e-book)

Published by Springer,
P.O. Box 17, 3300 AA Dordrecht, The Netherlands.

www.springer.com

Printed on acid-free paper

CONTENTS

Foreword   vii
by Gerry Stahl

Preface   xiii

Chapter 1
Modeling for meaningful learning   1
    David H. Jonassen and Johannes Strobel

Chapter 2
Engaged learning: Making learning an authentic experience   29
    David Hung, Tan Seng Chee and Koh Thiam Seng

Chapter 3
The contributing student: Learners as co-developers of
learning resources for reuse in web environments   49
    Betty Collis and Jef Moonen

Chapter 4
Situated learning in the process of work   69
    Reinhard Oppermann and Marcus Specht

Chapter 5
Education in the knowledge age – Engaging learners
through knowledge building   91
    Seng Chee Tan, David Hung and Marlene Scardamalia

Chapter 6
Engaging learners through intuitive interfaces   107
    John G. Hedberg and Susan Metros

Chapter 7
Learning science through online threaded discourse   127
    Allan H.K. Yuen

Chapter 8
Engage, empower, enable:
Developing a shared vision for technology in education   149
  Geoff Romeo

Chapter 9
Engagement with ideas and understanding:
An essential for effective learning in the electronic age   177
  Alan Pritchard

Chapter 10
Creating ICT-enriched learner-centred environments:
Myths, gaps and challenges   203
  Kar Tin Lee

Chapter 11
Cybergogy for engaged learning:
A framework for creating learner engagement through
information and communication technology   225
  Minjuan Wang and Myunghee Kang

Chapter 12
Engaging learners through continuous online assessment   255
  Cathy Gunn

About the Contributors   275

Index   283

FOREWORD

Gerry Stahl

Drexel University, Philadelphia, USA

The theme of engaged learning with emerging technology is a timely and important one. This book proclaims the global relevance of the topic and sharpens its focus. I would like to open the book by sketching some of the historical context and dimensions of application, before the chapter authors provide the substance.

Engagement with the world - To be human is to be engaged with other people in the world. Yet, there has been a dominant strain of thought, at least in the West, that directs attention primarily to the isolated individual as naked mind. From classical Greece to modern times, engagement in the daily activities of human existence has been denigrated. Plato (340 BC/1941) banished worldly engagement to a realm of shadows, removed from the bright light of ideas, and Descartes (1633/1999) even divorced our minds from our own bodies. It can be suggested that this is a particularly Western tendency, supportive of the emphasis on the individual agent in Christianity and capitalism. But the view of people as originally unengaged has spread around the globe to the point where it is now necessary everywhere to take steps to reinstate engagement through explicit efforts.

Perhaps the most systematic effort to rethink the nature of human being in terms of engagement in the world was Heidegger's (1927/1996). He argued that human existence takes place through our concern with other people and things that are meaningful to us. This analysis reversed many philosophic assumptions, including the priority of explicit knowledge. Our understanding of stated facts requires interpretation based on our previous and primary tacit understanding of our world and our concerns. Our active engagement in the world is a prerequisite for any learning.

Vygotsky's (1930/1978) socio-cultural psychology can be seen as an expansion of Heidegger's critique of Western assumptions. Not only is explicit theoretical knowledge reliant upon tacit practical knowledge, but individual learning is reliant upon collaborative learning. Vygotsky showed how most learning begins with interpersonal interactions and is only viii

secondarily internalized as individual knowledge. So it is our engagement with other people—whether in our family, tribe, classroom or workplace—that provides the primary context, motivation and source of new knowledge.

In the past several years, a number of theories have elaborated the perspectives of Heidegger and Vygotsky in ways that are particularly relevant to issues of engaged learning. Situated learning (Lave & Wenger, 1991) has stressed that learning is a matter of participating in communities of practice. Distributed cognition (Hutchins, 1996) has shown how engagement with artifacts can be central to learning. Activity theory (Engeström, Miettinen, & Punamäki, 1999) emphasizes engagement in a whole activity structure including tasks, people, artifacts and social structures. Group cognition (Stahl, in press) argues that knowledge is primarily built in the interactions of small groups.

Dewey (1949/1991) is a major source of the current discussion of engaged learning. Adapting the philosophic critique of individualism in Hegel (1807/1967) and Marx (1867/1976) to his pragmatist viewpoint, Dewey drew out the consequences for education. He opposed behaviorist and didactic training that emphasized drill and practice in favor of engaging students in inquiry into open-ended problem contexts. Fifty years after Dewey, we are still trying to introduce engaged learning into the classroom.

Engagement with learning - There are many dimensions to engagement with learning. As a number of the chapters will stress and illustrate, the nature of the problems that students are given is critical. If we want students to engage with a problem, it must be one that they "care about" in Heidegger's terms; it must involve issues that make sense to them within their interpretive perspectives on the world. In terms of Vygotsky's zone of proximal development, it should be a problem that challenges their current understanding but is within reach of their understanding, given some support by the people who are working on the problem with them. This may mean that they work collaboratively on a problem that they could not master on their own, or that adequate computer support is provided to guide them the way a mentor might.

Of course, not every problem can be in an interest area of every student. One student might have a passion for science, another for reading, drawing, sports or music. By having students work together on stimulating problems that have been designed and supported to optimize chances of successful knowledge building, educational activities can lead to increased interest and engagement with a new learning domain. Engagement with problems, people and domains can have a synergistic effect.

People are engaged in many communities simultaneously: family, neighborhood, religious, school, friendship, online, etc. These are primary contexts and motivators of engagement. People tend to learn the culture of their communities quickly and effortlessly. Communities of various sizes and formats can be formed for purposes of engaged learning. In some cases students can be introduced to professional communities (e.g., NASA), in other cases mini-communities can be constructed that are based on the professional community but are more accessible to the students (e.g., model rocket clubs). Communities can be built online so that people with a particular interest can interact with others around the world. Groups can also be formed to create new engagements, such as classrooms in different countries corresponding with each other as a way of learning foreign languages. Engagement generally grows through involvement in such communities. Often, small groups form within larger communities so that participants can get to know each other better and establish a shared history. It is in the intense interactions within such small groups that knowledge is likely to be constructed and shared.

One should not think of engagement as an individual attribute. Communities are engaged with specific issues; that may well be why they originally formed and continue to persist. Small groups also engage in activities. The community or group engagement may not so much be motivated by the desires of their individual members as vice versa. Individual engagement is often a consequence of being involved in an engaged group. One is motivated by the group effort. If a researcher looks closely at the behavior of a group, what appears is not a clear causation in either direction between individual and group; they tend to constitute each other's engagement through subtle interactional moves.

Similarly, engagement is neither a purely intellectual, affective nor social phenomenon. Engagement may involve cognitive tasks and the manipulation of conceptual materials. But it is also a feeling that people have that they are participating in something that is important and interesting. Further, it is a social undertaking, done with, for or because of other people and groups. The impetus to do something, the options available and the methods for accomplishing it are likely to be defined by the culture of some community. What is learned, the motivation to learn it and its socially accepted value are intimately intertwined in ways specific to each case.

So engaged learning can involve engagement with problems, with a domain of knowledge, with communities and with small groups. It can be observed at the individual, small group and community unit of analysis. It appears as a blending of intellectual, affective and social relations.

Engagement with technology - These days, engagement with learning is likely to mean engagement with technology. This is because networked computers seem to offer open-ended possibilities for promoting and supporting engaged learning. They can connect geographically isolated and dispersed individuals into collaborative groups. They can provide scaffolding for learning without requiring the presence of a skilled mentor.

They can offer access to worldwide resources. They can incorporate computationally powerful tools.

Unfortunately, this tantalizing potential is not yet at hand. Commercially available media do not support engagement. They are largely designed based on the individual transmission model: they allow individuals to access facts and to transmit opinions. To go beyond this, we need to design technologies that can serve as mediators of person-to-person interaction that goes beyond superficial socializing and exchange of opinions to engagement in deep knowledge building (Scardamalia & Bereiter, 1996). But to do this, we need to understand computer-mediated collaborative learning interaction much better than we do now. It is a complicated process, sensitive to many factors and not predictable from any. It is easy to know what will prevent successful engaged learning, but hard to know how to foster it, particularly given today's technology. While computers are indeed computationally powerful, the technology for programming learning environments is frustratingly rigid. Educational innovators face a wicked problem in trying to realize the potential of emergent technologies.

The far-reaching goal set forth in this book, to design and promote technologies for engaged learning, requires a worldwide effort. Fortunately, the book simultaneously represents a global engagement with this task. The following chapters pursue the educational and technical potential from diverse international perspectives.

REFERENCES

Descartes, R. (1633/1999). *Discourse on Methods and Meditations on First Philosophy.* New York, NY: Hackett.

Dewey, J., & Bentley, A. (1949/1991). Knowing and the known. In J. A. Boydston (Ed.), *John Dewey: The Later Works, 1925-1953* (Vol. 16). Carbondale, IL: SIU Press.

Engeström, Y., Miettinen, R., & Punamäki, R.-L. (Eds.). (1999). *Perspectives on Activity Theory.* New York, NY: Cambridge University Press.

Hegel, G. W. F. (1807/1967). *Phenomenology of Spirit* (J. B. Baillie, Trans.). New York, NY: Harper & Row.

Heidegger, M. (1927/1996). *Being and Time: A Translation of Sein und Zeit* (J. Stambaugh, Trans.). Albany, NY: SUNY Press.

Hutchins, E. (1996). *Cognition in the Wild.* Cambridge, MA: MIT Press.

Lave, J., & Wenger, E. (1991). *Situated Learning: Legitimate Peripheral Participation.* Cambridge, UK: Cambridge University Press.

Marx, K. (1867/1976). *Capital* (B. Fowkes, Trans. Vol. I). New York, NY: Vintage.

Plato. (340 BC/1941). *The Republic* (F. Cornford, Trans.). London, UK: Oxford University Press.

Scardamalia, M., & Bereiter, C. (1996). Computer support for knowledge-building communities. In T. Koschmann (Ed.), *CSCL: Theory and Practice of an Emerging Paradigm* (pp. 249-268). Hillsdale, NJ: Lawrence Erlbaum Associates.

Stahl, G. (in press). *Group Cognition: Computer Support for Collaborative Knowledge Building.* Cambridge, MA: MIT Press.

Vygotsky, L. (1930/1978). *Mind in Society.* Cambridge, MA: Harvard University Press.

PREFACE

We live in exciting times where technology for education and learning has advanced not only in the technical arena, but in terms of the adoption of all kinds of technologies in everyday life and culture. Students, children, and adults alike seem to be more 'engaged' with devices such as handphones which are pervasive within more matured societies. However, in the adoption of such technologies, is 'learning' being advanced? The key question for us in this book is how learning, both in formal and informal setting, can be engaging or meaningful through the integral accomplishment of learning and educational technologies.

This book which is a series of chapters written by a renowned international collaborators attempts to address some of these issues. The timing of this book is also in tandem to a world-wide call for learner-centred or student-centred constructivist forms of learning, otherwise recognized as 'engaged learning' or 'meaningful learning'. Obviously, the assumption here is that engaged or meaningful learning occur through learner-centred constructivist approaches. We recognize that perhaps engaged learning can occur within the context of a very engaging sage-centred presenter where a captive audience is stimulated with many self-prompted questions arising from the speech. However, in this book, we limit our discussion to learner-centred approaches.

In the first chapter, David Jonassen and Johannes Strobel describe the modeling for meaningful learning. They argue that the goal of formal education should be meaningful learning and it is necessarily social, collaborative, intentional, authentic, and active. They also describe different components of individual models and collaborative mental models. The later part of the chapter focuses on how technologies can be used to support student construction of their own models and theories of how phenomena work.

Hung, Tan and Koh attempt to make sense of engaged learning in Chapter 2. They propose that approaches such as problem-based learning should be advocated because it is an authentic form of learning encouraging students to be self-regulated and thus metacognitive towards their own thinking and behaviors. They describe the engaged learning framework focusing on both problem and process which would be necessary for authenticity in learning experience. In Chapter 3, Collis and Moonen present engaged learning and the contributing student. They state that learners can and do become engaged in learning through their own motivations, without the need for a teacher or instructional designer. They have differentiated between learning in school context and learning in workplace. The chapter consists of examples from both higher education and professional learning and illustrates how contributing model relates to engaged learning.

In Chapter 4, Oppermann and Specht examine the new approaches in situated e-learning which aim to overcome shortcomings of learning to use IT applications within working environments. They noted that the idea of situated e-learning is a continuous process of acquiring, applying, refining and exchanging of competence often taking place in communities.

Education in the knowledge age: engaging learners through knowledge building, chapter by Tan, Hung and Scardamalia focus on the classroom pedagogies which use a computer-supported collaborative learning technology to support the collaborative learning knowledge building community. The chapter includes examples of knowledge building classrooms in Canada and Singapore to illustrate how teachers can engage students as knowledge producers.

Hedberg and Metros, in their chapter, acquaints the reader with key concepts associated with leaner engagement by examining the user interface from cognitive, semiotic, psychological, artistic and pedagogical perspectives. The authors, by using a three-phase model as a foundation of creating engaging user interfaces, explore the cognitive and visual elements of effective interface design that engage learners through intuitive and direct interaction.

Allan Yuen, in Chapter 7, presents learning science through online threaded discourse anchored on the approach of knowledge building by Scardamalia and Bereiter. He reports that online discourse can broaden the basis for learning and teaching science and help in advancing knowledge in different ways. In Chapter 8, Geoff Romeo indicates that after more than two decades of computers in education in Australian schools there is still confusion at all levels about why the technology matters and widespread reluctance to move beyond the tokenistic use of computers in classrooms. To address the technology integration issues, the scenario planning technique is introduced. He argued that the scenario planning stages of establishing a focal point, identifying organizational mental models, and conducting an environmental scan can greatly assist schools in developing a shared vision, and can greatly assist in the development of realistic teaching methods.

Alan Pritchard considers that engagement with ideas and understanding is an essential for effective learning in the electronic age. In his chapter a model of the learning process which puts engagement at the centre of the enterprise is presented and discussed in details. In Chapter 10, Lee emphasizes that creating ICT-enriched learner-centred environments requires a holistic approach that calls for changes at three levels – teacher, schooling environment and learning activities. She discusses the challenges in ICT use which include teachers encouraging students to become active participants; changing classroom dynamics; leadership in existence; and teacher having an individual sense of how they are able to successfully influence student learning. Some practical solutions are offered in her chapter.

Cybergogy for engaged learning: a framework for creating learner engagement through information and communication technology by Wang and Kang focus on issues related to online learning and engagement. They argue that there is a need to establish a framework for generating meaningful and engaging learning experiences for distance students with diverse cultural and linguistic backgrounds. The term "Cybergogy" as a descriptive label for the strategies for creating engaged learning online was introduced which has three overlapping/intersecting domains, namely, cognitive, emotive, and social in their chapter.

In the final chapter, Cathy Gunn describes the topic on engaging learners through continuous assessment. She begins with a brief overview of developments in online assessment practice over a ten year period, identifies further questions for educational research, and proposed a framework for integrating the use of online assessment into courses for maximum educational benefits. The chapter offers an evidence-based framework for successful implementation of online assessment which involves leaner engagement.

There has been astonishing technological development in recent decades. The issue at hand for educators is how to exploit the affordances of these technologies, using it as a mean to learn and make the learners engaged in meaningful way. We hope that this collection of works will give you international perspectives and some useful information on engaged learning with emerging technologies.

We would like to express our thanks to all the contributors for responding to our invitation to write about their work and sharing their experiences. We wish to thank the academic staff members of the Learning Sciences Technologies Academic Group and Learning Sciences Laboratory of the National Institute of Education, Nanyang Technological University including the Ministry of Education (Singapore) for the support of this book. Without the support of the contributors, members of the University and the Ministry, this book would not have been possible. This book is our joint achievement.

We acknowledge that many of the ideas discuss in this book arise from international collaborations and linkages of our colleagues without which we would not be able develop upon these concepts. The journey towards engaging learners meaningfully in deep conceptual issues, metacognitive and reflective stances, knowledge building, and how designers of learning environments should situate and organize technological tools, activities, and other forms of social, emotional, and cognitive impetus remain a challenge and continuing dialogue. We wish for all readers to enter into this dialogue with us. We hope that this collection of chapters is a meaningful experience for you.

David Hung
Myint Swe Khine

Learning Sciences and Technologies Academic Group
National Institute of Education
Nanyang Technological University
Singapore

January 2005

Chapter 1

MODELING FOR MEANINGFUL LEARNING

David H. Jonassen[1] and Johannes Strobel[2]
[1]University of Missouri, USA; [2]Concordia University, Canada

Abstract: In the first part of the chapter, we argue that the goal of formal education should be meaningful learning. Meaningful learning is necessarily social, collaborative, intentional, authentic, and active. The result of meaningful learning lies in its cognitive residue, the learner's mental model.

In the second part of this chapter, we describe different components of individual mental models and collaborative mental models. Mental models are rich, complex, interconnected, interdependent, multi-modal representations of what someone or some group knows.

Perhaps the most effective means for fostering the development of mental models is the construction of computational models. We argue that modeling is an essential skill for all disciplines engaging students in meaningful learning. So, the third part of the chapter focuses on how technologies can be used to support students' construction of their own models and theories of how phenomena work. Students can build models of domain knowledge, problems, systems, semantic structures, and thinking while studying. In addition to distinguishing between what is modeled, we also distinguish between kinds of modeling systems (deductive simulations, inductive simulations, qualitative causal models like expert systems, and semantic modeling tools), and their affordances for supporting the construction of mental models.

Keywords: modeling, model-based reasoning, constructivism, problem solving, mental models, conceptual change, cognitive tools, Mindtools, expert systems, systems modeling

1.   WHAT IS MEANINGFUL LEARNING?

Jonassen, Howland, Moore, and Marra (2004) argue that meaningful learning occurs when learners are active, constructive, intentional, cooperative, and working on authentic tasks. Human learning is a naturally <u>active</u> mental and social process. When engaged in learning in natural contexts, humans interact with their environment and manipulate the objects in that environment, observing the effects of their interventions and constructing their own interpretations of the phenomena and the results of the manipulation and sharing those interpretations with others. Through formal and informal apprenticeships in communities of play and work,

D. Hung and M.S. Khine (eds.), Engaged Learning with Emerging Technologies, 1-27.

learners develop skills and knowledge that they then share with other members of those communities with whom they learned and practiced those skills. In all of these situations, learners are actively manipulating the objects and tools of the trade and observing the effects of what they have done.

During that activity, learners are continuously <u>constructing</u> their interpretations of their actions and the results of those actions. What happens when I do this? What does that mean to me? Rather than rehearsing what something means to the teacher or the curriculum developers, meaningful learning focuses on what phenomena mean to the learner. That requires active manipulation of ideas and artifacts. Humans naturally construct meaning. In order to survive, humans have always had to construct meaning about their world.

Learning is most meaningful when it is <u>intentional</u>. All human behavior is goal directed (Schank, 1994). That is, everything that we do is intended to fulfill some goal, however important or insignificant. When learners are actively and willfully trying to achieve a cognitive goal, they think and learn more because they are fulfilling an intention. The intention may not be initially expressed by the learner, but it must be accepted and adopted by the learner in order for learning to be meaningful. When learners evaluate their learning in terms of their intentions, they understand more and are better able to use the knowledge that they have constructed in new situations.

Most contemporary theories of learning agree that meaningful learning requires a meaningful task, and the most meaningful tasks are those that emerge from or are at least simulated from some <u>authentic context</u>. When learners wrestle with authentic problems, they are not only better understood, but also are more consistently transferred to new situations because they have more meaning. Rather than abstracting ideas in rules that are memorized and then applied to other canned problems, we need to teach knowledge and skills in real life, useful contexts and provide new and different contexts for learners to practice using those ideas. And we need to engage students in solving complex and ill-structured problems as well as simple problems (Jonassen, 1997). Unless learners are required to engage in complex learning, they will develop oversimplified views of the world.

Finally, meaningful learning is often <u>collaborative</u>. Humans naturally work in learning and knowledge building communities, exploiting each others' skills and appropriating each others' knowledge. In everyday contexts, humans naturally seek out others to help them to solve problems and perform tasks. Schools generally believe that learning is an independent process, so learners seldom have the opportunity to "do anything that counts" in collaborative teams despite their natural inclinations. However, relying solely on independent methods of instruction cheats learners out of more natural and productive modes of thinking and learning. Collaboration usually requires conversation among participants. Learners working in groups must socially negotiate a common understanding of the task and the methods they will use to accomplish it. That is, given a problem or task, people naturally seek out opinions and ideas form others, so conversation should be encouraged.

It is important to point out that these characteristics of meaningful learning are interrelated, interactive, and interdependent. That is, learning and instructional activities should engage and support combinations of active, constructive, intentional, authentic, and cooperative learning because they are synergetic. Learning activities that represent a combination of these characteristics results in even more meaningful learning than the individual characteristics would in isolation.

It is ironic to point out that meaningful learning typically occurs in natural contexts and seldom in formal educational contexts. The inculcation of ideas, values, and socially accepted beliefs too often prevents natural learning experiences in schools. However, there exist formalized learning activities that do engage meaningful learning, just as there are teachers who have for years engaged students in meaningful learning. In this paper, we argue that technologies can and should become the toolkit for meaning making. Technologies afford students the opportunities to engage in meaningful learning when used as tools for constructing, testing, comparing, and evaluating models of phenomena, problems, the structure of ideas, and the thought processes engaged in their creation.

In this chapter, we argue that one of the most meaningful and engaging forms of learning is modeling, that is, using technology-based environments to build representational models of the phenomena that are being studied. Why is modeling so powerful?

2.   WHAT IS THE COGNITIVE RESIDUE FROM MODELING?

What is left after modeling? What evidence exists that someone has learned meaningfully, that is, what is the cognitive residue (Salomon, Perkins & Globerson, 1991)? The result of modeling is both an internal and an external model of the phenomena that have been explored and manipulated. Learners begin constructing their own simple mental models to explain their worlds, and with experience, support, and more reflection, their mental models become increasingly complex as they interact with the world in more complex ways. Ever more complex models will enable them to reason more consistently and productively about the phenomena they are observing. Our belief is that humans are natural model builders who build simplified and intuitive personal theories to explain their world. Through experience and reflection, they reorganize and add conceptual complexity as they learn, manifesting strength, coherence, and commitment to their existing mental models (Vosniadou, 1999).

Unfortunately, the concept of mental model is conceptually rich but operationally problematic. For instance, how do you assess someone's mental model, the cognitive residue of what they have learned? That is a particularly difficult question, because there is so little agreement on what mental models are. There are many conceptions of mental models, beginning with Johnson-Laird (1983) and Gentner and Stevens (1983). All of these various conceptions have resulted in what Rips (1986) refers to as "mental muddles." Are mental models semantic models, simulations, procedural knowledge in the form of inference rules, or what? We believe that mental models are all of these, that is, they are rich, complex, interconnected, inter-dependent, multi-modal representations of what someone or some group knows. We describe these components next.

Individual Mental Models

Individual, internal mental models consist of multiple, interdependent, and integrated representations of some system or set of phenomena. In order to represent an individual's mental model, several forms of evidence are needed, including structural knowledge, procedural knowledge, reflective knowledge, spatial/imaginal knowledge, metaphorical knowledge, executive knowledge, and a host of beliefs about the world (Jonassen & Henning, 1999).

Structural Knowledge. Structural knowledge is the knowledge of the structure of concepts in a knowledge domain and can be measured in a variety of ways (Jonassen et al, 1993). Industrial and organizational psychologists tend to regard structural knowledge measures as the definition of metal models (Kraiger & Salas, 1993). Using structural knowledge methods to portray mental models assumes that they can be represented as networks of nodes and links. While we believe that networks of interconnected constructs underlay mental models, they cannot function adequately as the sole means of representation. They provide only the semantic structure for mental models. We develop a mental model about processes and their underlying assumptions that include an associative structure, but the model is not merely an accumulation of entities.

Performance/Procedural Knowledge. In order to assess someone's mental model, it is essential that she or he use the model to operate on the part of the environment that is being modeled. Utilizing an individual's model to test its predictive and explanatory power is perhaps the most essential component of the model. Jonassen and Henning (1999) assessed think-aloud protocols while individuals solved a troubleshooting problem. In addition to providing performance problems that need to be solved, learners should be required to articulate their plan for solving the problem, and they should be observed on how well they adhere to the plan, what strategies they use for dealing with discrepant data and events, and finally what kinds of generalizable conclusions they can draw from the solution.

An increasingly common method for assessing mental models is the teach-back procedure, in which learners or users are asked to teach another learner (typically a novice) how to perform certain tasks or how to use a system. Students often produce a variety of representations, such as a list of commands, verbal descriptions of task components, flow charts of semantic components, descriptions of keystrokes (van der Veer, 1989).

Image of System. Wittgenstein (1922) described propositions as imaginal models of reality. Most humans generate mental images of verbal representations. Mental models definitely include mental images of the system being explored. So, it is important to elicit the learner's mental image of a prototype of the system s/he is constructing. Requiring learners to represent their visual model or system model can provide rich data about any learner's understanding Taylor & Tversky, 1992).

Metaphors. In addition to imaginal representations, humans naturally tend to relate new systems to existing knowledge, often by associating them with other physical objects. Metaphors are important means for understanding peoples' mental models because the metaphors contain imaginal, structural, and analogical information about their understanding (Jonassen & Henning, 1999).

Executive Knowledge. It is not enough to have a runnable model of a domain or process, but in order to solve ill-structured problems it is essential to know when to run which model. Knowing when to activate mental models allows the learner to allocate and apply necessary cognitive resources to various applications. So it is necessary to assess the strategies that learners generate for solving problems (Jonassen & Henning, 1999).

Beliefs. Beliefs about the world may be the most compelling components of mental models. Beliefs are the reflected and unreflected assumptions underlying parts of the model. Belief represents the space where we connect the model with our own person (Durkheim, 1915). As theories emerge in humans, they rely on their own, fairly materialistic views of the world. These natural ontologies for representing phenomena provide coherent but often incorrect views of the world. The revolutionary conceptual change that is required for learners to give up these theories and adopt a more principled ontology of beliefs is very difficult (Chi, 1999). So, assessing an individual's beliefs about the phenomena they are representing is necessary for uncovering misconceptions or distorted conceptions of the world.

Collaborative Group Mental Models

Group or collaborative mental models are those that are socially co-constructed by groups of individuals who are collaboratively focused on the same meaningful task.   Group or team mental models also consist of multiple representations of some system or phenomenon. In order to represent a group's mental model, several forms of evidence need to be assessed, including activity-based knowledge, social or relational knowledge, conversational or discursive knowledge, and the artifacts that are used and produced by the group.

Activity Based Knowledge. Activity theorists believe that activity and consciousness are one and the same. We cannot think without acting or act without thinking (Engeström, 1987; Jonassen, 2000). The simplest inference from this belief is that in order to understand what learners know, watch what they do. That observation may include visible elements of behavior that can be observed without intervening in the process or invisible elements that must be inferred with invasive procedures such as think-alouds or teach-backs. These methods provide invaluable evidence about the nature of the mental models that learners are constructing. And because that activity is so often performed collaboratively, the combined activity can provide evidence about what the group knows.   Team mental models are constructed in collaboration, requiring an extensive amount of discursive knowledge (described next).

Conversational/Discursive Knowledge. Social negotiation of meaning is a primary means of solving problems, building personal knowledge, establishing an identity, and most other functions performed in teams. The most common initial step in problem solving is to contact a colleague and ask, "What do you think?" The primary medium of discourse is stories. These stories provide contextual information, function as a format for problem solution, and also express an identity. Stories provide a natural flow of conversation among the collaborators.   Stories often contain emotional overtones about the experiences, especially about first experiences as a performer (Jonassen & Henning, 1999).

Social/Relational Knowledge. Individuals in many everyday contexts experience ambiguity about their status within the larger organization (Barley & Bechty, 1994). Members of collaborative groups often build strong social relationships with other members of a well-defined community of practice. Examine most organizations and you find that members of work groups often socialize as well as function professionally. The social and relational knowledge that is fostered by this socialization helps to establish a group identity that helps to resolve ambiguity about their status within the organization.

Artifactual Knowledge. There is knowledge or cognitive residue evidenced in the artifacts that learners produce. That is, when students produce artifacts, especially while modeling systems, there is extensive evidence of their thinking in the products. The models that result from model building are artifacts that are full of knowledge, knowledge that represents some portion of the learner's mental model. Artifacts can also serve as discourse markers. Objects that are left around intentionally can serve as important lessons to others.

Summary

An important goal of all educators is to help learners to develop their theories about how the world works, that is, to construct mental models. Model using and especially model building reflect the construction of mental models. In the following section, we describe how to employ technologies to support mental model construction.

3.   MODELING MENTAL MODELS

Science and mathematics educators (Confrey & Doerr, 1994; Frederiksen & White, 1998; Lehrer & Schauble, 2000; White, 1993) have long recognized the importance of modeling in understanding scientific and mathematical phenomena. In this chapter, we attempt to expand upon that belief system by arguing that modeling is an essential skill in all disciplines, that is, it is an essential cognitive skill for meaning making in all domains. We also argue that in addition to modeling domain knowledge (the primary focus of math and science education work to date), learners can apply modeling skills in different ways: by modeling domain knowledge, by modeling problems (constructing problem spaces), by modeling systems, by modeling semantic structures, and by modeling thinking processes (i.e. cognitive simulations). In addition to distinguishing between what is modeled, we also distinguish between kinds of modeling systems and their affordances for supporting the construction of mental models. Why is modeling so important?

The mental models that most people have constructed of phenomena in the world (scientific, social, cultural, political, and even phenomenological) are naive, uninformed, and often inconsistent with established theories.

While developing personal theories and integrating them into mental models may be a natural cognitive process, that does not imply that people are very good at it.   Personal theories and mental models are replete with misconceptions and inadequate conceptions. However, all mental models are dynamic, changing with each effort to re-represent what is known based on interpretations of interactions with the world. Learners should be supported in their construction of more complete and viable models of the phenomena they are studying. What often makes human models weak and oversimplified is that they fail to identify relevant factors and are not dynamic, that is, they do not represent change in factors over time.

Modeling as a process is also important because it is one of the most conceptually engaging cognitive processes that can be performed. Solving design problems are potentially more engaging, however, technologies to date better afford modeling processes than designing activities which are less constrained and more complex.

The underlying assumption of this chapter is that constructing computational models of the world using computer-based modeling tools can serve to externalize learners' mental models of the phenomena that they are studying.   Several researchers have demonstrated the relationship between modeling and mental models (Frederiksen & White, 1998; Mellar, Bliss, Boohan, Ogborn, & Tompsett, 1994; White, 1993).   The most effective way to support the construction of mental models is to engage learners in using a variety of tools for constructing physical, visual, logical, or computation models of the phenomena. Most of these tools are technology-mediated. Jonassen (2000) has argued that constructing models is among the most effective and engaging ways to use technologies to engage critical think by modeling with technology. In this paper, we are explicity focusing on the effects of modeling on mental model constuction. That is, using or building physical and computational models using technologies provides learners the opportunities to operationalize and externalize their mental models. It is important here to now distinguish between learners using or interpreting models, which are common in classsooms, and building models.

There are two basic ways that models can be used to facilitate mental model construction, manipulating model-based environments and building models that represent the learner's understanding. In this paper, we will describe a number of model-based environments like ThinkerTools, EcoBeaker, Agent Sheets and other microworlds, where students can input data and manipulate the system characteristics, testing the effects of theory manipulations. Most simulations and microworlds are of this type. They are exploratory environments that afford learners the opportunities to test the causal effects of manipulations, but the underlying model that defines the system parameters is not revealed to the learner. Learners can infer parts of the model through manipulating the environment. These are known as black box systems. The model is in a black box and cannot be seen.

The second kind of model-based system that can be used to facilitate mental model construction is the tool that is used by learners to build representations of their mental models. These tools provide a framework for describing content that constrain the ways that learners view and understand the system. Systems modeling tools, expert systems, and semantic modeling tools (described in detail later) are glass box systems, where learners can not only investigate the underlying model, they can change it. In fact, the learners construct the model. While it is conceptually important to distinguish model-using from model-building, no research exists that compares the cognitive effects of model-using vs. model-building. We hope to provide some of that research in the future and believe that the cognitive residue from building models will be significantly greater than from using model-based systems.

4.   WHAT IS BEING MODELED

If modeling can aid the articulation of mental models, then learners should learn to model a variety of phenomena. In this section, we briefly describe the range of phenomena that can be modeled using different tools. An underlying assumption is that modeling different phenomena (domain knowledge, problems, systems, semantic structures, and thought processes) is necessary for constructing advanced, complete mental models.

Most of these models are what Lehrer and Schauble (2000) refer to as syntactic models. These are formal models, each of which imposes a different syntax on the learner that conveys a relational correspondence between the model and the phenomena it is representing. The purpose of syntactic models is to summarize the essential function of the system being represented.

Modeling Domain Knowledge

The primary focus of mathematics and science educational use of modeling has been for the purpose of modeling ideas in math and science domains. Learners can use a variety of tools for representing and experimenting with domain concepts. Sometimes those models are physical, functional models of body parts, such as the elbow, used by children as young as first graders (Penner, Giles, Lehrer, & Schauble, 1997). More commonly, middle school and high school students are using computer-based modeling tools, such as microworlds, systems modeling tools, or other qualitative modeling tools, to construct their models of scientific systems. For example, Figure 1

Although many computer-based modeling tools support the construction of quantitative models of problems, constructing qualitative models of problems is equally, if not more, important. Qualitative representations assume many different forms and organizations. They may be spatial or verbal, and they may be organized in many different ways. Qualitative representations are more physical than numerical. Physical representations of problems consist of entities that are embedded in particular domains (e.g. physics), and the inferencing rules that connect them and give them meaning are qualitative (Larkin, 1983).

Context 'This knowledge base is intended to simulate the processes of calculating molar conversions. '

D1: 'You know the mass of one mole of sample.'
D2: 'You need to determine molar (formula) mass.'
D3: 'Divide sample mass by molar mass.'
D4: 'Multiply number of moles by molar mass.'
D5: 'You know atomic mass units.'
D6: 'You know molar mass.'
D7: 'Divide mass of sample by molar mass and multiply by Avogadro's number.'
D8: 'Divide number of particles by Avogadro's number'
D9: 'Convert number of partcles to moles, then convert moles to mass'
D10: 'Convert mass to moles using molar mass, and then convert moles to molecules using Avogadro's number.'
D11: 'Convert from volume to moles (divide volume by volume/mole), and then convert moles to moles by multiplying by Avogadro's number.'

Q1: 'Do you know the number of molecules?'   A 1 'yes' 2 'no'
Q2: 'Do you know the mass of the sample in grams?'   A 1 'yes' 2 'no'
Q3: 'Do you know the molar mass of the element or compound?' A 1 'yes' 2 'no'
Q4: 'Do you know the number of moles of the sample?'   A 1 'yes' 2 'no'
Q5: 'Do you want to know the number of molecules?'   A 1 'yes' 2 'no'
Q6: 'Do you want to know the mass of the sample in grams?'   A 1 'yes' 2 'no'
Q7: 'Do you want to know the molar mass of the compound?'   A 1 'yes' 2 'no'
Q8: 'Do you want to know the number of moles of the sample? 'A 1 'yes'2 'no'
Q9: 'Do you know atomic mass units?'   A 1 'yes' 2 'no'
Q10: 'Do you know the volume of a gas?'   A 1 'yes' 2 'no'

Rule1:   IF q2a1 AND q8a1 THEN D2
Rule2:   IF (d1 OR q3a1) AND q2a1 AND q8a1 THEN D3
Rule3:   IF q4a1 AND q3a1 AND q6a1 THEN D4
Rule4:   IF q3a1 THEN D1
Rule5:   IF q3a1 THEN D5
Rule6:   IF q9a1 THEN D6
Rule7:   IF qq3a1 AND q2a1 AND q5a1 THEN D7
Rule8:   IF q1a1 AND q8a1 THEN D8
Rule9:   IF q1a1 AND q6a1 THEN D9
Rule10: IF q2a1 AND q5a1 THEN d10
Rule11: IF q10a1 AND q1a1 THEN d11

Figure 3. Excerpt from expert system rule base on stoichiometry

Qualitative representations rather focus on the design of processes (system thinking) and the system as a whole of connections/causal relations, quantitative representations rather focus on the numerical value of singular entities within the system and the formulas underlying in the process. Physical vs. non-physical representations distinguish more models of the natural (hard) sciences from social sciences/humanities.

Qualitative representations function to:

- explicate information that is stated only implicitly in problem descriptions but is important to problem solution
- provide preconditions on which quantitative knowledge can be applied
- qualitative reasoning supports construction of quantitative knowledge not available initially, and yield a set of constraints that provide guidelines for quantitative reasoning (Ploetzner & Spada, 1993).

In fact, Ploetzner, Fehse, Kneser, and Spada (1999) showed that when solving physics problems, qualitative problem representations are necessary prerequisites to learning quantitative representations. When students try to understand a problem in only one way, they do not understand the underlying systems they are working in. Figure 3 illustrates a qualitative model of a simple stoichiometry (molar conversion) problem in chemistry using an expert system. That is, the learners constructed a production rule system that describes the logic needed to solve the problem. Qualitative representations support the solution of quantitative problems. The best problem solutions may result from the integration of qualitative and quantitative models. That integration is best supported in systems modeling tools, such as Stella, that provide quantitative representations of the relations between problem components expressed qualitatively.

Figure 4 illustrates a Stella model of a stoichiometry problem, providing both quantitative and qualitative representations of the problem. In the model in Figure 4, the main parts of the model are contained in the flows (N_2O and H_2O production) and the converters (mass NH_4NO_3, total mass, etc,) which the students define by providing numerical values or formulas to describe relationships between the factors. The underlying assumption of systems models is change in the processes over time.

Modeling Systems

Another way of thinking about subject matter content is as systems. Rather than focusing on discrete facts or characteristics of phenomena, when learners study content as systems, they develop a much more integrated view of the world. There are several, related systemic conceptions of the word,

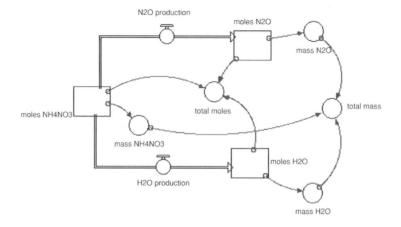

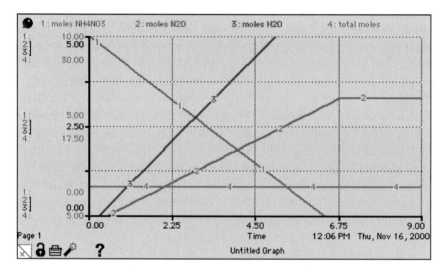

Figure 4. Systems dynamics model of stoichiometry problem in Stella.

including open systems thinking, human or social systems thinking, process systems, feedback systems thinking, systems dynamics, control systems or cybernetics, activity theory, and living systems. All of these conceptions similar attributes, including irreducible wholes, self-producing pattern of organization determined by dynamic interactions among components, interdependent parts, goal-driven, feedback controlled, self-maintaining, self- regulating, synergetic, and teleological. Requiring learnes to organize what they are learning into relevant systems that interact with each other provides learners with a much more holistic as well as integrated view of the world. There are a variety of computer-based tools for supporting systemic thinking. Based on systems dynamics, tools like Stella, PowerSim, and VenSim provide sophisticated tools for modeling systems. These tools enable learners to construct systems models of phenomena using hypothetical-deductive reasoning. Students must construct the models before testing them. Figure 5 illustrates a systemic view of the circulatory system constructed with Model-It, a simplified systems modeling tool developed by

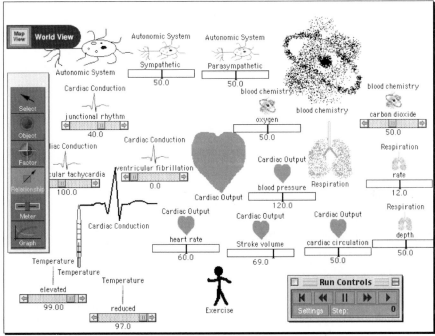

Figure 5. Modeling the circulatory system with Model-It.

the HI-CE group at the University of Michigan for junior high school students. This tool scaffolds the articulation of relationships among variables. Rather than entering formulae to describe relationships, students must identify the direction of the relationship and the potential effect of on variable on another.

Another class of tool enables learner to inductively construct models of systems. Microworlds such as NetLogo, AgentSheets, and Eco-Beaker enable learners to construct rules about the nature of the behavior in systems and to immediately test the effects of those rules. Figure 6 models the growth of miniature organisms in and environment and to perturb that environment and retest the growth patterns. In this case, the model shows the effects of a hurricane on the growth of Bryzoa. These tools represent a complexity theoretical view of the world, rather then a mere systems. That is, they explore the self-organizing nature of phenomena in the world.

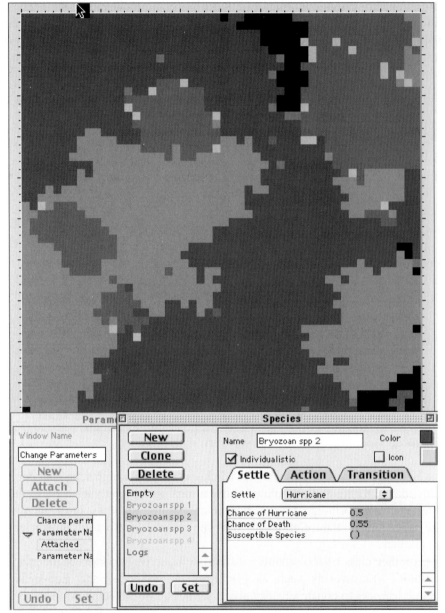

Figure 6. Modeling the effect of a hurricane on Bryzoan using EcoBeaker.

Modeling Semantic Structure

It is generally accepted by psychologists that knowledge in long term memory is organized in a variety of structures, known as cognitive structures or semantic networks. Cognitive structure is "...a hypothetical construct referring to the organization of the relationships of concepts in long-term memory" (Shavelson, 1972, pp. 226-227). These structures describe how concepts are interrelated. These organizations, from a schema theoretical view, provide meaning to concepts. That is, meaning idea is determined by the associations between concepts. While this is but one theoretical interpretation meaning, it is a dominant one that is supported by a number of computer based tools.

The more popular form of semantic organization tool is the concept mapping or semantic networking tool. The semantic networks in memory and the concept mapping tools that represent them are composed of nodes (concepts, constructs, or ideas) that are connected by links (statements of relationships between the constructs). Figure 7 shows a concept map that is part of a much larger map address British romantic poetry. The central concept is the title of a poem, which is linked to important characteristics of that poem. Clicking on any of the other concepts shows all of the associations to that concept. The aggregation of all of these individual maps represents someone's semantic network related to the domain.

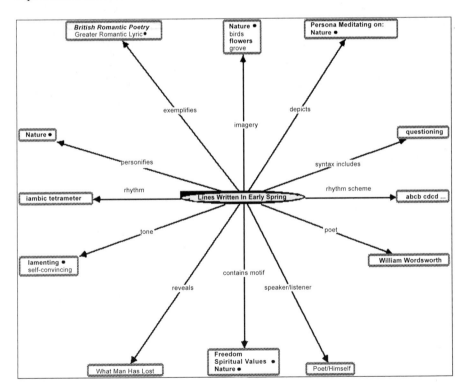

Figure 7. Concept map or semantic network about a poem.

Another tool for helping learners to articulate the semantic structure of ideas within a domain is the common database. Databases are used ubiquitously to organize information about every aspect of our lives. They can also be used by learners to organize information that they are studying. Figure 8 illustrates a database about cells created by biology students. This database, including fields about function, shape, location, tissue system, and other attributes of cells, provides a structure for interrelating these attributes. Students can compare and contrast cell types by searching and sorting the database.

cell type	location	function	shape	related cell	specialization	tissue syst
Astocyte	CNS	Supply Nutrients	Radiating	Neurons, Capillaries	Half of Neural Tissue	Nervous
Basal	Stratum Basale	Produce New Cells	Cube, Columnar	Epithelial Cells	Mitotic	Epithelial
Basophils	Blood Plasma	Bind Imm.E	Lobed Nuclri,Gra	Neutrophil, Eosinoph	Basic Possible Mast	Connective, li
Cardiac Muscle	Heart	Pump Blood	Branched	Endomysium	Intercalated discs	Muscle
Chondroblast	Cartilage	Produce Matrix	Round			Connective
Eosinophil	Blood Plasma	?, Protazoans, Aller	Two Lobes, gran	Basophil, Neutrophil	Acid, Phagocytus (?)	connective, li
Ependymal	Line CNS	Form Cerebralspinal	Cube		Cilia	Nervous
Erythrocytes	Blood Plasma	Transport O2, Remo	Disc	Hemocytoblast, Pro	Transport	Connective
Fibroblast	Connective Tissue	Fiber Production	Flat, Branched		Mitotic	Connective
Goblet	Columnar Epithelia	Secretion	Columnar	Columnar	Mucus	Epithelial
Keratinocytes	Stratum Basal	Strengthen other Cell	Round	Melanocytes		Epithelial
Melanocytes	Stratum Basale	U.V. Protection	Branched	Keratinocytes	Produce Melanin	Epithelial
Microglia	CNS	Protect	Ovoid	Neurons, Astrocytes	Neurophage	Nervous
Motor Neuron	CNS(Cell Body)	Impulse Away from	Long, Thin	Sensory Neuron, Neu	Multipolar, Neuromus	Nervous
Neutrophil	Blood Plasma	Inflammation, Destru	Lobed Nuclei	Basophil, Eosinophil	Phagocytos, Neutral	Connective, li
Oligodendrocyte	CNS	Insulate	Long	Neurons	Produce Myline Shea	Nervous
Osteoblast	Bone	Produce Organic Mat	Spider	Osteoclasts	Bone Salts	Connective
Osteoclast	Bone	Bone Restoration	Ruffled Boarder	Osteoblasts	Destroy Bone	Connective
Pseudostratified	Gland Ducts, Respir	Secretion	Varies	Goblet	Cilia	Epithelial
Satellite	PNS	Control	Cube	Schwann, Neurons	Chemical Env.	Nervous
Schwann	PNS	Insulate	Cube	Neurons, Satellite	Form Myelin Sheath	Nervous
Sensory Neurons	PNS(Cell Body)	Impulse to CNS	Long, Thin	Motor Neuron, Neuro	Unipolar, Action Pot	Nervous

Figure 8. Database on cells.

What makes modeling semantic structure different from modeling domain knowledge? Semantic nets are clearly a form of representation of domain knowledge. But the tools force students to use organizational formalisms unlike those they normally use. These formalisms explicitly signal the interrelationships between these ideas. They form a semantic foundation for understanding a domain.

Modeling Thinking

Another kind of modeling entails developing models of thinking processes. Rather than modeling content or systems, learners model the kind of thinking that they need to perform in order to solve a problem, make a decision, or complete some other task. That is, learners can use computer-based modeling tools to construct cognitive simulations. "Cognitive simulations are runnable computer programs that represent models of human cognitive activities" (Roth, Woods, & People, 1992, p. 1163). They attempt to model mental structures and human cognitive processes. "The computer program contains explicit representations of proposed mental processes and knowledge structures" (Kieras, 1990, pp. 51-2). The primary purpose of cognitive simulations is to attempt to externalize mental processes for analysis and theory building. Most often used by knowledge engineers to construct elaborate tutoring systems, Jonassen has found that even young learners can reflect on their thinking in order to build these simulations. Jonassen and Wang (2003) describes the process of constructing a cognitive simulation of metacognitive reasoning using an expert system shell. Figure 9 shows selected factors from that knowledge base. Students were required to reflect on how they used executive control and comprehension monitoring activities while study for their seminar. Lippert (1988) argued that having students construct small knowledge bases is a valuable method for teaching problem solving and knowledge structuring for students from sixth grade to

---

ASK:"Why am I studying this material?
Assigned = Material was assigned by professor
Related = Material is useful to related research or studies
Personal = Material is of personal interest"

ASK: "How well do I need to know this material?
Gist = I just need to comprehend the main ideas.
Discuss = We will discuss and interrelate the issues.
Evaluate = I have to judge the importance or accuracy of these
ideas.
Generate = I have to think up issues, new ideas, hypotheses about the material."

ASK: "How fast of a reader am I?"
CHOICES:slow, normal, fast

ASK: "How many hours do I have to study?
None = Less than an hour
Few = 1 - 3 hours
Several = 4 - 8 hours"

ASK: "How many days until class?"
CHOICES Days: more_than_7, 2_to_6,less_than_2

ASK:"How do I compare with the other students in the class?
Superior = I think that I am better able than my classmates to comprehend the material.
Equal = I am equivalent to the rest of the class in ability.
Worse = I am no as knowledgeable or intelligent as the rest of
the class."

Figure 9. Metacognitive factors in cognitive simulation

adults. Learning is more meaningful because learners evaluate not only their own thinking processes but also the product of those processes.

We have also been experimenting with systems dynamics tools for constructing cognitive simulations. Figure 10 illustrates a Stella model of memory (thanks to Ran-Young Hong). Stella is a systems dynamics tool for representing the dynamic relationships between systems phenomena. Both expert systems and systems dynamics tools enable the learners to construct and test the assumptions and functioning their models.

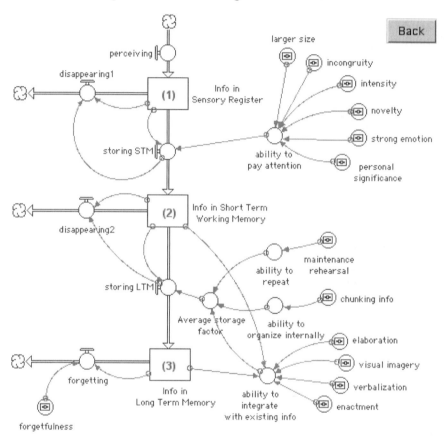

Figure 10. Stella model of memory.

5.   TYPES OF MODEL-BASED LEARNING SYSTEMS

As can be seen from the previous section describing the aspects of systems that can be modeled, there are many kinds of tools available for modeling a wide range of phenomena. These tools vary in their characteristics, functionality and affordances. Each uses a somewhat different structure and syntax for modeling phenomena. Each can be substituted for another, though not always with positive consequences.

Different combinations of critical, creative, and complex thinking are engaged by each kind of tool (Jonassen, 2000).

We briefly describe different kinds of modeling tools.

Building Deductive Simulations

A class of systems modeling tools, including Stella, PowerSim, VenSim, and Model-It enable learners to build and test models of closed systems controlled by feedback. Based on systems dynamics, learners build conceptual representation using a simple set of block icons to construct a map of a process: stocks, flows, converters, and connectors (see Fig. 10). Stocks illustrate the level of some thing in the simulation. In Figure 10, *info in long term memory* and *info in short term memory* are stocks. Flows control the inflow or outflow of material to stocks. *Storing* and *forgetting* are flows. Flows often counterbalance each other, like positive and negative influences in causal loops. For example, *forgetting* is a negative, controlling influence on *info in long term memory*. Converters convert inputs into outputs. They are factors or ratios that influence flows. *Forgetfulness* is a converter. Converters are used to add complexity to the models to better represent the complexity in the real world. Finally, connectors are the lines that show the directional effect of factors on each other by the use of arrows. These models are dynamic, that is, characterized by action or change in states. So a dynamic simulation model is one that conceptually represents the changing nature of system phenomena in a form that resembles the real thing. These simulations are syntactic representations of reality. What distinguishes these models from the next class is that the model is conceived and implemented before testing. The model is hypothetical/deductive.

This kind of model can also be built using spreadsheets. The model in Figure 11, for example, was built by students to test the effects of a series of resistors. The model is explicated n the formulae that are entered into each cell. If this model were built by the teacher for students to manipulate and test effects, it would function more as a microworld, where students explore black box simulations.

Building Inductive Simulation Models

Another class of modeling tool uses a more inductive approach for constructing simulations. Modeling tools like Agent Sheets, NetLogo, and GenScope enable learner to build more open system models of phenomena. Rather than identifying all of the components of the model before building it, students using these environments.

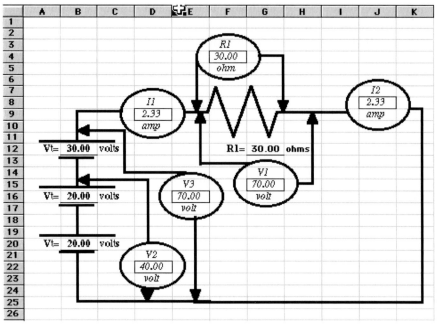

Figure 11. Resistor series model built in a spreadsheet.

Exploring Black Box Models or Simulations

Most simulations that are constructed for student exploration and experimentation do not explicate the underlying model. They enable learners to manipulate variables and test the effects of those manipulations. Students then generate hypotheses about the relationships between variables and further test those. Microworlds, like ThinkerTools (Figure 1; White, 1993), Boxer (deSessa, 1986), Geometric Supposer (Schwartz &Yerulshalmy, 1987) and others require learners to construct at least an implicit model of system in order to generate hypotheses and test them. They require learners to at least construct a mental model, but not necessary lead to a visualization of their mental model.

Expert Systems

Expert systems are artificial intelligence programs designed to simulate experts decision making for all sorts of problems. An expert system is a computer program that attempts to simulate the way human experts solve problems—an artificial decision maker. Constructed with facts and a series of IF-THEN rules, the builder must identify all the possible decisions or outcomes, all of the factors that may be involved in each decision, and then constructs the rules that connect all of the possible system conditions with all of the possible conclusions or results. Building expert systems is a knowledge modeling process that enables experts and knowledge engineers to construct conceptual models (Adams-Webber, 1995). While many of the systems modeling and other tools rely on quantitative representations of relationships among factors, experts systems rely on qualitative descriptions of causal relationships.

Semantic Modeling Tools

Tools for representing the semantic relationships within a domain of concepts, such as semantic networking/concept mapping tools and databases, enable learners to represent the semantic associations between domain concepts. These tools, however, are unable to model dynamic, causal relationships, only associational information about a domain of related concepts. These tools provide matrix and spatial representations of concepts and their interrelationships that are intended to represent the knowledge structures that humans store in their minds (Jonassen, Beisssner, & Yacci, 1993). Why create semantic networks? Meaningful learning requires that students connect new ideas to knowledge that they have already constructed. Concept maps and databases help in organizing learners' knowledge by integrating information into a progressively more complex conceptual framework.

Critical Caveat About Modeling Tools

We argued early in this paper that the cognitive residue of modeling is a model of what is being meaningfully represented internally. Further, we argued that using or constructing models supports the construction of mental models. If that is so, then we must ask if the models that learners construct possess evidence in the model or in its construction processes of structural, procedural, reflective, imaginal, metaphorical, executive knowledge and beliefs about that knowledge. Often they do not because the modeling tools that learners use rely on specific kinds of representations. If mental models are underdeveloped as a result of modeling, it may be necessary to use more than one kind of modeling tool to represent phenomena. That is, mental model construction will likely be enhanced when learners use more than one tool to model a domain, problem, system, semantic structure, or thought process. How many tools and which combinations will best facilitate mental model construction will need to be determined by research. Likewise, the criteria for what makes a good model have not been empirically tested. Jonassen (2000) provides rubrics for assessing different kinds of models. No research, however, has related student quality of student-built models to the quality of mental models, in part because there are no reliable means for assessing mental models.

6.   RATIONALES FOR MODEL CONSTRUCTION

Schwarz and White (2005) argue that modeling is fundamental to human cognition and scientific inquiry. They believe that modeling helps learners to express and externalize their thinking; visualize and test components of their theories; and make materials more interesting. We briefly summarize some of the reasons for constructing models to support meaningful learning and mental model construction.

- Model building is a natural cognitive phenomenon. When encountering unknown phenomena, humans naturally begin to construct theories about those phenomena as an essential part of the understanding process.
- Modeling supports hypothesis testing, conjecturing, inferring, and a host of other important cognitive skills.
- Modeling requires learners to articulate causal reasoning, the basis for most models of conceptual change.
- Modeling provides a high level of conceptual engagement, which is a strong predictor of conceptual change (Dole & Sinatra, 1998).
- Modeling results in the construction of cognitive artifacts (mental models) by constructing physical artifacts.
- When student construct models, they own the knowledge. Student ownership is important to meaning making and knowledge construction. When ideas are owned, students are willing to exert more effort, defend their positions, and reason more effectively.
- Modeling supports the development of epistemic beliefs. At the very root of learning are people's beliefs about what knowledge and truth are and how we come to develop these beliefs. From a biological perspective, we accept that humans are marvelously adapted to learning because of the size of their cortex. But what drives people to learn? Sociologists and psychologist talk about fulfilling needs, which supplies a solid conative reason for learning. But epistemologically, what motivates our efforts to make sense of the world? According to Wittgenstein, what we know is predicated on the possibility of doubt. We know many things, but we can never be certain that we know it. That uncertainty can only be mollified by efforts to know more about the world. Modeling tools enable learners to externalize and test their epistemological beliefs about the meaning of epistemological constructs, such as knowledge and truth and how those beliefs change over time
- Modeling provides shared workspaces provide a strong reason to collaborate.

7.   SUMMARY

In this chapter, we have argued that mental models provide the best evidence for meaningful learning. Further, we argued that the most effective way to use technologies to foster mental model development is through the use and construction of computational models using model-based software. By modeling domain knowledge, modeling problems being solved, modeling systems, modeling semantic structure, and modeling thinking processes, learners can more readily and more effectively build their internal mental models of the phenomena they are studying. Considerable research is required to explicate which tools and which form of model-based learning (model-using or model-building) are more effective for facilitating mental model development.

REFERENCES

Adams-Webber, J. (1995). Constructivist psychology and knowledge elicitation. *Journal of Constructivist Psychology, 8* (3), 237-249.

Confrey, J., & Doerr, H. M. (1994). Student modelers. *Interactive Learning Environments, 4* (3), 199-217.

DiSessa, A., & Abeson, H. (1986). Boxer: A reconstructible computational medium. *Communications of the ACM, 29*, 859-868.

Dole, J.A., Sinatra, G.M. (1998). Reconceptualizing change in the cognitive construction of knowledge. *Educational Psychologist, 33*, 109-128.

Durkheim, Émile. (1915) The Elementary Forms of the Religious Life. Translated by Joseph Ward Swain. New York and London: The Free press.

Engeström, Y. (1987*). Learning by expanding: An activity theoretical approach to developmental research*. Helsinki, Finland: Orienta-Konsultit Oy.

Frederiksen, J. R., White, B. Y. (1998). Teaching and learning generic modeling and reasoning skills. *Journal of Interactive Learning Environments, 55*, 33-51.

Gentner, D., & Stevens, A.L. (1983). *Mental models*. Hillsdale, NJ: Lawrence Erlbaum Associates.

Johnson-Laird, P.N. (1983). *Mental models: Towards a cognitive science of language, inference, and consciousness*. Cambridge, MA: Harvard University Press.

Jonassen, D.H. (1997). Instructional design models for well-structured and ill-structured problem-solving learning outcomes. *Educational Technology: Research and Development, 45* (1), 65-95.

Jonassen, D.H. (2000). *Computers as Mindtools for schools: Engaging critical thinking*. Columbus, OH: Merrill/Prentice-Hall.

Jonassen, D.H. (2003). Using cognitive tools to represent problems. *Journal of Research on Technology in Education, 35* (3), 362-381

Jonassen, D.H., Beissner, K., & Yacci, M.A. (1993). *Structural knowledge: Techniques for representing, conveying, and acquiring structural knowledge.* Hillsdale, NJ: Lawrence Erlbaum.

Jonassen, D.H., & Henning, P. (1999). Mental models: Knowledge in the head and knowledge in the world. *Educational Technology, 39* (3), 37-42.

Jonassen, D.H., Howland, J., Moore, J., & Marra, R.M. (2003) *Learning to solve problems with technology: A constructivist perspective,* 2nd. Ed. Columbus, OH: Merrill/Prentice-Hall.

Jonassen, D.H. & Wang, S. (2003) Using expert systems to build cognitive simulations. *Journal of Educational Computing Research, 28* (1), 1-13.

Kraiger, K., & Salas, E. (1993, April). *Measuring mental models to assess learning during training.* Paper presented at the Annual Meeting of the Society for Industrial/Organizational Psychology, San Francisco, CA.

Larkin, J.H. (1983). The role of problem representation in physics. In D. Gentner & A.L. Stevens (Eds.). *Mental models* (pp. 75-98). Hillsdale, NJ: Lawrence Erlbaum Associates.

Lehrer, R., & Schauble, L. (2000). Modeling in mathematics and science. In R. Glaser (Ed.) *Advances in instructional psychology: volume 5. Educational design and cognitive science* (pp. 101-159). New Jersey: Lawrence Erlbaum.

Lippert, R. C. (1988). An expert system shell to teach problem solving. *Tech Trends, 33*(2), 22–26.

McGuinness, C. (1986). Problem representation: The effects of spatial arrays. *Memory & Cognition, 14*(3), 270-280.

Mellar, H., Bliss, J., Boohan, R., Ogborn, J., & Tompsett, C. (1994). *Learning with artificial worlds: Computer-based modeling in the curriculum.* London: Falmer Press.

Penner, D.E., Giles, N.D., Lhrer, R., & Schauble, L. (1997). Buildig functional models: designing and elbow. *Journal of Research in Science Teaching, 34* (2), 125-143.

Ploetzner, R., & Spada, H. (1998). Constructing quantitative problem representations on the basis of qualitative reasoning. *Interactive Learning Environments, 5,* 95-107.

Ploetzner, R., Fehse, E., Kneser, C., & Spada, H. (1999). Learning to relate qualitative and quantitative problem representations in a model-based setting for collaborative problem solving. *Journal of the Learning Sciences, 8*(2), 177-214.

Rips, L.J. (1986). Mental muddles. In M. Brand & R.M. Harnish (Eds.), *The representation of knowledge and beliefs* (pp. 258-286). Tuscon, AZ: University of Arizona Press.

Salomon, G., Perkins, D.N. & Globerson, T. (1991). Partners in Cognition: Extending Human Intelligence with Intelligent Technologies. *Educational Researcher,* 20 (3), 2-9.

Schank, R.C. (1994). Goal-based scenarios. In R.C. Schank & E. Langer (eds.), *Beliefs, reasoning, and decision making: Psycho-logic in honor of Bob Abelson.* Hillsdale, NJ: Lawrence Erlbaum.

Schwartz, J.L., & Yerulshalmy, M. (1987). The geometric supposer: Using microcomputers to restore invention to the learning of mathematics. In D. Perkins, J. Lockhead, & J.C. Bishop (Eds.), *Thinking: The second international conference* (pp. 525-536). Hillsdale, NJ: Lawrence Erlbaum Associates.

Schwarz, C.V., & White, B. (2005). Metamodeling Knowledge: Developing Students' Understanding of Scientific Modeling. *Cognition and Instruction,* 23 (2), 165-205.

Schwarz, C.V., & White, B.Y. (in press). Developing a model-centered approach to science education. *Journal of Research in Science Teaching.*

Shavelson, R.J. (1972). Some aspects of the correspondence between content structure and cognitive structure in physics instruction. *Journal of Educational Psychology,* 63, 225-234.

Spector, J. Michael; Christensen, Dean L; Sioutine, Alexei V; McCormack, Dalton (2001) Models and simulations for learning in complex domains: Using causal loop diagrams for assessment and evaluation, in: Computers in Human Behavior. Vol 17(5-6) Sep-Nov 2001, 517-545

Taylor, H.A., & Tversky, B. (19920. Spatial mental models derived from survey and route descriptions *Journal of Memory and Language, 31,* 261-292.

van der Veer, G.C. (1989). Individual differences and the user interface. *Ergonomics, 32* (11), 1431-1449.

Vosniadou, S. (1999). Conceptual change research: The state of the art and future directions In W. Schnotz, S. Vosniadou, & M. Carretero (Eds.), *New perspectives on conceptual change* (pp. 1-13). Amsterdam: Pergamon.

White, B. (1993a). ThinkerTools: Causal models, conceptual change, and science education. *Cognition and Instruction, 10* (1), 1-100.

Wittgenstein, L. (1922). *Tractatus logico-philosophicus.* London: Routledge.

can be guided by others in co-regulation of learning activities such as discourse, supportive materials, procedural facilitators, etc.

In other words, self-regulated learning is usually associated with the attempts of students engaging in project work or problem-based learning as these efforts require learners to investigate a driving question or problem; construct explanations and artifacts; collaborate with others; and use technology to support inquiry (Patrick & Middleton, 2002).

Literature of self-regulated learning and metacognition is situated within the context of authentic activities where learners have opportunities to reflect and monitor their behaviors in the context of solving problems with social others. Situated within contexts such as communities of learners, students are 'simulated into' situations where they have to plan and monitor their actions and activities, including the use of appropriate tools and strategies in order to achieve these goals.

Metacognitive activities within the concept of communities of learners can be both explicit and implicit. By explicit, we mean the structuring of activities where learners need to engage in explicit processes of reflection such as researching, sharing, and performing (Brown & Campione, 1996). Students begin by researching complex domain-specific issues and share what they have learned in their sub-groups to others. Through reciprocal teaching, students are exposed to comprehension and monitoring strategies which guide them in the sharing process.

In other examples, Computer-Supported Intentional Learning Environments provide scaffolds in the form of procedural cues to assist learners in conjecturing, providing personal theories, find more information, etc. (Scardamalia & Bereiter, 1991). The Scientific and Mathematical Arenas for Refining Thinking (SMART) program facilitates the generation of ideas, multiple perspectives, researching and revising, testing one's ideas, going public with one's ideas, and reflecting on the process, and looking for newer challenges (Barron, et al., 1998). The above two examples anchor around authentic problems and ideas.

In the next section of this paper, we discuss the pedagogical approach of problem-based learning (PBL) and consider how learning can be anchored or centered around authentic problems with the potentials for self-regulated learning and metacognitive activities on the part of the learners. We discuss how PBL can be situated within the concept of communities of learners and not just as a stand-alone pedagogy.

5.   PROBLEM BASED LEARNING

"The principal idea behind problem-based learning is … that the starting point for learning should be a problem, a query or a puzzle that the learner wishes to solve" (Boud, 1995, p. 13). Problem-based learning starts primarily with a focus on real-life problems and activities, rather than intense disciplinary knowledge (Hung, 2002). The approach attempts to move students towards the acquisition of knowledge and skills through a staged sequence (serving as a scaffolding process) of problems presented in context, together with associated materials and support from necessary sources, for example, teachers and experts.

PBL which originated with Medical school as real-world case studies has these objectives (Barrows, 1986) for the students:

- construction of clinically useful knowledge;
- development of clinical reasoning strategies;
- development of effective self-directed learning strategies; and
- increased motivation for learning, and becoming effective collaborators.

The fundamental approach as adopted in PBL as practiced in medical schools is as follows (Bereiter & Scardamalia, 2000):

- Problems play a central role in the educational process;
- Dialogue is a central vehicle for problem solving;
- Finding out what needs to be found out is critical to the learning process;
- Small groups work together to solve the problem;
- Information gathering and other tasks as distributed among group members; and
- The focus is on a cognitive outcome rather than producing an artifact or product thus distinguishing it from project-based learning.

Barrows (1986) has identified two factors that affect the probability that any of these objectives might be achieved. The first factor is the nature of the case: whether it is a complete case, a vignette, or a full problem simulation. The second factor is the locus of control of learning: whether it is teacher-centered, student-centered, or mixed. In medical school, the patients are real patients. Barrows worked with the doctors in gathering the details of case studies used for PBL.

There are three reasons why the problems must address real issues. First, because the students are open to explore all dimensions of the problem, there is a difficulty in creating a rich problem with a consistent set of information. Second, real problems tend to engage learners more – there is a larger context of familiarity with the problem. Finally, students want to know the outcome of the problem (Savery & Duffy, 1998).

The original conceptions of PBL as derived from Barrows (1986) within the Medical school context had a strong linkage with the medical community of practice. Developed in the mid-50s, it is now spread into more than 60 medical schools. Traditionally, in the first 2 years of medical school, students were given the traditional lectures such as in anatomy and physiology. The PBL approach transforms this method into one in which upon reaching medical school, students are divided up into groups. A group of five to seven medical students, for example, and a facilitator meet to discuss a problem (Barrows, 1986). The facilitator provides the students with a small amount of information about a real patient's case, and then the group's task is to evaluate and define different aspects of the problem and to gain insight into the underlying causes of the disease process. Hypotheses are generated and issues are also raised. The group members may choose to divide themselves up to investigate the various issues and discuss upon the findings subsequently. The students re-gather to share what they have learned, to reconsider their hypotheses, or to re-construct new ones based on their consolidated understanding. The facilitator's role is to help the students' learning processes by modeling hypothesis-driven reasoning and other forms of metacognitive skills (Savery & Duffy, 1998) for the students and by encouraging them to be reflective. As students become more experienced with the PBL method and take on more of the responsibility for identifying learning issues, the facilitator is able to fade this type of support, or scaffolding.

Barrows is adamant that the facilitator's role and interactions be kept at the metacognitive level when engaging learners' on issues and with the problem at hand. The facilitator should constantly ask questions such as: "Do you know what this means?"; "What are the implications of this?"; or "Is there anything else?". Through this process, students are encouraged and expected to similarly think critically and monitor and regulate their own understanding (Savery & Duffy, 1998).

"Through problem-based learning, students learn how to use an iterative process of assessing what they know, identifying what they need to know, gathering information, and collaborating on the evaluation of hypothesis in light of the data they have collected." (Stepien & Gallagher, 1998, p. 44)

> [P]roceeding through the PBL process requires the learner's metacognitive awareness of the efficacy of the process. In this regard, PBL is inherently self-regulated. Yet, PBL does not exist in a vacuum. Rather, it is a social system within a larger cultural context. The knowledge that the learner seeks is embedded in and derives from social sources—in this case, the world of medical practice. From this perspective, the learner is seen as both transforming and as transformed as the processes of practice and their underlying symbol systems are internalized through dialectical activity … In this sense, learning is not an accumulation of information, but a transformation of the individual who is moving toward full membership in the professional community. This identity-making is

marked by observing the facility with which cultural tools, or the ways of thinking and using language, are invoked. The sociocultural context of PBL is the group meeting that simulates the social process of medical problem solving in a scaffolded way. (Hmelo & Evensen, 2000, p. 4)

Hung (2002) synthesized that the process of PBL requires that students adopt active and metacognitive learning strategies though posing their own problems, questions, and seeking the respective solutions. PBL approaches converge with the notion of communities of learning engaged in disciplinary engagement. Engle & Conant (2002) discuss the elements of disciplinary engagement as (1) problematizing subject matter; (2) giving students authority to address problems, (3) holding students accountable to others/peers and shared disciplinary norms, and (4) providing students with the relevant resources. These elements are congruent to the processes underpinning PBL. Students are encouraged to question theories and challenge previously accepted facts by presenting evidence of their conjectures. The basic approach taken is to engage learners in inquiry processes similar to experts and practitioners in the discipline.

Similar to PBL approaches is project work science or PBS. The American Association for the Advancement of Science (1993) and the National Research Council (1996) have in the last few years been recommending that students be engaged in the activities of scientific inquiry – asking questions, conducting experiments and investigations, collecting data, interpreting results, and reporting findings (Roth, 1995).

Project-based science (PBS) is one example where authentic learning occurs, emphasizing inquiry and social constructivist learning activities. PBS is characterized by (1) a driving question, (2) investigations, (3) artifact development, (4) collaboration among students, teacher, and others in the community, and (5) use of technology tools to support inquiry (Singer, Marx, Krajcik, & Chambers, 2000).

By adopting a driving question that contextualizes the science project, PBS makes the inquiry process authentic (Patrick & Middleton, 2002). "The driving question uses students' real-world experiences to contextualize scientific ideas and subquestions and anchoring events to help students apply their emerging scientific understandings to the real world, thus helping them see value in their academic work." (Singer, Marx, Krajcik, & Chambers, 2000, p. 167)

Between PBL and PBS, the starting point is an authentic problem or driving issue which learners can possibly relate to. In both, students collaborate with peers within their groups and with others outside the classroom. Due to challenging driving questions and problems, students are compelled to address subquestions to an overarching question and develop strategies to monitor their progress. Assisting in this developmental process and transformation from novice ways to methods which experts adopt is fundamental to understanding how we learn (Bransford, Brown, & Cocking, 1999)

Self-regulated learning and metacognitive strategies involved in PBS is particularly interesting (Patrick & Middleton, 2002). Cognitive and meatcognitive strategies are needed when students have to think systematically and deeply about questions and subquestions; use the appropriate technological tools to create models; connect different pieces of information; represent their ideas in different ways; monitor their progress; work together with others; etc. Thus, success in PBS requires the cognitive, metacognitive, motivational, and collaborative engagement that comprises self-regulated learning (Patrick & Middleton, 2002).

6.   IMPLICATIONS FOR ENGAGED LEARNING ENVIRONMENTS

Designing authentic learning environments is an important concern for teachers and educators. Inherently, these authentic activities are fundamentally learner-centered in nature allowing opportunities for learners to reflect and plan for their actions. Such monitoring and regulatory behaviors are crucial for learners. Tenets for engaging students in authentic learning experiences whether in PBL, PBS, or in any similar such settings include the following (as discussed in the above settings):

- Meaningful problems – usually project based;
- Staging activities – structured activities and investigations that introduce learners to investigation techniques, background knowledge, and processes needed in inquiry similar to particular disciplinary practices;
- Supportive tools – cognitive and reflective tools and other forms of social collaboration tools which enable learners to think and collaborate;
- Embedded information cases – embedding a library of resources that is linked directly to an investigation process; and
- Monitoring and Planning – allowing learners to record the process and intermediate products of an extended activity.

In order to facilitate self-regulatory and metacognitive behaviors in our students, the problem selected and the process of solving the problem ought to be authentic to the learner. Authenticity, in other words, is both at the *problem* and *process* levels. Not only should the *problem* be an authentic one, but at the *process* level, we mean the use of authentic tools and strategies to solve ill-structured problems within a social context. Moreover, by *process*, self-regulated learning in authentic learning situations such as PBL can be facilitated under the following conditions:

- Adopting the kinds of thinking and questioning processes of experts;
- Appropriating the kinds of tools and strategies used in communities of practices;
- Developing artifacts and products related to the problem; albeit in a simplified form as those produced by experts;
- Dividing the problem into sub-problems;
- Peer sharing and critique;
- Experts' consultation and advise;
- Access to relevant sources of information and materials;
- Opening ideas for challenge;
- Opportunities to reflect upon trials and experiments; and
- Opportunities to explain issues, findings, and conclusions.

The above conditions for authentic learning situations are realized in our proposed engaged learning framework described below.

7.   A PROPOSED ENGAGED LEARNING FRAMEWORK

Summarizing the above discussion, we derive the engaged learning framework – *Problem, Ownership, Collaboration, Monitoring, Experts, and Tools* (see Figure 1) – the five tenets of Authentic Learning Environments. In essence, the framework involves the following tenets:

1. the design of *Problem* task which needs to evolve based on the learners' learning goals and needs to understand;
2. *Ownership* of learning towards the problem at hand and an engaged responsibility towards the ideas and concepts being explored;
3. *Collaboration* with others as a central means of problem solving;
4. *Monitoring* and regulatory processes which lead to closure of experimentation and ideas' discourse;
5. the role of *Experts* and facilitators in the learning process; and
6. the role of supporting *Tools* in the generation of ideas and problem solving.

We would stress that 'authenticity' in learning cannot be based on problem authenticity alone. "Authenticity" is *both **problem** and **process***. Hence the design of authentic problems should include both problem design and process design. The set of design principles for authentic problems can be seen as follows:

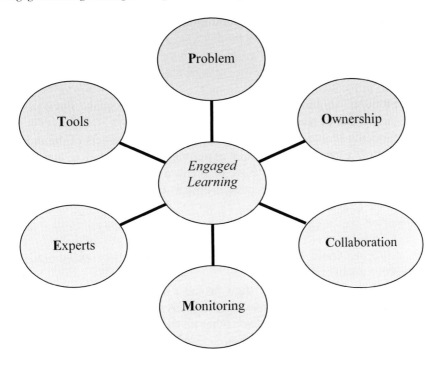

Figure 1. The Engaged Learning Framework

Problem Design – Problem (P)

Problems should be ill-structured with real life as anchoring problems/context. These problems should contain relevant learning issues also related to the syllabus which students have to learn in the schools. In this sense, problems should be identified collaboratively by teachers and students. The problem should be an integration of disciplines in problem solving so that students are given the opportunity to practice linking knowledge and skills of different disciplines in problem solving.

Ownership of inquiry where learners feel that the development and solution of the problem is meaningful is crucial to the design of authentic learning environments. Experts who are linked with learners in projects should coach and model the disciplinary thinking process through the use of support tools. Opportunity must be given to learners to reflect on the problem solving process together with facilitators and experts.

Process Design – Ownership (O), Monitoring (M), Experts (E), and Tools (T)

Ownership

   i.   Students should identify their own learning goals through the facilitation of teachers and experts;

   ii.   Students should be engaged in all the different aspects of the inquiry process such as investigation, experimentation, reflection, etc.; and

   iii.   Students need to know how to break down the problem into sub-problems and to engage in the problem solving process.

Collaboration

   i.   Students could be working in groups where they collaboratively solve problems.

   ii.   Students need to divide their projects up into respective roles and sub-tasks in order to achieve the objectives; and

   iii.   Students can account to each other on the work done.

Monitoring

   i.   Monitoring should be holistic which emphasizes on process rather than product, involving more than one form of evaluation techniques;

   ii.   Self-regulatory processes are needed on the part of the learners in order to monitor their progress in the problem solving process; and

   iii.   Monitoring should be done as a process similar to multiple evaluation in-situ which is at different crucial points of the problem solving cycle to assess learning as well as to inform the extent of support to provide in subsequent activities.

Experts

   i.   Experts together with teachers should provide a well guided inquiry/problem solving framework for problem solving;

   ii.   Experts and teachers should provide mediating tools and techniques for inquiry that are modeled after those used by the experts;

   iii.   Experts and teachers should provide sufficient/appropriate support for inquiry process, metacognition, collaboration and communication to bridge the gap between what the experts' knowledge and skills and that of the students'; and

   iv.   Experts and teachers should provide opportunities for students to play multiple roles in solving problems.

Tools

i.   The problem solving process should be done collaboratively through *open* communication tools between the students, teachers, and experts; and

ii.   The problem solving context should be collaborative and communicative through tools that are modeled after those used by experts.

Importantly, the engaged learning framework can be seen as a staged process similar to cognitive apprenticeship methods where problems are provided in terms of increasing complexity and diversity. The degree of progress in terms of the levels of ownership, monitoring behaviors, collaboration, expert-participation, tool-support can also be similarly conceived as progressive.

8.   TECHNOLOGIES WHICH SUPPORT ENGAGED LEARNING

Mindtools (Jonassen, Peck, and Wilson, 1999) are one example where learners actively engage in the creation of knowledge through tools such as concept-maps, reflecting their comprehension of the concepts rather than focusing on the presentation of knowledge. Jonassen proposes a model of constructivist learning environment that aims to engage learners in active and meaningful learning. The kernel of the constructivist learning environment is the issue, problem or project that serves as the focus of the learning episode. Jonassen believes in using interesting and authentic problems to motivate the learners towards the learning goal. Jonassen proposes using ill-structured problems arising out of real life context, which usually contain some emergent aspects that are definable by the learners. One major difference between expert and novice problem solvers lies in their experience in domain-specific problem solving. Experts possess knowledge and past experiences that are often encoded as stories; when met with a new situation or problem, they can readily search their memories for related cases. Jonassen proposes using related cases to supplant student experience and to provide multiple representations of content that reflect the complexity of the domain knowledge. In a constructivist learning environment, relevant and appropriate information, including web-based materials, could be made accessible as embedded hyperlinks at appropriate juncture.

To help engage the learners in higher order thinking, Jonassen suggests the use of cognitive tools, including visualization tools, knowledge modeling tools, performance support tools and information gathering tools. These tools help to facilitate cognitive processes and support learners in performing problem solving tasks. Premised on the notion of social constructivism, which emphasizes learning through collaborative construction of socially shared knowledge, Jonassen suggests using computer-mediated communication tools to support dialogue and collaboration within a communities of learners, who share similar knowledge and values and are pursuing similar learning goals. Collaborative tools include simple discussion forum and scaffolded environments such as Knowledge Forum. Besides devoting our effort to the design of a constructivist learning environment, Jonassen argues that a crucial factor for successful implementation of the learning activities is the social and contextual support. Without social and contextual support, which includes the physical infrastructure readiness and training to instructors and learners, the learning activities may be rendered ineffective.

Another example of technologies for engaged learning is anchored instruction. Anchored Instruction situates classroom learning in real life problem-solving scenario in order to engage students in problem solving. By anchoring learning in real life contexts, we are encouraging students to apply the knowledge they learn in classrooms to solve real-world problems, thus linking the "school knowledge" with everyday applications. An example of anchored instruction is the series of video-based program called *The Adventures of Jasper Woodbury Mathematical Problem Solving Series* developed by the Cognition and Technology Group at Vanderbilt.

Unlike traditional instructional videos that record "talking heads" to emulate lectures, each Jasper video contains a short realistic story that represents sufficiently complex problems. Since learning is demand-driven, the detective-like adventures help to motivate the students to engage in problem-solving tasks. Using "embedded data design" principle, the videos contain all the data necessary to solve the adventure with purposeful inclusion of irrelevant data to simulate the complexity of real life problems. Jasper adventures also contain "embedded teaching" episodes that model expert's approaches to solving problems. Leveraging on digital video technology, the video can be viewed and revisited as the learners solve the problems. While traditional mathematics teaching focuses on teaching of heuristics and problem solving steps, followed by "practice questions" that have single correct answer and one best method of getting the solution, the Jasper videos challenge the students to identify the problems, generate sub-goals, source for relevant information, cooperate with peers in planning and problem solving, compare perspectives, present possible solutions, select best solution and justify for the final solution. By taking up the challenge, the students apply their mathematics knowledge and concepts, critical thinking, and communication skills.

In summary, Table 2 describes the kinds of tools which can support the engaged learning framework.

Table 2. Technological supports to engaged learning framework

	Design considerations and tools for Engaged Learning
Problem	There is a need to provide or problem that is co-formulated by the students and teacher(s). The problem can be simulated into a learning environment after being co-formulated. The specific goals must be related to real-life cases according to the realities of the community of practice. Videos such as in anchored instruction can be adopted to describe the problem.
Ownership	The problem or case example must be interesting to the community (both students and teachers, and even experts)
Collaboration	The cases/problems are situated in a real life context. The learners, teachers, and practitioners each play a different but realistic role in solving the problem.
Monitoring	Students need to have tools to monitor and reflect on their learning experiences such as reflection logs, peer critiquing tools, and other forms of monitoring aids.
Experts	There should be plenty of opportunity for experts such as practitioners to operate within the learning environment. These activities can be scaffolding in terms of increasing complexity and diversity.
Tools	Tools are used throughout the process, in particular, social-constructivist tools for collaboration / communication between the students, teachers, and experts, in particular the co-formulation of problems, co-setting of goals, co-experimentations, co-explanations, and co-explorations of "what-if" questions. Mindtools and other forms of constructivist learning tools (e.g., concept mapping and visualization-simulation tools) are useful here. Information resources of precious cases, problems, and related information are crucial. Learners should receive appropriate feedback from each other, the teachers, and experts through the supports provided.

9. CONCLUSION

To orchestrate an engaged learning approach, it must start with the design of the anchoring problem. However, the process of problem solving should also be authentic. Authenticity should then be seen as both problem and process. The entire engaged learning framework of learning should be an authentic co-construction process on the part of learners, teachers, and experts where ownership in problem and process is an integral part of the learning experiences. Most importantly, the engaged learning framework differs from traditional learning in that learners are engaged in self-regulatory behaviors and that personal and collaboration knowledge construction are the tenets for authentic and engaged learning.

REFERENCES

Bakhtin, M. M. (1984). *Speech genres and other late essays*. Austin: University of Texas Press.

Barron, B.J.S., Schwartz, D.L., Vye, N.J., Moore, A., Petrosino, T., Sech, L., Bransford, J., & the Cognition and Technology Group at Vanderbilt (1998). Doing with understanding: Lessons from research on problem- and project- based learning. *Journal of the Learning Sciences, 7*(3/4), 271-313.

Barrows, H. S. (1986). A taxonomy of problem-based learning methods. *Medical Education, 20*, 481-486.

Bereiter, C., & Scardamalia, M. (2000). Process and product in Problem-Based Learning (PBL) research. In D.H. Evensen (Ed.) *Problem-Based Learning: A research perspective on learning interactions* (pp. 185-195). Mahwah, NJ: Lawrence Erlbaum Associates.

Boud, D. (1995). *Enhancing learning through self assessment.* London: Kogan Page.

Boud, D. & Feletti, G. (Eds.) (1997). *The challenge of problem-based learning.* Stirling: Kogan Page.

Bredo, E. (1994). Reconstructing educational psychology: Situated cognition and Deweyan pragmatism. *Educational Psychologist, 29*(1), 23-35.

Brown, A., & Campione, J. (1996). Psychological learning theory and the design of innovative environments: On procedures, principles, and systems. In L. Shauble & R. Glaser (Eds.). *Contributions of instructional innovation to understanding learning.* Hillsdale, NJ: Lawrence Erlbaum Associates.

Brown, J., Collins, A., & Duguid, P. (1989). Situated cognition and the culture of learning. *Educational Researcher, 18*(1), 32-42.

Butler, D. (2002). Qualitative approaches to investigating self-regulated learning: Contributions and challenges. *Educational Psychologist, 37*(1), 59-63.

Dewey, J. (1964). Science as subject matter and as method. In R.D. Archambault (Ed.). *John Dewey on Education: Selected writings* (pp. 121-127). Chicago: University of Chicago Press.

Edelson, D.C. (1998). Realising authentic science learning through the adaptation of science practice (pp. 317-331). In B.J. Fraser & K. Tobin (Eds.), *International Handbook of Science Education.* Dordrecht, NL: Kluwer Academic Publishers.

Edelson, D., Gordin, D., & Pea, R. (1999). Addressing the challenges of inquiry-based learning through technology and curriculum design. *Journal of the Learning Sciences, 8* (3 & 4), 391-450.

Engle, R.A., & Conant, F.R. (2002). Guiding principles for fostering productive disciplinary engagement: Explaining an emergent argument in a community of learners. *Cognition and Instruction, 20*(4), 399-483.

Habermas, J. (1984). *The theory of communicative action: The critique of functionalist reason. Vol 2.* Cambridge: Polity Press.

Hmelo, C., & Evensen, D.H. (2000). Problem-Based Learning: Gaining insights on learning interactions. In D.H. Evensen (Ed.) *Problem-Based*

Learning: A research perspective on learning interactions (pp. 4-8). Mahwah, NJ: Lawrence Erlbaum Associates.

Hung, D. (2002). Situated cognition and Problem based learning. *Journal of Interactive Learning Research, 13*(4), 393-414.

Jonassen, D., Peck, K., & Wilson, B. (1999). *Learning with Technology: A constructivist perspective.* NJ: Merrill.

Jones, B.F., Valdez, G., Nowakowski, J. & Rasmussen, C. (1995). Plugging in: Choosing and Using Educational Technology. Washington DC: Council for Educational Development and Research.

Lave, J. & Wenger, E. (1991). *Situated learning: Legitimate peripheral participation.* Cambridge, England: Cambridge University Press.

Maturana, H. & Varela, F. (1987). *The tree of knowledge: The biological roots of human understanding.* Boston: Shambhala.

Myer, D.K., & Turner, J.C. (2002). Using instructional discourse analysis to study the scaffolding of student self-regulation. *Educational Psychologist, 37*(1), 5-13.

National Research Council (NRC). (1996). *National Science Education Standards.* Washington, DC: National Academy Press.

Newmann, F.M., & Wehlage, G.G. (April, 1993). Five standards of authentic instruction. *Educational Leadership, 50*(7), 8-12.

Patrick, H., & Middleton, M.J. (2002). Turning the kaleidoscope: What we see when self-regulated learning is viewed with a qualitative lens. *Educational Psychologist, 37*(1), 27-39.

Paris, S.G., & Paris, A.H. (2001). Classroom applications of research on self-regulated learning. *Educational Psychologist, 36*(2), 89-101.

Patrick, H., & Middleton, M.J. (2002). Turning the kaleidoscope: What we see when self-regulated learning is viewed with a qualitative lens. *Educational Psychologist, 37*(1), 27-39.

Roth, W-M. (1995). *Authentic school science: Knowing and learning in open-inquiry science laboratories.* London: Kluwer Academic Publishers.

Savery, J. & Duffy, T. (1998). Problem Based Learning: An instructional model and its constructivist framework. In R. Fogarty (Ed.). *Problem Based Learning: A collection of articles* (pp. 73-92). IL: SkyLight Training and Publishing, Inc.

Scardamalia, M., & Bereiter, C. (1991). Higher levels of agency for children in knowledge building: A challenge for the design of new media. *Journal of the Learning Sciences, 1*, 37-68.

Scardamalia, M., & Bereiter, C. (1999). Schools as knowledge-building organizations. In D. Keating & C. Hertzman (Eds.), *Today's children, tomorrow's society: The developmental health and wealth of nations* (pp. 274-289). New York: Guilford.

Singer, J., Marx, R.W., & Krajcik, J. (2000). Constructing extended inquiry projects: Curriculum materials for science education reform. *Educational Psychologist, 35*(3), 165-178.

Stepien, W., & Gallagher, S. (1998). Problem-Based Learning: As authentic as it gets. In R. Fogarty (Ed.). *Problem Based Learning: A collection of articles* (pp. 43-49). IL: SkyLight Training and Publishing, Inc.

Wittgenstein, L. (1958). *Philosophical investigations.* Cambridge: Basil Blackwell.

Zimmerman, B. (1994). Dimensions of academic self-regulation: A conceptual framework for education. In D.H. Schunk & BJ. Zimmerman (Eds.), *Self-regulation of learning and performance: Issues and educational implications* (pp. 3-21). Hillsdale, NJ: Lawrence Erlbaum Associates.

Chapter 3

THE CONTRIBUTING STUDENT: LEARNERS AS CO-DEVELOPERS OF LEARNING RESOURCES FOR REUSE IN WEB ENVIRONMENTS

Betty Collis and Jef Moonen
University of Twente, The Netherlands

Abstract: Learners can and do become engaged in learning through intrinsic motivations without the need for a teacher or instructional designer. In the workplace, for example, workplace learning is typically seen as a process of such self-guided learning, based on the needs of the task at hand. In the school and higher-education setting however, it is the teacher who has a major role in shaping the conditions within which students can become engaged in their own learning. In this chapter we review several sets of conditions of good instruction that are argued to increase the engagement of learners and we describe a particular pedagogical model which we call the "contribution" model which reflects those conditions. The majority of the chapter consists of examples from both higher education and professional learning situations which illustrate how the contribution model relates to engaging learning.

Keywords: contributing student, pedagogy, learning activities, learning design, Web-based tools, course-management system, assessment, change, knowledge building, knowledge sharing

1.   INTRODUCTION

Learners can and do become engaged in learning through their own intrinsic motivations, without the need for a teacher or instructional designer. In the workplace, for example, workplace learning is typically seen as a process of such self-guided learning based on the needs of the task at hand. In the school and higher-education setting however, it is the teacher who has a major role in shaping the conditions within which students can become engaged in their own learning. In this chapter we review several sets of conditions of good instruction that are argued to increase the engagement of learners and we describe a particular pedagogical model which we call the

D. Hung and M.S. Khine (eds.), Engaged Learning with Emerging Technologies, 49-67.

"contribution" model which reflects those conditions. The majority of the chapter consists of examples from both higher education and professional learning situations which illustrate how the contribution model relates to engaging learning through:

> Exploration and discovery
> Knowledge creation and sharing
> Collaboration and contribution, and
> Authentic assessment

All of these relate to a major shift in learning activities, from learning as responding to instructions based on pre-selected study materials, toward learning via activities during which learners become co-designers of study materials for themselves and others. We will argue that this involves a number of deep changes in ideas about teaching, learning, assessment, and self-responsibility.

Through the examples, the need for network technology and Web environments with appropriate tools is an on-going theme. Without such appropriate tools the contributing-student approach to engagement is not scalable and may not be even feasible in practice.

The questions underlying this chapter are therefore:

> What is a "contributing student" pedagogy, how does it stimulate learner engagement, and what is involved in carrying it out in practice?

2.   INSTRUCTIONAL PRINCIPLES AND PEDAGOGICAL MODELS

In this section we begin by reviewing a series of key instructional principles which we relate to two important underlying views of the learning process.

2.1   Instructional principles

Based on his own work over the years and also on a deep knowledge of the learning-theory and instructional-design literature, Merrill has recently (2002) consolidated five "first principles of instruction". Merrill's premise is that, when applied in a course, these principles will facilitate learning in direct proportion to the degree of their implementation. The first principles of instruction are

1. "Learning is facilitated when learners are engaged in solving real-world problems.
2. Learning is facilitated when existing knowledge is activated as a foundation for new knowledge.
3. Learning is facilitated when new knowledge is demonstrated to the learner.
4. Learning is facilitated when new knowledge is applied by the learner.
5. Learning is facilitated when new knowledge is integrated into the learner's world." (Merrill, 2002, p. 45)

These principles can be seen reflected in many other sets of principles relating to the design of quality courses, and the stimulation of learner engagement. However, other researchers add additional perspectives such as in relation to different target groups. For example, Cross (1981) and Knowles (1984) over two decades ago indicated that adult learning should:

-Use the experience of the learners
-Involve the learners in the planning of their instruction
-Involve the learners in the evaluation of their instruction
-Challenge the learners to advance

The first of these clearly relates to Merrill's second principle and the last could be seen as implicitly underlying the principles, but the two principles relating to engaging the learners in the planning and evaluation of their instruction do not seem to be part of Merrill's orientation. While both Cross and Knowles were focusing on adult learners in general, Chickering and Gamson (1987) discuss principles of effective course design in higher education in which at least one of their principles also relates directly to learners taking an active role in the construction of their own learning:

-Encourage contact between learners and faculty
-Develop reciprocity and cooperation among learners
-Encourage active learning
-Give prompt feedback
-Emphasize time on task
-Communicate high expectations
-Respect diverse talents and ways of learning

Of this list, "encourage active learning" underlies Merrill's first, fourth, and fifth principles but "develop reciprocity and cooperation among learners" may go further in the direction of Cross' and Knowles' types of engagement. The other points in the Chickering and Gamson list reflect a level of pedagogical detail that Merrill does not explicitly discuss. This may be only a matter of choice in terms of the amount of detail to include in a list of principles. Or it might represent a more-fundamental distinction that can underlie pedagogical models.

2.2   Pedagogical models[1]

A pedagogical *model* relates to the abstract concepts about the learning- and teaching process that underlie an instructional approach. Sfard (1998) identifies two basic types of pedagogical models, the *Acquisition Model* and the *Participation Model*. Table 1 summarises Sfard's interpretation of these two fundamental pedagogical models.

Table 1. Two metaphors for learning (adapted from Sfard, 1998, pp. 6-7)

	Acquisition	Participation
Key definition of learning:	Learning as knowledge acquisition and concept development; having obtained knowledge and made it one's own; individualized	Learning as participation, the process of becoming a member of a community, "the ability to communicate in the language of this community and act according to its norms" (p. 6); "the permanence of having gives way to the constant flux of doing" (p. 6)
Key words:	Knowledge, concept, misconception, meaning, fact, contents; acquisition, construction, internalization, transmission, attainment, accumulation;	Apprenticeship, situatedness, contextuality, cultural embeddedness, discourse, communication, social constructivism, cooperative learning
Stress on…	"The individual mind and what goes into it" (p. 6); the "inward movement of knowledge" (p. 6)	"The evolving bonds between the individual and others" (p. 6); "the dialectic nature of the learning interaction: The whole and the parts affect and inform each other" (p. 6)
Ideal	Individualized learning	Mutuality; community building
Role of instructor	Delivering, conveying, facilitating, clarifying	Facilitator, mentor, "Expert participant, preserver of practice/discourse" (p. 7)
Nature of knowing	Having, possessing	Belonging, participating, communicating

---

[1] This section is adapted from Collis & Moonen, 2001, pp. 20-23, 87-89.

subsequently used as a resource bank, added to, or analysed. Students can be asked to select several of the submitted resources (not ones they submitted themselves) and do something further with the resources contributed by others--discuss, reflect, categorise, or relate.

Case studies

Case studies illustrating issues being studied in the course are uploaded into a course Web site. The origin of the cases can be in the instructor, but in the contributing-student approach they will more often contributed by the students themselves, reused from contributions made by students in earlier cycles of the course, or they can be found externally (for example, on the Web). The students can work in groups to discuss the cases, using groupware tools or Web-board discussion tools in the course Web site. They are asked by the instructor to follow a certain structure in their discussions. After the deadline for the activities is passed, the discussions of each group become open to the other groups. As a follow-up activity, each group compares its main ideas to those of the other groups and comments on points of agreement and alternative interpretations. If students meet face-to-face, they can have a culmination of this activity as a group discussion; however, their comments are retained on a course Web site as a resource, for students who were not present at the face-to-face discussion or for students outside of that particular cycle of the course. The instructor may wish to retain several of the strongest points of discussion, and make those available in the course Web site for the next cycle of students, as a starting point for their analyses of the cases.

Creating study resources

A major project for a course could be that students work in groups and each group choose a topic relevant to the course. The group must then prepare a report (using what ever type of technology is most appropriate--word processing, HTML, audio, video, or their combination). The intention of the activity is to extend and complement the textbook in relation to the topic in a way that is helpful to all of the students in the course. Draft versions of the report are made available via the Web site, for feedback from the instructor and other groups of students. The final version is also available via the Web site, in enough time before the end of the course so that students can read and submit comments about each other's work. The reports can be interlinked in the course Web site, to each other and to the other resources in the course, and can be available for the following cycle of students in the course. Students in the following cycle of the course can update and revise the previous reports, as a new contribution-oriented learning activity.

Creating test items

For some or each topic in a course, students are engaged in an activity in which they must construct several multiple-choice test items, along with a scoring key and appropriate feedback for each of the choices. All items are available via the course Web site as study materials for other students. As a subsequent activity, students must evaluate the questions that have been submitted. The instructor indicates that the final examination of the course will contain some of the contributed questions, so it is worth the students' time to study each others' questions as a review before the examination.

Discussion activities

Student use a Web-board or computer-conferencing tool to participate in written discussions relating to issues being discussed in the course where their contributions can be made at a time convenient to themselves but within the deadline for the completion of the discussion. Students can take turns having the role of moderator of the discussion. The instructor sets expectations for how often students should contribution, and for characteristics of the contribution such as length, a requirement that it explicitly mentions the ideas of the message to which it is responding, or that the submission also includes a reference to the course text or one of the course Web-based resources. Students earn marks for their submissions and moderating tasks. Dineen, Mayes, and Lee (1999) show how via such task-directed discussions students can see their results as a new form of courseware, available via an indexed multimedia database. And discussion does not have to be an end in itself. Fischer, Troendle, and Mandl (2003) demonstrate how learning groups can use a shared document repository and whitebook to discuss and support each other during each phase of a communal problem-solving activity.

All of these kinds of contributions can involve a follow-up activity where peer assessment takes place, as well as where learners compare and contrast their own ideas with those of others. Tsai, Lin, and Yuan (2002) for example demonstrate how peer feedback helps students through each step of a complicated development process. All of the above types of activities engage the students in way consistent with a contributing-student orientation, as long as there is explicit reuse made of each other' contributions as learning resources. Students are active in a way which directly contributes to the course as a whole, not just their own learning. Also, this sort of approach avoids the problems of lack of fit or the "not invented here" reaction that accompanies so many computer-based learning products. These study materials were "invented here", in a cost-effective way, as the course proceeds. The products developed as a result of the process of participating in the course are by definition a good fit to the course and to the local communication norms and culture.

Sets of examples illustrating these sorts of activities in the higher-education context can be found in Collis and Moonen (2001), Oliver and McLoughin (1999), and in the collection of "learning designs" available from the University of Wollongong in Australia (http://www.learningdesigns .uow.edu.au/; last accessed 11 November 2003). In the corporate-learning context, a contribution-oriented approach can also work well in practice (Margaryan, Collis, & Cooke, 2004). Examples of contribution-oriented activities from a corporate learning setting for engineers in the oil industry include:

- In a course on health-risk assessment in the workplace, participants arrange a visit to a site of their choice in their workplaces and diagnose the situation in terms of potential health or safety hazards. Each step of the process involves interactions in the actual workplace, summarized via the course Web environment, and used by the other participants as resource materials for analyzing their own work. The activities in this course progressively build upon one another, the final product being a health-risk assessment plan for each participant's own workplace, ready to put into action.

- In a course that involves a face–to-face component with a pre–classroom component carried out via the Web environment the pre-classroom component learners involves learners identifying a problem in their workplace related to the course concept and within the scope of their job roles to solve and to discuss these with their workplace managers. They must submit a description of the problem three weeks before the classroom session to the course site so that everyone can see them. The course instructor and other learners can provide feedback on the problems or help the participants modify the problem statements before they bring them to the classroom. Once physically together, the learners form small groups based on their interactions via the Web site, to further tackle each others' submitted problems by peer-assist activities.

- In another course the activities all relate to the participants' analysis of commercial opportunities in their own workplaces. Once these analyses are submitted to the course environment, follow-up activities occur where the participants reflect on summaries of each others' submissions and compare and contrast these with their own workplace situations.

These sorts of contribution-oriented activities also are effective for learners involved in school or healthcare practica. LaMaster and Tannehill (1999) for example show how peer mentoring when pre-service teachers provide each other with support and guidance via posting questions and sharing experiences with peers as well as with teachers with practical experience can lead to contributions becoming learning resources for others.

In summary, there are many educational benefits to a contributing-student approach. These include the benefits of:

- Learning from the work of other learners. Bandura (1986) called this vicarious learning where learners can access the dialogues and discussions of other learners to gain insight into the problems they might have encountered and the strategies they used in coming to a solution.

- Using the work and experiences of other students as model answers or as a basis for peer feedback, peer reflection, or peer teaching.

- The motivation that comes when students know that their submissions are meaningful to the communal learning experience of the course and will be used by others for learning activities.

- Expanding the range of examples and resources available for the course and for reuse in subsequent versions of the course or other courses, through the judicious reuse of selected submissions of the students.

- Dialogue and interaction with others during activities that use collaboration learning and knowledge sharing (Collis & Moonen, 2004).

5.   ROLES OF TECHNOLOGY

Technology is a critical tool in contribution-oriented activities. A contribution-oriented pedagogy can be used in a distance-education course or can be used as part of a course with face-to-face sessions. While networks and computer technology are, in principle, not necessary for the approach, the technology makes it feasible, scalable, and manageable for both instructor and students alike. Without the technology, in particular the Web technology, application of a contribution-oriented pedagogy as described in this article will be difficult to apply. A Web-based system with appropriate upload, collaborative, and communication functionalities provides the common medium into which contributions are placed, for further sharing as well as for feedback and assessment. Figure 1 shows how a course Web environment can grow in terms of materials contributed to it during the course itself. The activities mentioned in the figure are typical for a contribution-oriented approach. These activities are usually initiated by the instructors, but are essentially conducted by students individually or within a student's group in the course. Users of the contributions may also be other students in other cycles of the course or students in other courses or learners who are not in a course context at all but who could refer to the materials via a database in the same way as they now use a library or a Web search engine.

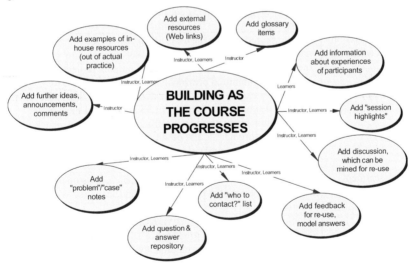

Figure 1. Building as the course progresses, through contributions (Collis & Moonen, 2004)

Table 3 presents the ideas in Figure 1 in terms of different components of a Web-based course-management system.

Table 3. Supporting the contribution-oriented aspects of a course with different components of a course-management system (adapted from Collis & Moonen, 2001, pp. 83-85)

Component	To support a contribution-oriented pedagogy
1. For general course organization	-Have students add links to resources related to the course, and to the work and homepages of experts related to the course
2. For support of lectures or contact sessions	-Extend the lecture after the contact time by having all students reflect on some aspect and communicate via some form of structured comment via the Web page; or students can add to the lecture materials themselves, or take responsibility for some of the lecture resources. The instructor uses the students' input as the basis for the next session or activity -Capture student debates and discussions, make available as video on demand, and use as basis for asynchronous reflection and further discussion
3. For self-study and exercises; practical sessions	-Facilitate students using each other's submissions as learning resources once these are available as part of the Web environment. Select certain submissions as model answers and reuse with subsequent groups. -Structure communication and interaction via the WWW site so that students are guided as to how to respond productively to each other's work and questions. Guide students to take responsibility for answering each other's questions (with monitoring by the instructor)
4. For multi-session projects or activities	-Make shared workspace tools along with other communication and reporting tools available in the Web site to allow group members to work collaboratively on complex projects -Use work submitted previously as the starting point for a new project, for example, to add new examples to or otherwise update or tailor a submission from the previous cycle of the course -Guide students to provide constructive on-going feedback to each other, through the use of structured communication forms and by having their partial products accessible via the course Web site
5. For assessment	-Integrate new forms of assessment, such as all students maintaining their own portfolios, within the course Web environment -Include peer-assessment activities as activities that are themselves marked and graded
6. For general communication	-Add a Web board for discussion about course topics as a major activity in the course; have students take responsibility for moderating the discussions, adding links to external resources to justify their comments when appropriate -Involve experts from outside the course in responding to the contributions of the students.

With a contribution-oriented pedagogy, the resources contributed can become new content objects in themselves, depending on how they are used in subsequent activities and other course processes. Tools for adding metadata to selected contributions to annotate and package them for reuse in other courses are important additions to course-management systems (Strijker, 2004).

6. CHALLENGES AND OPPORTUNITIES[3]

Given the rapid growth in the personal use of the World Wide Web by both students and instructors to find resources (used for contribution purposes) that can extend or supplement printed resources such as textbooks (used for acquisition-oriented learning), the trend toward students contributing URLs of resources found on the Web to a collection for shared use by their classmates is already developing. Course-management systems are in common use in universities, and these are bringing many of the types of contributions shown in Figure 1 into practice (De Boer, 2004). However, this growth brings with it some serious issues. Several of these are:

- *Issues relating to changes in the role of the instructor*: Contribution activities will involve many changes for the instructor. The instructor moves from presenter to manager of activities. His or her feedback is given to contributions from the learners which may include material new to the instructor. The instructor has to study the new material in the contributions before they can be responded to. The time needed to monitor and manage a contribution-oriented pedagogy is likely to exceed the time needed in an acquisition-oriented approach.

- *Issues relating to assessment and evaluation*: Students should be graded on their contributions. The assessment of student contributions, particularly as they involve peer interactions and inclusions of materials from non-traditional sources, require new approaches to grading and assessment. These new approaches are likely to be more time consuming for the instructor than traditional assessment methods in which all students answer the same questions and can be marked against the same answer key. This means that the aims of the contributions have to be clearly specified in pre-set grading criteria. Distinctions between individual and peer-related criteria must be specified; if an assignment, for example, requires a first student to reflect on the

---

[3] This section is adapted from Collis & Moonen, 2004 (in press)

feedback made by a second student, but the feedback from the second student has not occurred, how will the first student be able to respond to the reflection activity? How will be this affect his marks for that activity? As Macdonald (2003) notes, a discussion about assessment "leaves various uncomfortable questions in the air" (p. 390).

- *Issues related to new expectations for the students*: Not all students welcome a switch to a contribution approach. They sometimes complain that "it is the instructor's job to 'teach them'", that looking for additional study materials takes too much time ("Why don't you just give them to us?"), they want to expect study materials to be definitive ("What do I need to know for the test?"), and thus having to evaluate materials found on the Web or created by their peers is not something for which they have the desire or skills (Collis & Moonen, 2001, p.107). Contribution-type activities also call for higher-order skills on the part of the students. Bennet, Dunne, and Carre (1999) identify key skills related to management of self, management of information, management of others, and management of task and include higher-level aims relating to critical thinking as well as self regulation. These key skills emerge slowly over time and cannot be assumed to be adequately available for students confronted with a contribution task. Careful instructions and scaffolding from the instructor are necessary for a contribution approach to be manageable in practice.

- *Issues related to plagiarism and privacy*: The risk of plagiarism, intentional or indirect, increases the more that students can see each others' work or make use of resources contributed by other students. Strict guidelines must be established to prevent submissions that closely resemble previous submissions. And as a parallel issue, students may not wish their work to be available to others in their class, for various reasons such as maintaining their own advantage in terms of grades or avoiding embarrassment. In some institutions, the student has a right to privacy and must explicitly indicate that he agrees to his work being made available to others. This can complicate the sharing and collaboration process as well as add increased managerial burdens on the instructor.

7. CONCLUSION

We began by looking at Merrill's five first principles of instruction. Contribution-oriented activities relate very well to Merrill's first, second, fourth, and fifth principles. The first two principles, "Learning is facilitated when learners are engaged in solving real-world problems" and "Learning is facilitated when existing knowledge is activated as a foundation for new knowledge" are directly applied when contribution-oriented activities relate to real-world problems and make use of real-world resources found by the learners, via the Web or via direct contacts with real–world settings. When activities build upon each other, the second principle of activating existing knowledge in the construction of new knowledge is applied. The fourth and fifth principles, "Learning is facilitated when new knowledge is applied by the learner" and "Learning is facilitated when new knowledge is integrated into the learner's world" are inherent in well-designed contribution-oriented activities. In addition, the extra features of good learning identified by Cross and Knowles which call for involving the learners in the planning and evaluation of their instruction, can also be strongly reflected. The contribution-oriented approach reflects Sfard's "participation" pedagogy, and also her call for a combination of both acquisition and participation. The approach is only feasible and scalable if well-designed and accessible Web-based tools are available because otherwise there is no convenient, shared repository of contributions. Reuse or access independent of time and location require a network system and Web tools. Course-management systems that limit learners in what and where they can make a contribution (perhaps only allowing submissions in a "drop box") are not well designed for a contribution approach. Learning-content management systems (LCMSs) which assume all content is supplied by external, professional sources will also not be adequate for the contribution approach.

The most interesting contribution-oriented activities are those that are combinations of discovering and creating, comparing and discussing, and building on other learners' products. The value of the contribution-oriented pedagogy lies in the creation or finding and selection of existing resources, their combination, structuring, and argumentation why a selection was made, as well as the reflection upon the thinking processes behind this. In such a way the participants really contribute to a course, not only for themselves, but, by making results of their work and learning available for others, for the whole participating community, and, given the potential of re-use of the most valuable contributions, to a much wider community.

REFERENCES

Bandura, A. (1986). Social foundations of thought and action. Englewood Cliffs, NJ: Prentice Hall.

Bennett, N., Dunne, E., & Carre, C. (1999). Patters of core and generic skill provision in higher education. Higher Education, 37(1), 71-93.

Brophy, J., & Alleman, J. (1991). Activities as instructional tools: A framework for analysis and evaluation. Educational Researcher, 20 (4), 9-24.

Chickering, A.W., & Gamson, Z.F. (1987) Seven principles for good practice in undergraduate education AAHE Bulletin, 39(7) pp. 3-7.

Collis, B., & Moonen, J. (2004) Contribution-oriented pedagogy. In P. Rogers (Ed.), Encyclopedia of distance learning, Vol. 1 (pp. 415-422). Harrisburg, PA: Idea Group.

Collis, B., & Moonen, J. (2001) Flexible learning in a digital world: Experiences and expectations. London: Kogan Page.

Cross, K.P. (1981). Adults as learners. San Francisco: Jossey-Bass.

De Boer, W. F. (2004). Flexibility in the changing university. PhD dissertation, Faculty of Behavioural Science, University of Twente, The Netherlands.

Dineen, F., Mayes, J. T., & Lee, J. (1999). Vicarious learning through capturing task-directed discussions. Learning Technologies Journal (ALT-J), 7(3), 33-43.

Dopper, S., & Dijkman, B. (1997). Action learning geschikt voor deeltijdonderwijs [Action learning appropriate for part-time students]. Onderzoek van Onderwijs [Research in Education], 23, 57-59.

Fischer, F., Troendle, P., & Mandl, H. (2003). Using the Internet to improve university education: Problem-oriented Web-based learning with MUNICS. Interactive Learning Environments, 11(3), 193-214.

Jonassen, D.H., Peck, K. L, & Wilson, B. G. (1999). Learning with technology - A constructivist perspective. Upper Saddle River, NJ: Prentice-Hall.

Kearsley, G., & Shneiderman, G. (1998). Engagement theory: A framework for technology-based teaching and learning. Educational Technology, 38 (5), 20-24.

Knowles, M.S. (1984). The adult learner: A neglected species (3rd Ed.). Houston, TX: Gulf Publishing.

LaMaster, K., & Tannehill, D. (1999). Preservice teachers as mentors using telecommunications. International Journal of Educational Telecommunications, 5(1), 25-46.

Laurillard, D. (1993). Rethinking university teaching: A framework for the effective use of educational technology. London: Routledge.

Macdonald, J. (2003). Assessing online collaborative learning: Process and product. Computers & Education, 40, 377-391.

Margaryan, A., Collis, B., & Cooke, A. (2004). Activity-based blended learning. Human Resource Development Interaction, (HRDI) (in press).

Merrill, M.D. (2002). First principles of instruction. Educational Technology Research and Development, 50(3), 43-59.

Oliver, R., & McLoughlin, C. (1999, 26 June). Curriculum and learning-resources issues arising from the use of Web-based course support systems. Paper presented at ED-MEDIA '99, Seattle.

Reigeluth, C. M. (1996). Instructional design theories. In Tj. Plomp & D. Ely (Eds.), International encyclopedia of educational technology. Second edition (pp. 163-169). London: Elsevier.

Sfard, A. (1998). On two metaphors for learning and the dangers of choosing just one. Educational Researcher, 27(2), 4-13.

Simons, P. R. J. (1999). Three ways to learn in a new balance. Lifelong Learning in Europe, IV (1), 14-23.

Strijker, A. (2004). Learning objects in context: Human and technical perspectives. PhD dissertation, Faculty of Behavioural Science, University of Twente.

Tsai, C.-C., Lin, S. S. J., & Yuan, S.-M. (2002). Developing science activities through a networked peer assessment system. Computers & Education, 38, 241-252.

Chapter 4

SITUATED LEARNING IN THE PROCESS OF WORK

Reinhard Oppermann[1] and Marcus Specht[2]

[1]*Fraunhofer Institute for Applied Information Technology and University Koblenz-Landau, Germany;* [2] *Fraunhofer Institute for Applied Information Technology, Germany*

Abstract: New approaches in situated e-learning aim to overcome shortcomings of learning to use IT applications within working environments. Situated learning supports the learning on demand process both in individual and co-operative working contexts. The support provides opportunities for consultation to solve critical working situations but also for reflecting work processes by creating, editing and using annotations and demonstrations for oneself and for exchanging them within a group of domain workers. The concept will be described and exemplified in realistic working settings.

Discovery learning on demand and exchange of information between workgroup members (communities of practice) are currently very important ways how people learn in working environments. However, none of the traditional means for on-demand help (like call-centres, help desks or on-line help facilities) assists workers in retrieving instructions in the task environment and in retaining or retrieving their discoveries when they are needed again, or tap into the knowledge that other workgroup members have already acquired. Such traditional methods remain distant from the current task, environment and understanding of the learner or the learner group. Instead, situated e-learning methods allow for on demand instruction embedded into the work process as well as for exploitation and exchanging learning and consultation experiences on an individual and a group level. The underlying idea of situated e-learning is that learning is not seen as a set of momentary and isolated events but as a continuous process of acquiring, applying, refining and exchanging of competence often taking place in communities.

Keywords: situated learning, learning on demand, learning process, learning and relearning, learning context, learning and consultation, reflection in action, learner models

1.   INTRODUCTION

Learning becomes an integrated part of life and an integrated part of work. Learning happens planned and unplanned, controlled and

D. Hung and M.S. Khine (eds.), Engaged Learning with Emerging Technologies, 69-89.
© *2006 Springer. Printed in the Netherlands.*

uncontrolled, consciously and unconsciously, single and collectively. Today's working life and its widespread use of technology requires more than ever acquiring permanently new domain knowledge and tool knowledge. The learning process is assumed to be iterative, i.e., the learner proceeds in his or her competence through several trials of acquisition and utilisation of knowledge. The first step to acquire knowledge may be (a) exploratory, (b) supported by technical or human consultants, (c) error prone, (d) including indirect solutions, and (e) including dead ends. This first step of learning provides the user with rudimentary knowledge about errors, risks, and solutions. Making only one experience is not sufficient for a full understanding and it is not robust to forgetting. It has to be reinforced and extended by re-use in later similar situations. Learning is knowledge-dependent. I learn what I already know - at least a little bit.

Four aspects of learning build the main characteristics of our understanding of learning:

- learning is ubiquitous and situated: it can happen in every working or living environment, everywhere and everywhen; but learning best performs when situated in an authentic task context with real problems and real solutions,
- learning is a combination of active exploration and instruction: people learn by trying things out and by consulting technical or human help facilities,
- learning is an iterative phenomenon; it evolves step by step using earlier knowledge for progressive understanding and use
- learning is an individual and a social activity: people learn on their own but they also appreciate the support and knowledge exchange in social interactions.

Learning embedded in a situation of task accomplishment is not a new phenomenon arising together with e-learning. The situation has been focused as a context for understanding and supporting human actions and a context for understanding and supporting human learning. Situated action (Suchman 1987) and situated learning (Lave and Wenger 1991) are well established concepts. Together with electronic working tools situated e-learning can be integrated into the working environment and in the working process. Methods of situated e-learning can best be applied for work at computerised workplaces. The more electronic components become embedded into appliances of everyday life or the more devices accompany the user in everyday life like smart phones the more situated e-learning can be assumed to be applicable in many situations. Situated learning is a kind of learning where the given characteristics of the location, the time, the environment, the tasks and the other human partners constitute cognitive, motivational and social determinants for the acquisition of knowledge and skills. Situated learning is often discussed together with contextualised learning. Contextualised in our understanding includes the progressive aspect of situations, i.e., its history, whereas the situation focuses the momentary constellation of the parameters mentioned above. Situated learning increases the quality of learning (effectiveness, efficiency and satisfaction) and increases the reusability and progressiveness of learning results. This makes situated learning attractive for vocational learning and for learning on the job where the learning demand increases and requires continuous learning effort integrated in the working process.

2.   LEARNING ON THE JOB

Learning in this chapter will be regarded as learning with the support of computer based tools. Many aspects of learning characteristics can be generalised beyond computerised workplaces. In particular learning in communities and the preference of learning from technical instruction together with supporting peers at the workplace seem to be of general importance. The notion of a computerized workplace is changing rapidly. Whereas the computerized workplace some years ago has been a desktop PC with keyboard and mouse and a screen in new workplaces today the personal computer is often supplemented or even replaced by PDAs or mobile devices and we foresee that in the near future the personal computer as known disappears in the background and gets supportive or assistant character. Nevertheless most of the underlying processes about learning and the support of learning on the workplace get even more important. By the possibility to embed computer based learning and training at the workplace without interrupting a task gives new possibilities and challenges to system designers and human resource development.

We want first to discuss some underlying findings and important understandings of the underlying learning processes.

Training and learning on the job. The learning process is assumed as being integrated into the task accomplishment (Dutke and Schönpflug 1987, 295f.; Paul 1995, 168). A substantial part of learning does not happen during the training but during task performance. "...people learn best when engrossed in the topic, motivated to seek out new knowledge and skills because they need them in order to solve the problem at hand" (Norman and Spohrer 1996, 26). "...information that is accessed but never put to use dur-ing the learning process may be difficult to retrieve and use when the need arises in the real world" (Schank and Kass 1996, 28). For learning about electronic system features a 'guided exploration' facility was proposed to support this kind of learning (Carroll and Rosson 1987); (Carroll 1990). Guided exploration owes its origins already in the concept of 'discovery learning' out of the late '60s and early '70s (Williams and Farkas 1992, 41).

Prior knowledge plays an important role in learning. Numerous studies have shown the impact of prior knowledge on learning in various disciplines such as physics (McCloskey 1983; Galili, Ben Dall et al. 1993), cognitive psychology, especially in reasoning (e.g. Lovett and Anderson 1996; Whittlesea and Wright 1997), reading comprehension (see Hazan 1995 for a review), and in learning computer applications (Carroll 1990). (Whittlesea and Wright 1997) claim that "the vast majority of human behaviour is controlled by past experience of which they are unaware at the time of performance and creates consequences for future behaviour of which they are equally unaware. Prior knowledge activation can facilitate learning (Rumelhart 1980); (Carroll 1990); (Waern 1993); (Hazan 1995); (Lovett & Anderson 1996). The closer learned and used knowledge can be connected the higher the benefit for the learner. A good fit of learned and used knowledge can be assumed when the learner can define and observe the context of the acquisition and the exploitation of knowledge in the authentic learning history.

Not any breakdown or new situation creates the need for acquiring new knowledge, i.e., to learn. Users in contrast do avoid explicit learning. As Carroll and Rosson cite: "I want to do something, not learn to do everything" (Carroll and Rosson 1987, 83); they resume: "adults resist explicitly addressing themselves to new learning" (op.cited, 101); see also (Knowles 1973; Kidd 1977). In particular, if the critical situation is supposed to occur only once the user is not motivated to *learn* a solution. It is sufficient if he or she is enabled to get the job done, for instance by the help of step by step instructions not meant to induce a knowledge acquisition with the user. Williams and Farkas give an example where a user who has exceptionally to produce a footnote instead of known endnotes for a particular journal will not accept the "compel (...) to 'learn' or 'remember' the procedures that he or she explicitly needs now in order to create the footnotes" (Williams and Farkas 1992, 44). For recurrent problems and tasks new knowledge will be acquired.

Learning support therefore must be integrated into the learning and usage phases of new applications and new tasks.

Support from on-line help. For working with computerized systems when problems arise, breakdowns occur or solutions are unknown, addressing technical on-line-help is often insufficient for the user. The sup-

The selection of the right learning support in the right time is therefore dependent on a variety of parameters of the situation and goals of the application in the working context.

Empirical findings show that adaptation to learner models and parameters of the learning situation lead to more effectiveness, efficiency and motivation for learning. Adaptive educational hypermedia systems collect information from user assessment, feedback, the current task or user goal and other implicit and explicit acquisition methods. In a contextualized learning system additionally the current user context with a variety of environmental parameters can be taken into account. Those environmental sensors enable the application to collect much more information about the behaviour of a user. Even more, by the integration of environmental sensors and user sensors new applications can collect direct feedback from user sensors dependent on the variation of environmental parameters measured by environmental sensors like shown in Figure 1. A good example for such an application can be a training system that monitors the user's moves while handling a complex machine and giving direct feedback for training purposes. Such systems are already used in medical training applications like echo tutor (Grunst, Fox et al. 1995).

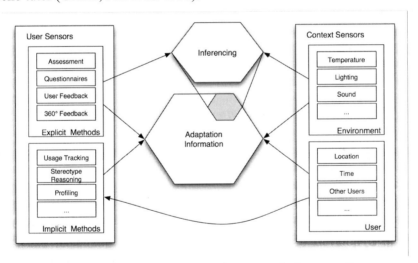

Figure 1: User Sensors and Environmental Sensors for more valid inferences and validation of implicit user tracking methods

For the adaptation to individual users the system in that sense can have shorter feedback cycles and adapt not only to the individual learner model and explicit user feedback but also to implicit feedback loops from a variety of contextual parameters. First simple examples for new adaptive methods in content delivery are location based services and museum information systems like hippie (Oppermann and Specht 2000). Beside new adaptive methods this can additionally have an important impact on the interaction with the learning system. New forms of augmented reality training systems in this sense are not restricted to the request of information but enable the learner to explore the learning subject and its artefacts either in virtual reality training simulations (Rickel and Johnson 1997) or in a tracked real training environment (Fox 2001). From our point of view this is not only a different way of accessing learning materials but can be seen as support for constructivist learning approaches in combination with an adaptive intelligent system that tracks the users learning activities in a given situation and responds to them.

Another example for the extension of adaptive methods comes from the field of adaptive augmented reality systems where not explicit learning takes place but natural or artificial items attract the interest of the human and information technology provides content. Typical environments for such on-the-way learning are museums. The LISTEN system (Goßmann and Specht 2001) tracks the user with a resolution of 5cm and 5 degrees, which allows to identify if a user looks onto a detail A of an artwork in a gallery or onto a detail B or beside the artwork. Additionally the system can present information to the user embedded in the physical environment with 3D audio technology. So the user experiences the sound of presentations coming from the environment or from specific objects in the environment. Based on those location tracking sensors and the presentation possibilities new adaptive methods can be realized. Some examples are:

- *Adaptation of presentation to position and object distance.* The user's position in space relative to an object in the physical space is mapped onto the direction and the volume of the sound for the presentation of the information.

- *Selection of presentation style based on position.* If a user moves in a room the user will get different presentation styles from the system. If the user moves into the centre of a room more general information about the room as a whole is presented and a sound collage for the single objects in the room is generated with directed sound sources coming from the objects. If a user moves close towards an object and focuses that object the volume of that piece of the collage is turned up and more detailed information of the object will be selected.

- *Adaptation to movement and reception styles.* Several kinds of common behaviour can be identified with people walking through the environment (e.g. clockwise in museums). By using the fine grained tracking technology the system can learn about preferred user movement and perception styles. The information about the time of listening to object descriptions can be combined with the movement. The selection and dynamic adaptation of tour recommendations can be adapted to the stereotypical type of movement and his/her preferred perception style.

- *Adaptation to time and lighting conditions and position of user* is a complex adaptive method taking into account environmental factors, the time, and the user position for the explanation of artworks in LISTEN. The sound presentation can be adapted to the changing lighting conditions during the day (based on sensor data) for explaining certain details that can only be visible during a certain time period or from a certain position in the room.

The contextualization of learning experiences and information is not only important on a level of presenting single contents but is additionally important on the level of integrating and synchronizing learning activities in blended learning and the integration of pre-existing learning experiences.

In this sense we perceive m-learning as a natural evolution of e-learning: New technologies allow for a better support of learning than classical ways of e-learning where the text book often was just replaced by a computer screen. While in the current discussion about e-learning blended learning approaches are often mentioned as a solution for the integration of e-learning in existing educational scenarios, we see m-learning and situated learning as a good chance to develop e-learning one step further. Often in blended learning scenarios intermixing computer based and face-to-face learning in the learning process describe the way towards a certain educational goal. Nevertheless this often neglects the problem of synchronization of learning steps. How should an intelligent learning environment get aware of the users progress? How should remote peers support a user when s/he is in an actual learning/working context? Many of those questions can be answered when the computer disappears in the environment or gets mobile in a first step. Learners could use contextualized learning tools just like a mobile telephone where they could not only call an expert for advice but also use a variety of other learning tools for helping in an actual situation. In this sense we understand m-learning and the contextualization as a natural way of integrating learning technology in the learning process on demand. That this does not only work with planned instruction can be seen with examples of system that use more accidental learning like in museum environments (Oppermann and Specht 1999).

Learning support must be integrated into the learners' context and take into account the context of use to disappear.

4.   ANNOTATION FACILITIES AND SITUATED ANNOTATION AUTHORING

For the support of learning we propose annotation facilities that exploit given learning steps for later own or peer consultation as an augmentation of the learning process. Annotation means support the reflection in action as proposed by (Schoen 1990). Annotations incorporate the results of the reflection about working processes or working tools and preserve these reflections for applying and continuing them in later situations.

With embedded memos and if necessary screen captures users can record problems they encounter or solutions they find when using software applications. They can annotate the recordings with textual or verbal comments, store them in a personal archive (individual 'demotheque'), and leave stickers on any part of their working environment with pointers to the memos and recordings that are relevant in the respective area. Users can send memos and video clips to a consultant for on-line help that contain questions or log problems with the software. Memos and registered action sequences that describe representative solutions in a video clip can be made available and exchanged among a group of users via an embedded 'demotheque' - for an example of such a system in the area of medical training on the job see (Hillgren and Bjorgvinsson 2002).

Intuitive and simple tools can support the user in making memos and recordings. Tools can support the user in structuring the demotheque and retrieving earlier solutions for the current problem situation. If learning is a process referring to earlier learning steps as explained above a demotheque supports the steps of the learning process, i.e., the transfer from the solution finding to the solution applying episode. Once the user has found a solution he or she can store the results and the process towards the results.

There are situations where the user learns a particular feature of an application that only implies 'declarative knowledge' (see Anderson 1976). A simple description of handling details, parameter settings or other *static* features is helpful if this description is at hand on demand. For this purpose an individual explanation facility that may be called an 'individual memo' is sufficient. In individual memos the user enters his or her comments–either text or voice–, sticks it to the relevant interface element of the application and re-activates it on demand.

There are other situations where the *process* is important to (re-)acquire 'procedural knowledge'. While individual memos support static features of the learning task, video clips support the (re-)understanding of *dynamic* features. A 'living' clip is easier to grasp than a formal description[2]. A recording cannot replace experience but it can exploit the user's own former practice to support his or her recapitulation of solutions in later situations.

A self-exploration and a demonstration by an expert always take place under time and attention constraints[3]. The user has to follow the instruction of the expert and make sure to memorise the solution for later application. With a recorded demonstration the emotional stress not to miss or forget relevant details can considerably be reduced. Sometimes a recording is not sufficient to reveal the rational of a solution. Annotation facilities may help to denominate the general concept of a solution, the reasons for a solution, warnings to misleading assumptions, or hints to unexpected side effects to support its transfer to similar tasks[4].

The benefit of the static (memo sticker) or dynamic annotations (video) can be expected in two learning phases. First, the annotations integrated into the application enhance traditional software training. Users can pass the training with less mental stress, will be able to ignore or forget relevant details of the tutorial without serious negative consequences, and will benefit from the fact that the training exercises and demos during the training are also contained in the demotheque and can still be consulted later. Second, in later phases when users find their own solutions or consult experts, the demotheque can be seen as leveraging the problem solving effort of users and consultants, and as a partial embodiment of the organization's tacit collective knowledge.

The problem of exploiting own and peer experience is of great practical relevance. People learn continuously but they have difficulties in finding and using prior established competence. Annotations in a demotheque provide a self-learning support facility to bring the user in touch with his or her

---

[2] see Palmiter, S. and J. Elkerton (1991). An Evaluation of Animated Demonstrations for Learning Computer-based Tasks. In: S. P. Robertson/G.M. Olson/J.S. Olson (eds.): CHI'91 Conference Proceedings, 257 - 263. and Palmiter, S., J. Elkerton, et al. (1991). Animated Demonstrations vs Written Instructions for Learning Procedural Tasks: A Preliminary Investigation. International Journal of Man-Machine Studies 34 (1991), 687 - 701. showed that a film with animated demonstrations are superior for learning both in speed and accuracy during training sessions of highly graphical systems.

[3] see Eales, R. T. J. and J. Welsh (1995). Design for Collaborative Learnability. Computer Support for Collaborative Learning '95. October 17-20, 1995 Indiana University, Bloomington, Indiana U.S.A..

[4] see Alpert, S. R., M. K. Singley, et al. (1995). "Multiple Multimodal Mentors: Delivering Computer-Based Instruction via Specialized Anthropomorphic Advisors." Behaviour & Information Technology **14**(2): 69 - 79., 72.

learning history and to open the access to the competence of peers. The learners might exchange their problems and solutions by this means. They can exchange problems and solutions through a database network so that co-operative work is supported more effectively than by a mail system.

The human's ability exploited by a demotheque is what is called "episodic memory". Episodic memory is an individual's memory for the unique personal experiences. Episodic memory can be contrasted with "semantic memory", which is a person's memory for facts. While people are relatively poor at remembering facts, they are often very good at remembering sequences of past episodes. A demotheque presents crucial information as a virtual key about an episode that helps people to remember additional information about that episode.

Written or spoken memos and commented or mute interaction recordings can be produced by the learner on the fly. An easy to use interface can allow for creating, editing and storing memos or recordings. Memos can, e.g., be produced by clicking on a memo icon, i.e., a needle in the toolbar of the application and dragging the needle to the element of the application's interface the memo is meant for. With releasing the mouse button a small yellow[5] "Post-it" window appears as shown in figure 2 and allows for editing a new memo and also referring to earlier ones. The needle signifying the memo to the given element of the application is displayed to the user for later use.

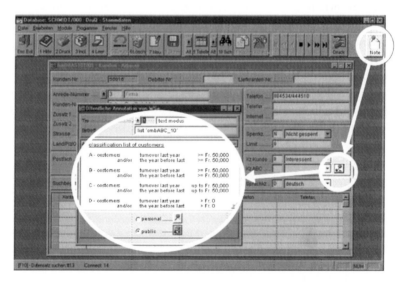

Figure 2. Annotation button ("note"), annotation display and annotation edit window

---

[5]   Analogous to the yellow Post-it™

Video clips can be produced by identifying portions of an interaction sequence containing problems the learner has encountered or solutions s/he has found when using the application. The sequence can be defined from a continuous stream of background recording of, say, 2 hours interaction time automatically stored by the system during the task accomplishment or exploration. The learner can verbally, graphically or in writing comment on them, and store sequences as episodes in a multimedia database called 'demotheque'.

5. COMMUNICATION FACILITIES

For a maintenance field we have developed another prototype for situated learning. During maintenance tasks the service man often occurs situations where he faces new problems or finds new solutions for technical machineries. For situated support by remote peer experts he might want to document features of the machinery as textual, verbal or video annotations. For such annotations we have developed a mobile collector for a tablet PC. The content of the mobile collector can in situ be sent to the remote peer expert for consultancy or be stored in the 'demotheque' for own later use in similar maintenance situations.

As mentioned in several examples above learning in the working environment takes place in a social context. People have similar tasks using similar applications. They consult and support each other and exchange experiences and solutions. Technical support should enable the users to send and receive typical solutions (demo recordings) found by an individual. For exploiting distributed experiences the learners can exchange episodes that describe questions, problems with the tool, or breakdowns when using the tool. Recordings can also be sent as a request for off-line help to a consultant to make both the learner and the consulted expert (or power user) more independent from verbal explanations of errors or recommendations. Episodes that describe users' personal experiences of solutions can be made available to a group of users in a cooperative 'demotheque'. The cooperative 'demotheque' contains such recordings that are not only of individual value but also expected to be of use for a community of users, i.e., being typical for the user group, their tasks or their tools. Support facilities will be provided for different interaction types between a user and a consultant. The user can (a) explore problems and solutions on his or her own (no social interaction at all), the user can (b) consult somebody face-to-face (typically a peer expert, a power user or a member of the decentralised local support unit) or the user can (c) consult somebody remote (typically a specialist of the central user support unit). The consultation can happen synchronously and asynchronously. Table 2 shows supporting illustration facilities for different (inter-action) types.

Table 2. Kinds of (inter)actions for different time and site conditions

User-consultant interaction Time of interaction	user alone	face-to-face	remote
synchronous			consultation with shared screen about recordings about the current errors or problems and the current solutions
asynchronous	(explorative) learning with a recording or memo about the past (errors or problems)and for the future (solutions)	consultation with recordings or memos about the past (errors or problems) and for the future (solutions)	consultation with the user's recordings or memos about the past and presence (errors or problems) and the consultant's recording or memos for the future (solutions)

Memos and recorded interaction sequences can be supported by retrieval facilities. It is not sufficient for the learner to know that there is an explaining memo or demo. The learner also has to be supported in finding them in the later context with a similar error or problem as occurred earlier when s/he created the memo or demo. The retrieval task will be addressed by several approaches. Memos will be directly displayed by an icon (needle) indicating the existence and the status of the memo, i.e., whether it is meant to be a personal or a public one. Recordings cannot be presented directly mainly because they do not refer to an interface element of the application but to a process of interaction with several functions of the application. Indirect access will be provided to help the learner to find appropriate demos, e.g., via the title the user has specified when creating the demo, the time the demo was stored, and the document, the application and the function of the application the demo refers to. The exploitation of memos and recorded interactions can be increased by agent technology that supports the organisation, retrieval and application of memos and demos in the new context. Each situation of exploration, error, problem, or solution is specific. The transfer of experience from one learning episode to another has to take into account the limited similarity of characteristics and select appropriate reference memos or demos. This selection and presentation can be supported by an intelligent agent.

In the following table the methods of learning support tools are shown on a glance:

Table 3. Components of learning support tools

Individual memos:	The user can stick an electronic description to system elements to explain system features used for individual needs.
Recording interactions:	The user can replay and explore his or her own interaction history (e.g., an error situation).
Defining relevant demos:	The user can select a relevant episode and keep it for similar future situations in a personal 'demotheque'.
Annotating demos:	The user can add comments and warnings referring to what he or she has done. Different modes of annotations should help to avoid information overload of a single sense organ.
Retrieving demos:	The user can select different access methods to retrieve the relevant episode from the demotheque. The retrieval can be supported by an agent.
Selecting Views:	The user can select different kinds of views to exploit a relevant episode from the 'demotheque' for supporting the re-learning of a solution and for supporting the transfer of the solution to the current task.
Exchanging questions and answers:	A remote consultation can be supported to enable the user and the consultant to exchange questions and answers independent of their time and space constraints.
Exchanging solutions:	The users of a co-operative work environment can exchange task and tool competence by providing and requesting solutions typical of the workspace.

6. SUMMARY AND CONCLUSION

Ubiquitous computing and ubiquitous learning are different phenomena but they can benefit from each other. Ubiquitous computing provides computing power everywhere and everywhen without focusing computers as dedicated machines at dedicated locations. Ubiquitous computing aims at integrating computing power into environments in working and every day sectors. Ubiquitous learning also considers learning as not restricted to dedicated periods and dedicated institutions as educational tasks with active teachers and receptive students but ubiquitous learning considers the acquisition of knowledge and skills as continuous activities during problem solving, task accomplishment and serendipity driven activities. Situatedness of learning can build a symbiosis of computing facilities and learning readiness in the context where the subject develops new knowledge and competence. From the technology side mobile and networked systems are needed together with software tools for receiving and creating snippets of learning units integrated into the individual process of activities. From the mental side of the individual a constructive understanding of work and competence development is needed together with a responsible social role in cooperative teams. Examples have been shown for this kind of learning and learning support in the area of step by step acquirement of explorative tool and procedure competence with technology by integrated notes and demo exchange facilities, in the area of situated on demand information in arranged environments during mobile activities (e.g. exhibitions and museums) and in the area of maintenance where service personnel gets consultation and documentation support for its own and community problem solving capability. Both are needed: technological progress in designing and maturing flexible and intuitive solutions of systems as well as mental and social strategies and habits of creative and progressive competence production.

REFERENCES

Ackerman, M. S. and T. W. Malone (1990). "Answer Garden: A tool for growing organizational memory." Proceedings of the Conference on Office Information Systems **11**: 31-39.

Alpert, S. R., M. K. Singley, et al. (1995). "Multiple Multimodal Mentors: Delivering Computer-Based Instruction via Specialized Anthropomorphic Advisors." Behaviour & Information Technology **14**(2): 69 - 79.

Anderson, J. R. (1976). Language, Memory, and Thought. Hillsdale, N.J.: Lawrence Erlbaum Associates.

Bannon, L. J. (1986). Helping Users Help Each Other. User Centered System Design. New Perspectives on Human-Computer Interaction. D. A. Norman and S. W. Draper. Hillsdale, N.J., London, Lawrence Erlbaum Associates: 399 - 410.

Berlin, L. M., R. Jeffries, et al. (1993). Where Did You Put It? Issues in the Design and Use of a Group Memory. In: Proceedings INTERCHI '93, pp. 23-30.

Brancheau, J. C., D. R. Vogel, et al. (1985). An Investigation of the Information Center from the User's Perspective. Data Base 17 (1985), 1, 4 - 17.

Brezizinski, R. (1987). When it's Time to Tear Down the Info Center. Datamation 33 (1988), 21, 73 - 82.

Brockmann, R. J. (1990). Writing better Computer User Documentation: From Paper to Hypertext. New York: John Wiley & Sons.

Carroll, J. M. (1990). The Nurnberg Funnel: Designing Minimalist Instruction for Practical Computer Skill. Cambridge, MA: MIT Press.

Carroll, J. M. and M. B. Rosson (1987). Paradox of the Active User. Interfacing Thought. Cognitive Aspects of Human-Computer Interaction. J. M. Carroll. Cambridge, Mass., London, The MIT Press: 80-111.

Dutke, S. and W. Schönpflug (1987). When the introductionary period is over: Learning while doing one's job. Psychological Issues of Human-Computer Interaction in the Work Place. M. Frese, E. Ulich and W. Dzida. Amsterdam, Elsevier Science Publishers B.V. (North-Holland): 295 - 310.

Eales, R. T. J. and J. Welsh (1995). Design for Collaborative Learnability. Computer Support for Collaborative Learning '95. October 17-20, 1995 Indiana University, Bloomington, Indiana U.S.A.

Fox, T. (2001). Präsentation neuer interaktiver Lehrmedien in der Sonographie. Dreiländertreffen DEGUM -SGUM - ÖGUM, Nürnberg.

Fox, T., G. Grunst, et al. (1994). HyPLAN: A Context-Sensitive Hypermedia Help System. Adaptive User Support. Ergonomic Design of Manually and Automatically Adaptable Software. R. Oppermann. Hillsdale, New Jersey, Lawrence Erlbaum Associates: 126 - 193.

Galili, I., S. Ben Dall, et al. (1993). "The effects of prior knowledge and instruction on understanding image formation." Journal of research in science teaching 30(3): 271-301.

Goßmann, J. and M. Specht (2001). Location Models for Augmented Environments. Ubicomp Workshop on Location Modelling for Ubiquitous Computing, Atlanta, USA.

Grunst, G., T. Fox, et al. (1995). Szenische Enablingsysteme - Trainingsumgebungen in der Echokardiographie. In: Ulrich Glowalla/Erhard Engelmann/Arnould de Kemp/Gerhard Rosbach/Eric Schoop (Hrsg.): Deutscher Multimedia Kongreß '95. Auffahrt zum Information Highway, S. 174 - 178.

Hazan, Y. (1995). A comparison between the facilitative effects of three second language prior knowledge activation methods in relation to specific fields. School of Education, Tel-Aviv University, Israel.

Hillgren, P.-A. and E. B. Bjorgvinsson (2002). Readymade design at an Intensive Care Unit. Participatory Design Conference 2002, Malmö, Sweden.

Horton, W. K. (1990). Designing & Writing Online Documentation: Help Files to Hypertext. New York: John Wiley & Sons.

Kidd, J. R. (1977). How Adults learn. New York: Associated Press.

Knowles, M. S. (1973). The Adult Learner: A Neglected Species. Houston: Gulf Publishing Company, American Society for Training and Development.

Lave, J. and E. Wenger (1991). Situated Learning: Legitimate Peripheral Participation. Cambridge, Cambridge University Press.

Liechti, M. (1988). Das "Information Center" - wichtige Supportstelle im Betrieb, 1. Teil, io Management-Zeitschrift 57 (1988), 574-575.

Lovett, C. M. and R. J. Anderson (1996). "History of success and current context in problem solving: Combined influences on operator selection." Cognitive Psychology 31: 168-217.

McCloskey, M. (1983). " The intuitive physics." Scientific American 48: 114-122.

Moning, U. and B. Winkelmann (1993). Entwicklungsphasen von Information Center, Ergebnisse einer empirischen Untersuchung über betriebliche Endbenutzerunterstützung in der Schweiz. In: Wirtschaftsinformatik, 6 (1993), 532-541.

Nardi, B. A. (1993). A Small Matter of Programming. Perspectives on End User Computing. Cambridge MS, The MIT Press.

Norman, D. A. and J. C. Spohrer (1996). "Learner-Centered Education. Introduction." Communications of the ACM 39(4): 24 - 27.

O'Malley, C. E. (1986). Helping Users Helping Themselves. User Centered System Design. New Perspectives on Human-Computer Interaction. D. A. Norman and S. W. Draper. Hillsdale, N.J., London, Lawrence Erlbaum Associates, Publishers: 377 - 398.

Oppermann, R. and M. Specht (1999). "A Nomadic Information System for Adaptive Exhibition Guidance." Archives and Museum Informatics. Cultural Heritage Informatics Quarterly 13(2): 127 - 138.

Oppermann, R. and M. Specht (2000). A Context-Sensitive Nomadic Exhibition Guide. Handheld and Ubiquitous Computing. Second International Symposium, HUC 2000, 25-27 September 2000, Bristol, UK, Springer.

Palmiter, S. and J. Elkerton (1991). An Evaluation of Animated Demonstrations for Learning Computer-based Tasks. In: S. P.

Robertson/G.M. Olson/J.S. Olson (eds.): CHI'91 Conference Proceedings, 257 - 263.

Palmiter, S., J. Elkerton, et al. (1991). Animated Demonstrations vs Written Instructions for Learning Procedural Tasks: A Preliminary Investigation. International Journal of Man-Machine Studies 34 (1991), 687 - 701.

Paul, H. (1995). Exploratives Agieren. Ein Beitrag zur ergonomischen Gestaltung interaktiver Systeme. Frankfurt am Main, Peter Lang Verlag.

Rickel, J. and L. W. Johnson (1997). Integrating Pedagogical Agents in a virtual Environment for Training. Proceedings of the First International Conference on Autonomous Agents (Agents'97).

Rumelhart, D. E. (1980). Schemata: The building blocks of cognition. In; R.J. Spiro/B.C. Bruce/W.F. Brewer (Eds.): Theoretical Issues in Reading Comprehension. Hillsdale, N.J., London: Lawrence Erlbaum Associates, Publishers.

Santhanam, R. and S. Wiedenbeck (1993). Neither novice nor expert: the discretionary user of software. International Journal of Man-Machine Studies 38 (1993), 2, 201 - 229.

Schank, R. C. and A. Kass (1996). A Goal-Based Scenario for High School Students. Communications of the ACM 39 (1996), 4, 28 - 29.

Schoen, D. A. (1990). Educating the Reflective Practitioner. San Francisco, Oxford: Jossey Bass Publishers.

Suchman, L. A. (1987). Plans and Situated Actions. Cambridge: Cambridge University Press, UK.

Terveen, L. G., P. G. Selfrigde, et al. (1993). From "Folklore" To "Living Design Memory". In: Proceedings INTERCHI '93, pp. 15-22.

Waern, Y. (1993). "Varieties of learning to use computer tools." Computers in Human Behavior 9: 323-339.

Whittlesea, W. A. B. and L. R. Wright (1997). "Implicit (and explicit) learning: acting adaptively without knowing the consequences." Journal of experimental psychology: learning, memory, and cognition 23(1): 181-200.

Williams, T. R. and D. K. Farkas (1992). Minimalism Reconsidered: Should we Design Documentation for Exploratory Learning? SIGCHI Bulletin 24 (1992), 2, 41 - 50.

Chapter 5

EDUCATION IN THE KNOWLEDGE AGE – ENGAGING LEARNERS THROUGH KNOWLEDGE BUILDING

Seng Chee Tan[1], David Hung[2] and Marlene Scardamalia[3]

[1,2]Nanyang Technological University, Singapore; [3]University of Toronto, Canada

Abstract: In this Knowledge Age or innovation-driven age, knowledge is a key asset for a society to create value.   The health and wealth of societies depend increasingly on the capacity of people to innovate (Scardamalia & Bereiter, in press 2002).   Since schools are responsible for preparing the young for the future they have to be models of innovation, where teachers and students are "willing to take new routes, try different methods, and occasionally break the mould" (Shanmugaratnam, 2003). Too often, however, we find classroom pedagogies varying between two extremes: didactic knowledge transmission where teachers are the "sage on the stage", or constructivist approaches where students are actively engaged on activities.   The former approach is often criticized for treating students as a passive party, assuming that knowledge can be transmitted and assimilated into the student's mind. The latter approach, on the other hand, has the tendency to motivate students to complete tasks and activities, but not necessarily engaged with the knowledge creation process. In this chapter, we argue that we should engage our students directly in knowledge production, not so much of asking students to produce new knowledge or discoveries, but putting them into a development trajectory to be knowledge producers. Examples of knowledge building classrooms in Canada and Singapore schools will be used to illustrate how we can engage students as knowledge producers, who take on ownership of learning by collaboratively and continually improve upon their initial ideas to better ideas, thus advancing collective knowledge within the community.

Keywords: engaged learning, knowledge building, constructivist learning, Knowledge Forum, professional development, Computer-Supported Collaborative Learning

1.   CONSTRUCTIVIST EPISTEMOLOGY AND ENGAGED LEARNING

In the past two decades, constructivism has become a dominant epistemology, gradually replacing the objectivist and positivist paradigm in many parts of the world. Constructivism, deriving from multiple roots in the

D. Hung and M.S. Khine (eds.), Engaged Learning with Emerging Technologies, 91-106.

psychology and philosophy of the last century (Perkins, 1991), holds that meaning is imposed by our interpretation of the world; there are many ways to structure and interpret the world, and there are many meanings and perspectives for any event or concept (Duffy & Jonassen, 1992). Constructivist learning is manifested as different types of classroom activities: guided discovery, learning through problem solving, curiosity-driven inquiry, etc. (Bereiter & Scardamalia, 1996).

One of the strands of constructivist educational reform that involve educational technology is the notion of *engaged learning*. Engaged learning is based on studies from the North Central Regional Education Laboratory (NCREL), Stanford Research Institute (SRI), and other research institutions. The notion of engaged learning is represented in the indicators for engaged learning developed by Jones, Valdez, Nowakowski, and Rasmussen from NCREL (1994). There are 8 proposed indicators, which are summarized as follows:

1. Vision for learning: The vision is to nurture engaged learners who are actively involved and committed in their own learning, who develop a repertoire of thinking/learning strategies, and who develop new ideas collaboratively, with passion for learning.
2. Tasks: Learning tasks should be authentic and addressing personal interest, should be challenging yet not too frustrating, and should involve multidisciplinary knowledge.
3. Assessment: assessment should be performance based, which is integrated in the learning process and is culturally fair.
4. Instructional model: The instructional approach should be interactive and generative, gearing towards meaning construction.
5. Learning context: Learning should occur collaboratively, valuing multiple perspectives and diversity.
6. Grouping: grouping should be heterogeneous and flexible, providing equitable experience for all students.
7. Teacher roles: Teachers act as facilitators, guiding students in learning or acting as co-learners.
8. Student roles: Students act as explorers of new ideas, cognitive apprentice of their mentors, instructors to their peers, and producer of products of real use to themselves and to others.

Engaged learning adopts a problem-based or project-based learning approach (Meehan & Nolan, 2001). Developed by K-12 teachers, a project typically includes an authentic ill-structured problem, data or data collection activities, learning units, references, and report writing. Instructions are provided to teachers to help them in scaffolding the students towards completing the projects.

While moving away from the knowledge transmission model of the objectivist paradigm, problem-based or project-based learning may suffer from one common pitfall – focusing on activities rather than knowledge creation. No doubt starting with good intention, if the instructions are not executed appropriately, the end results might be students buzzing with activities – collecting data, preparing presentations, locating references, writing reports – but not engaged in deep understanding and creative work with ideas. These approaches engage students in interesting tasks through which they actively construct meaning, but often remain focused on the completion of fairly short-term tasks or projects with pre-defined rather than emergent goals. When the task is over there is need for someone to set the next motivating activity for them, as they have not internalized the processes through which ideas of value to a community are generated and continually improved. The agency for and power of knowledge creation remain in the hands of others, instead of the learners. In this chapter, we embrace the vision of engaged learning, but we suggest engaging students through knowledge building, that is, to "move ideas to the center" where students deal directly with the problems of knowledge (Scardamalia, 1999). In the following sections, we shall explain the knowledge building approach and Knowledge Forum, the supporting technology. We will then illustrate the notion of knowledge building with an example in professional education of a group of Master degree students.

2.   ENGAGING K-12 LEARNERS THROUGH KNOWLEDGE BUILDING

What is knowledge building and why might it be an appropriate method of education in the Knowledge Age?

"Knowledge building may be defined as the production and continual improvement of ideas of value to a community, through means that increase the likelihood that what the community accomplishes will be greater than the sum of individual contributions and part of broader cultural efforts." Scardamalia & Bereiter (2002)

Knowledge building engages learners (K-12 and beyond) directly in knowledge creation. The process involves theorizing, invention, and design, as in real world knowledge creating communities (e.g. scientific communities). It is collaborative in nature, with the goal of advancing "public knowledge" – ideas that are available to members in the community to work on and improve upon. Unlike many constructivist activities, the learners deal directly with the problem of knowledge. In the process they complete tasks and activities, but the driving force is their wonderment and efforts to deepen their understanding, not the requirement to complete an assignment.

Perhaps an example will best illustrate the knowledge building approach. In a study by Lamon, Reeve, & Scardamalia (2001), 22 students in one Grade 5/6 classroom at the Institute of Child Study Laboratory School of the University of Toronto were engaged in knowledge building in physical science over the course of an academic year.

"The teacher began by asking students to bring in questions and ideas from newspapers, television and other sources that interested them. As so often happens, events in the world coincidentally met with learning goals: At the beginning of this year the Swiss Air Flight 111 crashed off the coast of Nova Scotia and Ontario had an earthquake both of which became objects for ongoing discourse.

All questions were written on index cards and posted to a bulletin board in the classroom and each day several were discussed. As one example, there were reports that American currency had been on the Swiss Air Flight 111. Students wondered whether the money would disintegrate in salt water. One student's parent was in Scotland and was directed to bring back salt water from the Atlantic Ocean. Students submerged an American dollar into the salt water, put the container in the refrigerator and observed what happened to the money. This was the beginning of inquiry time, a single period each day of the week, with students' questions leading the work and little teacher guidance at this point. We have found that a slow period of getting started, where the children feel ownership of the questions and the teacher keeps the 'ends-in-view', is very productive as a way into sustained investigations by the children. The emphasis on conducting experiments as the dollar example shows was also important to students."

During this time students also began to create their Knowledge Forum database. The teacher had intended to call the database "Wings, Weather and the World" to follow the intended curriculum focus but students came up with the name "Chance, Challenge and Change" which they believed mapped onto their questions and concerns more closely so this was the name used…"

In the above example, the students took ownership in initiating questions and ideas that lead to problem investigations about physical science based on their feeling about some real life event. It was a collaborative process and ideas were made public in Knowledge Forum, an online forum, so that they can be built on and improved upon. The teachers are engaged along with students in identifying and refining goals and plans as they pursue investigations. The learning episode demonstrated the indicators of engaged learning (Jones, Valdez, Nowakowski, and Rasmussen from NCREL, 1994). Most importantly, the students were engaged directly in sustained investigation of problems related to concepts of physical science, instead of solving problems pre-selected by teachers. Like the NCREL's model of engaged learning, knowledge building uses technology (Knowledge Forum) to augment the generative and interaction processes among learners.

3.   TECHNOLOGY SUPPORT FOR KNOWLEDGE CREATION

Knowledge Forum can be regarded as a Computer-Supported Collaborative Learning (CSCL) tool, or more specifically a knowledge building environment (Scardamalia, 2003) that mediates the process of collaboration among learners; promotes inquiry, sense-making and reflective thinking; facilitates knowledge building; and provides record keeping. It is designed based on research studies by Scardamalia and Bereiter and Scandamalia (1996) aimed at fostering knowledge building communities in schools. It provides an environment where ideas are discussed and improved through discourse in a productive knowledge building community.

In Knowledge Forum, a graphical interface known as a View (Figure 1) allows conceptual organization of ideas. A main View can be linked to other Views which represent alternate representations of the same ideas or provide more detailed information. Messages (called Notes) are linked graphically, showing the flow and development of ideas. Learners can post, reflect, link, relate and question ideas posted by themselves or others, thus making the knowledge-construction process overt and traceable.

Another unique feature of Knowledge Forum is customizable scaffolds that facilitate knowledge building discourse. For instance, to support inquiry-based knowledge building, student may be asked to post notes using the following labels: "My theory", "I need to understand", "My theory doesn't explain", or "A better theory is". These are cognitive supports which model and encourage learners to engage in more in-depth inquiry rather than superficial chatting.

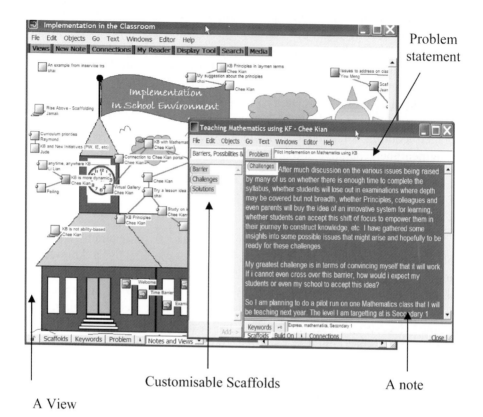

Figure 1. A discussion in Knowledge Forum®

Scardamalia (2004) explained the affordances of Knowledge Forum in supporting knowledge building process:

1. It fosters multiple perspectives, multiple literacies, and team work by providing a graphical medium where *views* (a new view is like a blank sheet of paper where graphics and notes can be added) can be created for discussion on different topics; allowing use of text, graphics, and multimedia to input ideas; allowing individual or group design of views and notes.

2. It creates connections and pubic knowledge by allowing ideas to be linked in various ways: building on, citation, annotation, and references.

3. It supports knowledge building through its customizable scaffolds and it emphasizes problem of understanding by providing a problem field at the header of a note.

4. It encourages rise above and improvable ideas by allowing review and revision of notes, publications of views, and a "rise above" function which allows users to synthesize or summarize ideas at a higher level.

5. It affords building of individual and group portfolios through creation of individual or group "views" that can be linked.

6. It makes ideas and artifacts as objects of inquiry. By putting ideas in Knowledge Forum, they are subject to review, critique or comment by other members. The historical interactions of these processes are automatically captured in the database. Thus ideas in mind (implicit knowledge) become "objects" that can be acted and improved upon.

7. It allows embedded and transformative assessment by allowing searching and tracking of contribution from individuals and groups, and concurrent feedback to these processes.

4. KNOWLEDGE BUILDING IN TRANSITION IN SINGAPORE SCHOOLS: SETTING THE CONTEXT

Knowledge building, supported by Knowledge Forum, has been introduced to K-12 schools in Singapore over the last few years, through collaboration with the Ontario Institute for Studies in Education. The initial implementations were disappointing. Knowledge Forum was not seen as an integral part of the curriculum and learning activities; students used it to chat about social issues rather than to present ideas and develop knowledge. When interviewed, students' responses exhibited no motivation or disposition for knowledge construction and knowledge building. Classroom practices were generally traditional where teachers' talk occupied most of the curriculum time.

As a result of these frustrations and the inability to penetrate into the traditional epistemologies and pedagogies of the standard classroom, we decided to begin the process among our graduate students who were school teachers. We hypothesized that if we could gradually enculturate these teachers into the process and epistemology of knowledge building, they would be able to make an impact with their learners in the classrooms. These graduate students needed to do a thesis as part of their Masters' course and the dissertations centered on a problem or issue (e.g. problems in knowledge building.) For example, one of the graduate student-teacher implemented knowledge building among the low-achievers in her school, and because these students had a more flexible curriculum where technology was central, knowledge building was a success.

As we reflected on the different attempts made by these graduate students, we recognized that professional development and deep integration of knowledge building into the life of the classroom are essential to the success of knowledge building pedagogy and technologies. In the sections below, we describe our attempts at developing a professional development framework for teachers.

5.   KNOWLEDGE BUILDING IN PROFESSIONAL DEVELOPMENT AMONG TEACHERS AS LEARNERS – A CASE EXAMPLE

In this example, we describe a class taught at the National Institute of Education in Singapore, which served as a basis for engaging professionals in a design process for next-generation educational environments. We elaborate the ways in which these professionals have been able to integrate knowledge building into their own work and into classrooms in Singapore and Canada.

The class consisted of 16 adult learners participating in a Master level course on knowledge building. Among the participants, there were 11 K-12 teachers, one Education Technology Officer from the Ministry of Education and four adult learners working in training industry. In addition, 12 other participants were purposefully invited to encourage greater diversity of ideas among the group. These nine participants include officers from the Ministry of Education, teachers, and post-graduate students. The instructors were the authors of this chapter, as well as the principal and two teachers from the Institute of Child Study, Ontario. We were also joined by several researchers from Canada. In the discussion that follows, participants refer to both the post-graduate students and the invited guests.

The course started with a 5-day workshop and sharing of case examples of knowledge building in Canadian and Singapore classrooms. The participants then discussed the theoretical and practical issues of knowledge building in Singapore context. We shall first summarize how it corresponds to the NCREL's indicators of engaged learning, followed by discussion of participant engagement in sustained knowledge building.

Vision for learning	The course fostered the creation of a knowledge building community; participants engaged in theoretical discussions and practical implementation of knowledge building in their schools or work place.
Tasks	During the five-day workshop, the participants were engaged in group discussions about knowledge building principles and issues. After, they explored the theoretical issues further, implementing the approach in their work place, or contributing to the knowledge of the community in other ways.
Assessment	The participants were assessed based on their continual contributions to the knowledge of the community, using Knowledge Forum database as the main medium for recording the contribution. There was no special paper or assignment to deliver; the participants were assessed based on their participation and contribution. The participants could choose their own way of contributing to the knowledge database – contributing new ideas, sharing experience in implementation, conducting a literature review, etc.
Instructional model	Knowledge building pedagogy, as discussed in the earlier section, was adopted.
Learning context	The approach was collaborative. All discussions or implementation of knowledge building were based on local context.
Grouping	As described above, the participants came from diverse background. Diversity of ideas was evident throughout the course, which will be elaborated below.
Teacher roles	The instructors shared their experience, encouraged diversity of views, and learned from and mentored participants who wanted to implement the knowledge building approach.
Student roles	The participants contributed new ideas and improved on ideas suggested by their peers so that the knowledge was useful to the community. A number of participants formed small teams to support each other in the implementation of the approach in their work place.

6.   ENGAGEMENT IN KNOWLEDGE BUILDING

In this professional education case, the participants were building knowledge on knowledge building (perhaps we can call it meta-knowledge building). In the following section, our discussion focuses on some indicators of engaged learning that arose from the interactions among the participants.

1. There was collective responsibility for contributing to community knowledge.
    Throughout the workshop, we saw active engagement of all participants (including MA students, guests, and instructors) discussing knowledge building issues. There were scheduled sessions during which the instructors shared their views or experience in knowledge building, but they were conscious about giving sufficient opportunities for the participants' voices to be heard. As such, the participants did not hesitate to seek clarification, voice different opinions, offer suggestions, propose solutions to problems, etc. This active participation occurred both in face-to-face interaction, as well as in online discussion via Knowledge Forum. Data on Knowledge Forum use showed that more than 450 notes were contributed within the 5-day workshop, with an average of about 14 notes contributed by each participant. The average number of notes read by each participant was about 240. This suggests engagement and collective responsibility by all members contributing to the knowledge database of the community.

2. Participants, as epistemic agents, initiated discussion of authentic issues in their local context.
    The instructors were mindful of the power relationship in class. While sharing of theories and experience were typically initiated by the instructors, they consciously engaged the participants in conversation. The instructors were addressed by first names instead of by professional titles (which is uncommon in an Asian classroom culture). The participants took ownership of the knowledge building tasks, often initiating discussion of real life issues in local context. For example, in the discussion of implementation issues of knowledge building in classrooms, the participations raised concerns on various pertinent issues: obstacles presented by exam-oriented culture, sustaining student motivation, limitation of curriculum time, using Knowledge Forum for mathematics education, challenge of scaffolding students, and viability

of other system besides Knowledge Forum. This particular forum was entirely "owned" by the participants, with about 120 notes contributed.

3. Diversity of ideas was professionally handled.

    In the class, it was common for participants to voice differing opinions, presenting arguments for their positions with good reasons. Respect for differing ideas was evident in discourse recorded in Knowledge Forum. The following extracts show several participants reacting to the comment on examination initiated by one participant (words in square bracket [ ] are scaffolds provided in Knowledge Forum):

A: [Opinion] My opinion is that we, the teachers, are bounded very much by the requirements of exams. [Evidence] The fact that schools are ranked based on their Exam results itself restricts and confines teachers to what needs and has to be taught.

B: [Opinion] KNOWLEDGE FORUM is supposed to help pupils get better results when they sit for examination at the end of the year - isn't it? [Elaboration] Idea : I teach a topic on Water - pupils have problem with water cycle and its processes like condensation, evaporation, etc. I get the pupils to discuss the topic of water cycle via KNOWLEDGE FORUM. And HOPEFULLY at the end of the year when they sit for the examination, they will be able to fare better, with a deeper understanding of the topic due to their active participation on the KNOWLEDGE FORUM - what do you all think?

C: [This theory cannot explain] why the philosophy and pedagogy of KNOWLEDGE BUILDING cannot find a place in our school and society. [My theory] Is that it does not reside in our culture because teachers and parents do not see the far reaching implications of education? That we are ultimately producing citizens of the future and not just people who can pass exams. Even though we idolise these "icons" of out antiquated education system.

D: [Opinion] I feel that we should also consider our students. Many of them have been 'inculcated' into an education system which has not really emphasised self-learning but has become rather 'exam focused'. Students tend to expect answers from teachers and any attempts to get them to do self-learning is a best met with apathy. They do not want to take responsibility for their learning as they want just the answers to get 'A's in exams.

4. Ideas were improved continually.
   One of the affordances of Knowledge Forum is making idea public to the members within a community, thus achieving inter-subjectivity among the members and ideas could continually be improved. The following extracts of discourse showed a typical example of idea improvement. The idea of co-constructing learning environment becomes more defined through the discussion.

   A: [My theory] The use of knowledge building in Classrooms would require a lot of classroom participation from the students. What I should do so that my students would be in a 'safe and secure' environment that they be able to express their views freely without being laughed at or put down.

   B: [My theory] Ask your pupils how they could contribute to creating such an environment. They may have some good ideas. Sometimes, we forget that our key stakeholders, our pupils, can help us find the answers.

   C: Students and teachers co-constructing a new learning environment interactively. This will be a new environment.

   D: [I need to understand] the term co-construction, are you referring to an environment as a design product whose creators are the teachers or are both pupils and teachers co-creators? [A better theory] would be perhaps viewing design as a dynamic process where the environment is never fully completed i.e. the environment is in a constant state of flux (it is not a terminal product) where the designers design and re-design based on the constant feedback of the users into the design process (based on the work of Finnish product designers).

5. There was sustained knowledge building.
   Though the MA students could choose how to contribute to the knowledge building database, the majority (more than 60%) took the challenging option of implementing knowledge building in their classrooms. A few participants who could not implement it due to constraints helped their peers to co-design the knowledge building activities. As a result, the participants moved from the forum that talks *about* knowledge building, to forums in individual classrooms where school students were engaged in knowledge building, and eventually their reflections of the implementation experience in the original forum

further enhanced the community knowledge. The following extracts showed some of their reflections three months after the workshop:

A: One of the first thoughts that came to my mind was how this knowledge building concept can be built into the peer mentoring programme in my school. Teachers tend to be privatised in their practice. One of my greatest challenges is to get teachers to break out of this and share...How can the tacit knowledge and experiences of the teachers involved in the peer mentoring programme be archived in some form so that it can benefit a larger circle of teachers who may not be directly involved in this programme? These are questions where technology such as Knowledge Forum can help.

B: I have discovered that before I can start a knowledge building community, I need to have a community built first. I have observed that the students in my class were more or less not so enthusiastic in posting on Knowledge Forum when I first started. This could be due to the fact that the students were 'new' to each other and thus 'shy' and not so willing to share.

C: From what I've attempted so far and my own readings of research on collaborative knowledge building, I feel there are four main challenges I have to overcome. Balancing the tension of a traditional direct instructional teacher-centred approach to teaching and learning vs a student-centered constructivist approach to teaching and learning. The challenge is to get the students to become independent learners and be interested in actively engaging themselves in productive discourse about the content. Often students expect answers from teachers and are lazy to look for answers themselves. I have to foster in my students a 'knowledge building attitude'...

Teachers in Singapore are not accustomed to adopting knowledge building dispositions such as collective responsibility and the pursuit for the improvement of ideas. Such actions and thinking dispositions are not commonly present in the schools and classrooms. When these teachers were gathered together around the Masters' class taught at the National Institute of Education, a knowledge building community evolved over a period of time. During this period, these teachers became gradually acquainted with both the theoretical and practical dimensions of knowledge building. It was only through experimentation with these concepts in their own settings that the value of knowledge building became apparent. These powerful concepts of responsibility and engagement became fruitful and an eye-opening experience for these teachers.

7.   CONCLUSION

To be a confident citizen in this Knowledge Age requires the ability to continually advance knowledge collaboratively. This is of great individual and social value, and applies not just to elite professionals, but to everyone.

The recent trend towards constructivist learning arises from changing demands as well as discontent with the didactic paradigm of instruction. Knowledge building is consistent with the social constructivist philosophy in engaging learners in meaningful learning. By engaging learners directly in working with knowledge, it avoids the pitfall of many constructivist approaches that focus on task completion. It empowers people to be knowledge agents, able to self initiate the creation of new ideas, to share ideas with the public, and to improve upon them. Moreover, learning provides access to existing knowledge and preserves the cultural capital of a society; knowledge building enhances the cultural capacity through new ideas and values that are continually generated and improved.

Our example tells a success story of fostering professionals in education in collaborative knowledge building by encouraging creation and continual improvement of ideas, making ideas accessible to participants in a knowledge building community, providing a shared workspace for collaborative works, and empowering participants to be epistemic agents. It is not an isolated success story; other cases of knowledge building have been reported (see Caswell & Lamon, 1998; Hakkareinen, 2003; Hewitt, 2001; Lamon, Reeves, & Scardamalia, 2001).

In short, we agree with the constructivist epistemology and the notion of engaged learning, but we advocate engaging learners through knowledge building.

REFERENCES

Bereiter, C., & Scardamalia, M.   (1996). Rethinking learning.   In D.R. Olson, & N. Torrance   (Eds.), *The handbook of education and human development: New models of learning, teaching and schooling* (pp. 485-513).   Cambridge, MA: Basil Blackwell.

Casewell, B., Lamon, M.   (1998).   Development of scientific literacy: The evolution of ideas in a Grade Four knowledge-building classroom. Paper presented at the Annual Meeting of the American Educational Research Association, San Diego, CA, April 13-17.

Drucker, P.   (1985).   Innovation and entrepreneurship: Practice and principles.   New York: Harper and Row

Duffy, T. & Jonassen, D. (Eds.) (1992). Constructivism: New implications for instructional technology. In T.M. Duffy & D.H. Jonassen (Eds.), *Constructivism and the technology of instruction: A conversation* (pp. 1-16). Hillsdale, NJ: Lawrence Erlbaum Associates.

Hakkarainen, K. (2003). Emergence of progressive-inquiry culture in Computer-Supported Collaborative Learning. *Learning Environments Research, 6*(2),199-220.

Hewitt, J. (2001). From a focus on tasks to a focus on understanding: The cultural transformation of a Toronto classroom. In Koschmann, T., Hall, R., & Miyake, N. (Eds.), CSCL 2 carrying forward the conversation: Computers, cognition, and work (pp.11-41). Mahwah, NJ: Lawrence Erlbaum Associates.

Jones, B., Valdez, G., Nowakowski, J., & Rasmussen, C. (1994). *Designing Learning and Technology for Educational Reform*. Oak Brook, IL: North Central Regional Educational Laboratory.

Lamon, M., Reeve, R. & Scardamalia, M. (2001, April). Mapping the growth of deeply principled understandings in a knowledge building community. Annual Meeting of the American Educational Research Association. Seattle, WA. Retrieved 22 March 2004 from http://ikit.org/lamon/mapping.html

Meehan, S., & Nolan, M. (2001). Handbook of engaged learning projects. Retrieved on 21 March 2004 from http://www-ed.fnal.gov/help/cover. html

Perkins, D.N. (1991). Technology meets constructivism: Do they make a marriage? *Educational Technology, 31*(5), 18-23.

Scardamalia, M. (1999). Moving Ideas to the Center. In L. Harasim (Ed.), *Wisdom & Wizardry: Celebrating the Pioneers of Online Education* (pp. 14-15). Vancouver, BC: Telelearning, Inc.

Scardamalia, M. (2004). CSILE/Knowledge Forum®. In *Educational technology: An encyclopedia*. Santa Barbara: ABC-CLIO.

Scardamaiia, M. (2003). Knowledge building environments: Extending the limits of the possible in education and knowledge work. In *Encyclopedia of distributed learning*. Thousand Oaks, CA: Sage Publications.

Scardamalia, M., & Bereiter, C. (2002). Knowledge building. In *Encyclopedia of education* (2nd Ed.). New York: Macmillan Reference, USA.

Shanmugaratnam, T. (2003). Speech at the MOE Work Plan Seminar at Ngee Ann Polytechnic on Thursday, 2 October 2003. Retrieved 31 March, 2004, from http://www.moe.gov.sg/speeches/2003/sp20031002. htm

Trilling, B., & Hood, P. (1999). Learning, technology, and education reform in the Knowledge Age or "We're Wired, Webbed, and Windowed, Now What?" *Educational Technology, 39*(3), 5-18.

U.S. Department of Labor, Secretary's Commission on Achieving Necessary Skills (SCANS). (1992). Learning a Living: a Blueprint for High Performance. Washington, DC: U.S. Department of Labor

Chapter 6

ENGAGING LEARNERS THROUGH INTUITIVE INTERFACES

John G. Hedberg[1] and Susan Metros[2]

[1]*Macquarie University, Australia;* [2]*Ohio State University, USA*

Abstract: This chapter acquaints the reader with key concepts associated with learner engagement by examining the user interface from cognitive, semiotic, psychological, artistic and pedagogical perspectives. Technology affords educators with a new way to present course content that is no longer text only, paper constrained, linearly organized and visually flat. Engaged learning can borrow from the interactive and community-based activities prevalent on the Internet. The use of gaming, role-playing, blogging, instant messaging and chat coupled with multimedia modalities that address multiple learning styles has the capacity or stimulate today's technology savvy learners. By employing these familiar methodologies to learning, educators can better meet the needs of a new student demographic that has grown up with computers, is predominantly visually oriented, watches rather than listens to music on MTV, uses Google as a key reference tool, shops online and accesses news through 24/7 online streaming feeds. These students expect to take part in experiential and authentic learning in unconventional and engaging ways. However, new ways of learning require new teaching methodologies. The traditional forms of teaching do not transition well to the engaging online environment. The authors, using a three-phase model as a foundation for creating engaging user interfaces, will explore the cognitive and visual elements of effective interface design that engage learners through intuitive and direct interaction. By deconstructing a series of educational interfaces that are functional, usable, communicative, and aesthetically appropriate, readers will learn to identify the visual and cognitive demands of a knowledge domain that creates engaging, interactive results.

Keywords: engagement, interaction, GUI, graphical user interface, design

1.   INTRODUCTION

If one of the primary goals of e-learning is to stimulate active involvement, then educators and instructional designers need to better understand the role of the graphical user interface in promoting and sustaining learner engagement. Engaged learners are intrinsically motivated to perform. They direct their efforts to understanding the tasks and

D. Hung and M.S. Khine (eds.), Engaged Learning with Emerging Technologies, 107-125.
© *2006 Springer. Printed in the Netherlands.*

challenges in a learning context; and they strive to construct knowledge and derive meaning from their prior experience and available resources. Graphical user interfaces (GUI) can help stimulate learner engagement or conversely, disengage and confuse learners if they are poorly designed.

The GUI is the lens through which the instructor or designer communicates with learners. Poor GUI design can place high cognitive demands upon the learner that can reduce interest and divert attention away from the primary learning tasks. This is not to suggest that all e-learning programs need to match the immediacy and visual intrigue of computer games, but there is certainly a need for clear design and a reduction of apparent complexity. GUIs must be intuitive and facilitate an array of interactions between learners, the instructor, the content and other resources within the program.

Many educators design or direct the design of e-learning materials with little understanding of the importance of functional, usable, communicative, and aesthetically appropriate user interfaces. Educators typically use the interface dictated to them by a given system. Few have the skills and knowledge necessary to either modify the existing interface or create a new user interface even with the help of a graphic designer who also may or may not have working knowledge of human factors. In any case, e-learning programs continue to mimic correspondence mail models of distancing education, failing to use the potential of modern telecommunication technologies to enhance independent and collaborative learning.

We suggest a three-phase model for designing engaging GUI. It stresses the importance of GUI design for facilitating essential e-learning interactions. First, we examine design intentions and learner engagement. Then, we discuss important human factors to consider while applying each phase of the model.

2.   DESIGN INTENTIONS

The desired learning outcomes and environment should drive the design of the GUI. However, popular course authoring systems, such as WebCT and Blackboard, do not support the design intentions of educators attempting to create innovative e-learning environments based on constructivist approaches to teaching and learning. Educators must work within the design models that are either implicitly or explicitly imposed by a particular authoring tool. For example, many GUIs used by current authoring systems consist of elements associated with traditional classroom instruction such as a syllabus, course documents, assignments and student rosters. It is the close approximation to objects found in traditional courses that make some authoring systems more appealing than others. Modern authoring tools also make it relatively easy for educators to post materials and publish an online course. They reduce the learning curve and allow educators to develop and deliver online coursework with limited time and resources. The problem is that such authoring tools often perpetuate the use of teacher-directed methods by lock-stepping the author into a set of constrained templates that do not readily support the development of innovative e-learning environments.

Supporters of constructivist learning theories criticize authoring tools that have inflexible inbuilt pedagogical support because the learning environment must be designed within the constraints proscribed by the authoring tool (e.g., Jonassen & Reeves, 1996). Murray (1999) proposed that such systems acknowledge concepts such as intrinsic motivation, context realism and social learning contexts, but many saw them as either not important, or as being too complex or incompletely understood to incorporate into instructional systems. We disagree. Not only are these concepts essential in engaging learners, but also examples of environments based on constructivist design principles that have proven to be effective especially when the problems that are posed are ill structured and require more than simple factual responses (e.g., Jonassen, 1997; Hedberg, et al, 1998; Herrington, et al, 1999).

Human-computer interface designers continue to wrestle with the challenge of affording a new generation of visually savvy learners with engaging online experiences. In her seminal book *Computers as Theatre,* Laurel (1993) suggested ways to use the notion of theatre, not simply as a metaphor, but as a way to conceptualize human-computer interaction. Laurel defines this type of engagement as, "what happens when we are able to give ourselves over to a representational action, comfortably and ambiguously. We gain a plethora of new possibilities for action and a kind of emotional guarantee" (p115). Laurel is referring to what Csikszentmihalyi (1996) termed *Flow State*, to describe the state of total engagement. Users attain *Flow State* when they have no conscious awareness of the passage of time. *Flow State* occurs when users enjoy a sense of playfulness, a feeling of being in control, a period of concentration when attention is highly focused, an interlude of enjoyment of an activity for its own sake, a distorted sense of time, and a rewarding match between the challenge at hand and one's personal skills.

The design intentions discussed here are derived from the main tenets of constructivism and focus on how engagement is achieved within the learning tasks and challenges presented to students. In the next section, we describe how the approach directly translates into clear descriptions of motivating tasks that are embedded in interactive e-learning strategies and communicated to students through the GUI. The emphasis on motivating tasks situated within well-designed and engaging interactions with the user interface provides the instructional designer greater surety that the final experience will be effective.

3.   CREATING AN ENGAGING INTERFACE: A THREE PHASE MODEL

Based on key concepts associated with learner engagement and engagement theory, we have proposed a design model for creating constructivist e-learning environments. The model suggests an iterative approach with a focus on integrative strategies (Figure 1). Recognizing that traditional design models concentrate on tasks and their descriptions, the added dimensions of task representation and motivation represents a shift in focus to a more integrative and holistic design process. The three major phases work to create a rich description of the learning experience and how it will serve different and diverse learners.

The approach begins with an initial description of the project space and how the educational content information is to be used by students. The term "project" can represent a course, a course component such as a learning object, a set of web-based support resources, a CD-ROM product, or other various combinations. The second phase defines a method for learners to access and manipulate the information. The purpose of the final phase is to actualize the learning experience by ensuring that the GUI and the visual metaphors are consistent with the prior steps to reinforce the core learning outcomes. To this end, the interface elements should visually communicate the educational objectives and goals.

A CD entitled "123 Count with me," developed by emLab at the University of Wollongong and published by the NSW Department of Education and Training in Australia illustrates the application of the model (Figure 2). The CD introduces basic mathematical concepts to K-2 teachers and shows them how they might use an innovative instructional strategy to group students and introduce basic mathematical thinking.

Phase One: Information Design and Project Space Definition

Phase one compiles information on learners' needs and describes the parameters of the project space. It encompasses the essential information to be included in the e-learning materials, distills what the target audience understands about the information and describes how the project should be structured for its intended audience. The purpose of this initial stage is to begin a holistic structuring of the information and to model it so that it will eventually form the basis of an organizing visual metaphor.

Isolating the key attributes within a learning experience is not trivial. It is difficult to clearly define the knowledge domain and how it should be presented for a particular audience. To understand the options, instructional designers need to ask their project originators and users three questions.

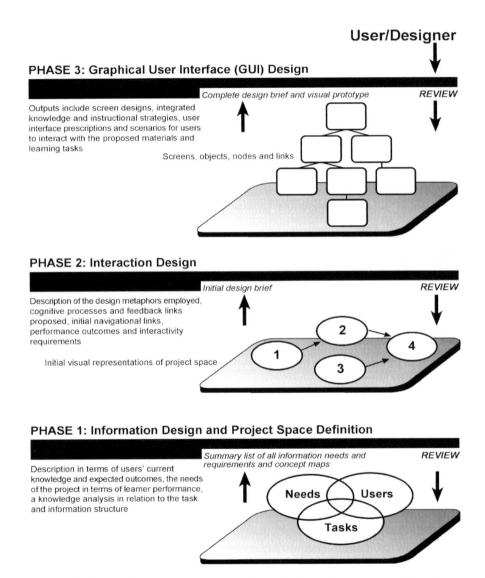

Figure 1. The design process used as the basis for interactive multimedia project development (based on Hedberg et al, 1994, Metros 2001).

Figure 2. Modeling the information and the message in "123 Count with me" through a spatial metaphor familiar to the intended audience. Teachers are familiar with a classroom metaphor.

1. *What is the topic (content) of this project?* Attempts to define the content often become a lengthy written list of ideas. The preferred method is to identify a simple visual representation, such as a concept map, that may serve as a useful structure for accessing the knowledge domain. A concept map can be used to ideate, plan, organize, and visualize the concepts and links that are included in the model's first phase (Ferry, Hedberg & Harper, 1997). Figure 3 is an early concept map used as the structuring device for the classroom panorama in "123 Count with me" Figure 2.

2. *Who are the intended users of this knowledge domain?* The content might be the same for different groups, but learners may want to "view, use or manipulate" the content in different ways. For example, novices may want help in understanding how a domain is structured and how elements are related. Experts may already have well-developed schemas and prefer to get right into

applying key concepts. The primary users should be given opportunities to suggest mechanisms to aid them in understanding the topic at hand

3. *Why is e-learning being undertaken?* Encouraging the commissioning client to state in a few sentences what he or she thinks the project will achieve is often enough to gain insight into the core-driving objective(s). We have found that the client's original stated objective almost always needs revision to better identify and describe the underlying purpose. The "real" purpose once enunciated will help to clarify and direct many subsequent decisions.

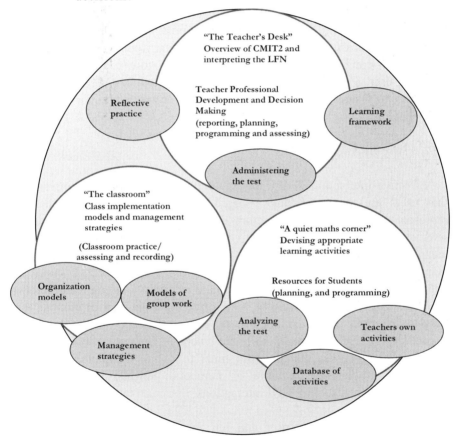

Figure 3. Concept Map of the organizational of content in "123 Count with me"

The answers to the three questions form the foundation for a particular e-learning project space. Using an iterative process, the designer can then elaborate the project space by presenting clients with progressively refined descriptions of five key attributes (a) the learning tasks, (b) the information structure, (c) the expert's perspective, (d) the cognitive demands of the intended user, and (e) the mental images and the effort required to interpret the images if placed within the graphical user interface.

In "123 Count with me," a concept map was created to represent the learning tasks and information structure (Figure 3). The remaining attributes were addressed in "concept and treatment" description of the project. In short, the teachers' desk served as a metaphor for the "expert" where novice users were encouraged to think about the teaching task and what mathematics learning is about. Multiple points of access either through menus or by clicking on elements in the panorama were designed to address the limited computer skills and reduce the cognitive demands on the intended user. Finally, the classroom metaphor reduces the mental effort necessary to figure out the product while reinforcing a familiar setting and experience.

Phase Two: Interaction Design

Effective interaction design that matches cognitive expectations ensures that users are motivated and engaged. Creating a GUI that effectively represents the information structure does not immediately lead to useful interactions. The use of interactive technologies does not ensure that meaningful interactions will occur. The challenge is to create interactions that are easily manipulated at the users' technology skill level. The point and click function in the "123" example ensures simple information manipulation. The user should be able to focus on the goal of the task they wish to undertake rather than the process of how the task must be done. This is particularly true in complex software where wizards are often required to sort out the processes that the user must follow to complete a task, like drawing a graph from a table of numbers. Norman (1988) provides guidelines for constructing GUI interactions.

1. *Visibility*: The user can tell the state of the device and the alternatives for action through observation. In the "123" example, learners are positioned within the same virtual classroom space that purposely reduces their choice of options. When learners make a choice, a window opens that makes their selection obvious (Figure 4).

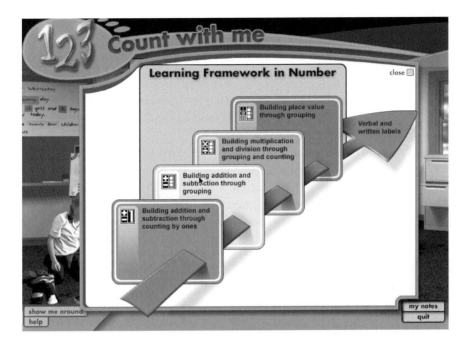

Figure 4. An example in "123" of how selecting a section covers the screen.

2. *An effective conceptual model*: There should be consistency in how program functions "work" leading to a coherent conceptual user model. Novice interface designers are often guilty of creating different actions for the same concept. This only confuses users when they go to do something in one section of the program and find that the actions are markedly different in another section of the same environment. In the "123" classroom, the introduction "show me around" and the help links use the same palette function which can be accessed by simply clicking on the term (Figure 5).

3. *Effective mapping*: There are clear relationships between actions and results, controls and their effects, and between system state and what is visible.

4. *Feedback*: There must be continuous feedback about the results of actions. Novice designers often create instructional materials that provide feedback on every user action; yes that answer is correct, no it is not, and so on. They fail to realize that almost every action creates some perturbation. For feedback to be effective, designers should employ a variety of feedback that link to specific learning outcomes.

In addition to Norman's guidelines, there are alternative techniques for reducing the load on a learner's working memory to enhance interaction design.

1. *Use visual conventions borrowed from the real world.* For example, "123 Count with me," emulates the file directory structure used by both Windows and Macintosh operating systems (Figure 6).

2. *Apply consistent visual metaphors.* This seems self-evident but it is easily contravened. The classic mismatch that is often quoted is the method for ejecting a disk on a Macintosh computer by dragging its icon into the trash. This confuses novice users as they think that they are going to delete files, or worse, erase the disk.

Figure 5. Example of the universal palette function in "123."

3. *Recognize the role of the learner as actor.* Successful human interface interactions can be considered a form of acting. The user is participating in a dialogue that is unfolding, often in real-time (Laurel, 1993; Hedberg & Sims, 2001). Considering the learner as an actor within a staged environment can ensure both planned and serendipitous interactions.

particularly important for e-learning because visual displays of information encourages diversity of individual viewer styles and promotes personalizing, reasoning, and understanding of content (Tufte, 1990). To maximize e-learning, the GUI must be integral to the system itself, rather than a decorative detail or afterthought.

Following Laurel's (1993) lead, we can better understand the attributes of a GUI by applying the metaphor of the theater. The physical portal of the stage can be compared to the physical dimensions of monitor's display. However, unlike the three-dimensional stage, the interface must rely on the "trickery of perspective" to create the illusion of depth. In the theatre, the director positions scenery, props, the effects of lighting, and the actors upon the stage. Within the GUI, the designer places various data elements within the interface inclusive of text, backgrounds, photographs, illustrations, animations, audio and video players, icons, bullets, banners, toolbars, etc. Much like the objects that populate the stage, GUI items come in a variety of shapes, sizes, colors, textures, and proportions. A stage filled with props and actors has little meaning unless they interact with each other and their environment as the plot unfolds. The same holds true for the GUI. The elements within the interface must interrelate through acts of balance, contrast, motion, and spatial arrangement, all the while communicating meaning. The virtual "choreography" leads the learner through a purposeful journey, complete with varied pace, directed foci, crescendos in action, and even mood swings. Both a play and e-learning applications share one goal–to engage the audience. The major difference is that a GUI must entice the learner to interact while the playgoer can sit back and passively watch.

To visually represent the e-learning environment, designers use typographic, photographic, illustrative design techniques to encourage interaction and convey meaning through the GUI. When defining the GUI, there is a wide range of choices to be made not only related to technique, but inclusive of style and medium. The choice of technique depends on the learning objectives and the project's overall "look and feel." Techniques range in style from literal to abstract, static to dynamic, content-driven to purely decorative. If the subject matter does not exist in reality, creators can fabricate visuals from scratch or digitally manipulate existing imagery.

Visuals are an important component of the GUI because they have the ability to focus learner attention, set ambiance, add texture and depth to the screen, and provide thematic consistency. Furthermore, if working illustratively, the designer must select a consistent medium. Pen and ink, paint, watercolor, pencil, marker, or the wide array of computer-generated media each provides a different look and feel. GUIs also can encompass three-dimensional worlds. Using specialized software, designers can craft explorable, architectural landscapes and model objects that learners can examine, dissect, and manipulate in 360-degrees.

Coinciding with the use of metaphor, GUIs often adopt a thematic look and feel based upon historical periods (the Wild West, art deco), cultural motifs (ancient Rome, Africa), physical locales (the classroom, a campus, a futuristic cityscape) and everyday objects (a book, an instrument panel, a game board). The emulation of familiar conventions reinforces consistency, takes advantage of previously learned associations, promotes understanding between diverse concepts and helps the learner grasp complex ideas. Ultimately, effective e-learning translates into learner engagement, a result of dynamic and authentic interaction. To further enhance the use of themes and metaphors, GUI designers can add perspective and apply Gestalt principles to trigger interaction and promote engagement.

Perspective adds dimensionality to what Tufte (1990, p. 12) refers to as "flatland," the two-dimensionality of a video screen. Perspective provides the illusion of depth and creates a visually engaging environment that models reality. The simplest form of perspective uses foreground and background space. The "123" classroom exemplifies this perspective through position, size, color, and detail of the various objects and individuals placed within the panorama (Figure 2). Adding shadows, shading, high/low lighting, location sensitive sound, shrinking and expanding animated objects can increase dimensionality. The illusion of depth also can be envisioned by rendering objects in three-dimensions and by employing isometric perspective.

The GUI designer can also apply select Gestalt principles to build a visual frame of reference that provides a reliable psychological basis for the spatial organization of graphic information (Berryman, 1979). An example of a Gestalt principle applied to the GUI is the practice of grouping together universal navigation commands such as site maps, and quit and home buttons. This Gestalt principle is called "Proximity." It states that perceptual groupings are favored according to the nearness of parts. Closer parts naturally form groups by visually uniting related elements. Figure 9creates three small groups within the classroom using this simple grouping stratagem.

Phase 1 conceptualizes the project space. Phase 2 applies a metaphor to design interactions. Phase 3 takes the process to fruition by visualizing the outcome. The outcome is usually expressed as a visual prototype. It can be as simple as a roughly sketched, paper-based storyboard or as sophisticated as computer-generated graphic screens with rudimentary programming included to demonstrate functionality.

4. CONCLUSION

Effective e-learning environments built upon solid foundations of learner needs and outcomes, metaphorically crafted cognitive processes, and instructional strategies communicated through effective graphical user interfaces that intrigue, challenge and engage the learner. Crafting of such projects requires a new approach in which the instructional designer, technologists, graphic designer, educator and student collaborate to insure that the end result is usable, functional and visually communicative and attractive. This can be accomplished by employing reasonable yet innovative conventions; such as organizing visual metaphors that scaffold access to the underpinning knowledge that support the desired level of challenge and engagement. As interactive technologies become the staple communication vehicle for innovative virtual worlds, effective GUI design will ensure that the learner's focus on learning rather than operating the software.

Development of an engaging GUI is not a trivial task. Creating appropriate challenges that are effectively represented by the visual design requires understanding of how learners need to access and manipulate available resources and an appreciation for the skills and knowledge of each design team member. The choice of authoring tools can also greatly affect the way information may be structured and manipulated. Popular authoring tools may actually reduce the interactivity and visual representations that are possible (Hedberg & Sims, 2001). Educators who wish to take a constructivist approach to teaching and learning may find it difficult to realize their design intentions if required to use certain authoring tools. While some tools facilitate the physical process of putting educational materials online, they may also inhibit the design of innovative and engaging GUIs. The three-phase model offers guidelines for modifying or creating original GUIs and gives educators a better understanding of the importance of functional, usable, communicative, and aesthetically appropriate user interfaces.

REFERENCES

123 *Count with me.* (2004) Sydney: NSW Department of Education and Training, Instructional Design Shirley Agostinho, John Hedberg, Kerry Long, Vicki Lowery and Rob Wright, Graphic Design, Karl Mutimer.

Berryman, G. (1979) *Notes on Graphic Design and Visual Communication.* Los Altos, CA.: William Kaufmann, Inc.

Csikszentmihalyi, M. (1996) Thoughts about education, In D. Dickinson (Ed.) *Creating The Future: Perspectives on Educational Change,*

Seattle, WA: New Horizons for Learning. Retrieved November 20, 2001 from http://www.newhorizons.org/crfut_csikszent.html.

Duffy, T. M., & Cunningham, D. J., (1996). Constructivism: Implications for the design and delivery of instruction. In D. H. Jonassen, (Ed.) *Handbook of Research for Educational Communications and Technology*, NY: Macmillan Library Reference USA. pp. 170-198.

Ferry, B., Hedberg, J. G., & Harper, B. M. (1997). *Using concept mapping to help pre-service teachers map subject matter knowledge*. Paper presented to the Australian Association for Research in Education 1997 Annual Conference, Brisbane, 30th November to 4th December.

Hannafin, M. J., & Land, S. M. (1997). The foundations and assumptions of technology-enhanced student-centered learning environments. *Instructional Science*, *25*, 167-202.

Hedberg, J. G., & Sims, R.(2001). Speculations on design team interactions. *Journal of Interactive Learning Research*, *12*(2/3), 189-214.

Hedberg, J. G., Harper, B. Lockyer, L. Ferry, B. Brown, C., & Wright, R. (1998). Supporting learners to solve ill-structured problems. In R. Corderoy, (Ed.) Flexibility: the Next Wave. Proceedings of the 15th Annual Conference of the Australasian Society for Computers in Learning in Tertiary Education. December 14th-16th, Wollongong, NSW: University of Wollongong. pp. 317-327.

Hedberg, J. G., Harper, B. M., Brown, C, & Corderoy, R, (1994). Exploring user interfaces to improve learner outcomes. In K. Beatie, C McNaught, & S. Wills, (Eds.), *Interactive Multimedia in University Education: Designing for Change in Teaching and Learning*. Amsterdam: North Holland, Elsevier, pp 15-29.

Herrington, A., Herrington, J. Sparrow, L. & Oliver, R. (1999). Investigating mathematics education using multimedia. *Journal of Technology and Teacher Education*, 7(3), 175-186.

Hicks, R. and Essinger, J. (1991) *Making Computers More Human: Designing for Human-Computer Interaction*. Oxford, UK: Elsevier Advanced Technology, pp. 75-76.

Jonassen, D. & Tessmer, M. (1996-1997). An Outcomes-based Taxonomy for Instructional Systems Design, Evaluation and Research. *Training Research Journal*, *2*, 11-46.

Jonassen, D. H. (1997). Instructional Design Models for Well-Structured and Ill-structured Problem-Solving Learning Outcomes. *Educational Technology Research and Development*, 45(1), 65-94.

Jonassen, D. H., & Reeves, T. C. (1996) Learning with Technology: Using Computers as Cognitive Tools. In D. H. Jonassen, (Ed.) *Handbook of Research on Educational Communications and Technology*. New York

Scholastic Press in collaboration with the Association for Educational Communications and Technology, Chapter 25.

Kearsley, G. and Shneiderman, B. (1999) *Engagement theory: A framework for technology-based teaching and Learning*, April 5,1999. Retrieved November 20, 2001 from http://home.sprynet.com/~gkearsley/engage htm.

Laurel, B. (1993). *Computers as Theatre*. Reading, MA: Addison-Wesley.

Lave, J. & Wenger, E. (1991). *Situated learning: Legitimate peripheral practice*. New York: Cambridge University Press.

Marton, F. and Saljo, R. (1976) On qualitative differences in learning: Outcome and process, *British Journal of Educational Psychology, 46*, 4-11.

Metros, S.E. (1999). Making connections: a model for online interaction," *Leonardo: Journal of the International Society for the Arts Sciences and Technology, 32*(4), 281-291,

Metros, S.E. (2001). Visually engaging online learners. *LlinE: Lifelong Learning in Europe, 6*(2), 85-95.

Murray, T. (1999). Authoring Intelligent Tutoring Systems: An analysis of the state of the art. *International Journal of Artificial Intelligence in Education, 10*, 98-129.

Nielsen, J. (1993). *Usability Engineering*. Boston, MA: Academic Press.

Norman, D. (1988). *The Psychology of Everyday Things*. New York, NY: Basic Books.

Savery, J. R., & Duffy, T. M. (1996). Problem Based Learning: An instructional model and its constructivist framework. In B. G. Wilson (Ed.), *Constructivist Learning Environments: Case Studies in Instructional Design*. Englewood Cliffs, NJ: Educational Technology Publications. pp. 135-148.

Tufte, E. R. (1990). *Envisioning Information*. Cheshire, CT: Graphics Press.

31. *Software Example*

Chapter 7

LEARNING SCIENCE THROUGH ONLINE THREADED DISCOURSE

Allan H.K. Yuen
Division of Information and Technology Studies
The University of Hong Kong, Hong Kong

Abstract: Taking the approach of knowledge building (Scardamalia & Bereiter, 1999), 793 students from six primary schools in Hong Kong were engaged in inter-school asynchronous online threaded discourse through Knowledge Forum (KF), a computer mediated communications platform designed to facilitate knowledge building and to explicate students' role as intelligent agents in the learning process. This paper aims to investigate the knowledge building and participation patterns using KF in online threaded discourse and to explore their relationship to student perceptions on learning. Data collection included student KF discourses, teacher and student interviews, KF system logs and pre-and-post activity questionnaires. The results demonstrate that online discourse can broaden the basis for learning and teaching science and help in advancing knowledge in different ways, and indicate four patterns of online participation and their relationship to student perceptions and academic performance.

Keywords: online discourse, knowledge building, learning community, science education, primary education, computer mediated communication, information and communication technology, curriculum innovation, learning culture, pedagogy

1. INTRODUCTION

During the past decade there has been an exponential growth in the use of information and communication technology (ICT), which has made pervasive impacts both on the society and education. In addition to the growth of ICT use, the emergence of the knowledge society has also brought about a much greater emphasis on economy and education, as Drucker (1999) pointed out, "the most valuable asset of a 21st century institution, whether business or non-business, will be its knowledge workers and their productivity" (p.79), and he also indicated factors determine knowledge worker productivity, such as autonomy, continuing innovation,

D. Hung and M.S. Khine (eds.), Engaged Learning with Emerging Technologies, 127-147.

and continuous learning. Education, as central to a knowledge society, must produce people who are able to create and gain advantages from the new knowledge (Bereiter, 2002). Because of the changing nature of the knowledge age, students need to develop ways of dealing with complex issues and problems that require different kinds of knowledge that they have ever learned.

In response to these challenges, a number of policies on ICT in education have been produced in many countries (Pelgrum & Anderson, 1999). Such policies reveal that educational innovations in ICT have been increasingly embedded within a broader framework of education reforms that aimed to develop students' capacities for self-learning, problem-solving, information seeking and analysis, and critical thinking, as well as the ability to communicate, collaborate and learn, abilities that figured much less importantly in previous school curricula (Law et al., 2000; Yuen, Law & Wong, 2003). Roschelle et al. (2000), drawn from findings of cognitive research on effective learning, highlighted ways of ICT can enhance student learning by supporting the four fundamental characteristics of learning: active engagement, participation in groups, frequent interaction and feedback, and connections to real-world context. ICT in particular the Internet technologies have been translated into a number of strategies for teaching and learning (Jonassen, Peck & Wilson, 1999). However, integrating ICT into school curricula is not a simple matter. In view of the challenges of ICT and knowledge society, this paper looks at issues of engaging science learning with online technology in primary schools.

2.   LEARNING SCIENCE AND LEARNING COMMUNITIES

How should science be treated in schools? Following the advocacy of teaching science in a wired world, Bigum (1998) argues: "it is important for science teachers to recognize that there are important changes in the world outside the science classroom as well as that within" (p. 21). It seems clear that computer-mediated communications (CMC) tools can provide a unique bridge between the classroom and the world beyond (Fishman, 1999), for they allow instruction to become more authentic and students engaging in collaborative projects (Rose & Winterfeldt, 1998). CMC are being increasingly used as resources to enhance teaching and learning in schools and higher education (Glaser & Poole, 1999; Harasim, Hiltz, Teles, & Turoff, 1996).

Brown (1999; p.19) pointed out "the most promising use of Internet is where the buoyant partnership of people and technology creates powerful new online learning communities" though the idea of learning communities has been introduced more than two decades (Caverly & MacDonald, 2002). Given the advancement of CMC technology, a number of ways have been

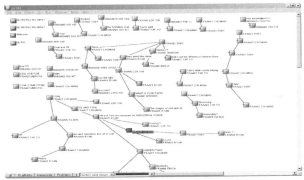

Figure 1: An example of KF threaded discussion

Knowledge Forum Client version 3.4 was used throughout the project. The central activity of the KF community is students' contributions to the communal knowledge bases, and contributions can take the following forms: (a) individual note (Figure 2), in which students state problems, advance initial theories or improve theories; (b) build-on, which allows students to connect new notes to existing notes; and (c) rise-above, which allows students to summarize and synthesize a group of related notes. In addition, customizable scaffolds to support discourse, such as "My theory", "I need to understand", and "New information", are also available to assist students in the process of knowledge building.

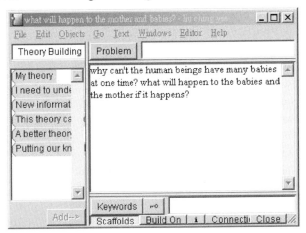

Figure 2: An example of KF note

Using the KF, students from different schools engaged in discussion and knowledge building, and thus collaborative learning communities were formed. Students from School A & School C participated in a project discourse about the formation of oil and coal; students from School B & School D participated in a project discourse around the theme of why there are twins; and School E & School F participated in a project discourse around the topic of the development of a well-planned city.

7.   DATA COLLECTION

In order to portray a picture of scientific knowledge building, online participation, student perceptions, and academic performance, the data were derived from five sources, namely, student KF discussions, interviews of students and teachers, system logs of the KF system, pre-and-post project questionnaires, and academic results before and after the semester.

First of all, student KF discussions (i.e. threaded KF notes) provided rich qualitative data about the knowledge building process. After the project, thirty students including students with high, medium or low participation rates of writing and reading KF notes and eleven teachers from six schools were invited for semi-structured group interviews. Student discussions and semi-structured interviews of students and teachers were analyzed to conceptualize various categories of variations in their perception, understanding and reflection of their participation in the process of scientific knowledge building.

The system logs provided data for scrutinizing all the online activities on KF and the participation between students and the technology. Table 2 shows the eight measures (labeled as PE1 to PE8) collected from the Analytic Toolkit for KF. The elements of "use of scaffolds" and "use of rise-above" were rare and they are not considered in the data analysis.

Table 2. Online participation elements

PE1	Number of nodes created
PE2	Number of editing
PE3	Number of new reading
PE4	Number of new keywords used
PE5	Number of reading of the same school
PE6	Number of reading of different schools
PE7	Number of new built-on within the same school
PE8	Number of new built-on across different school

In these participation elements, PE3, PE5, and PE7 are read-participation, and the other elements are write-participation, in which read and write are typical participation of online discussion.

A self-reported questionnaire consisted of 13 items was developed by the research team to collect student perceptions on aspects of learning and discussion in science curriculum. Responses of each item were set in four-point Likert scale anchored by strongly disagree, disagree, agree, and strongly agree. The Chinese questionnaire was administered to 793 students before and after the online discourse activity. Table 3 shows the English translation of the 13 items.

Table 3. Measurement items of student perceptions

SP1	Information collection and analysis are very important to learning.
SP2	Synthesizing personal as well as others' viewpoints is very important to learning.
SP3	Reinforcing ability of innovation could make learning easy.
SP4	Strengthening problem solving ability could be helpful in learning.
SP5	Knowledge solely comes from teachers.
SP6	The content of knowledge solely comes from textbooks.
SP7	Science knowledge is continuous renewed.
SP8	Science knowledge should first be verified by experiments.
SP9	New input could change our existing concepts of knowledge.
SP10	Discussion could widen the scope of viewpoints.
SP11	Discussion could improve learning abilities.
SP12	Students, teachers, parents and specialists should be included in discussion.
SP13	Discussion could deepen learning.

Finally, student examination results of the science subject before and after the 3-month online discourse were collected and converted into standard scores to indicate their pre-test and post-test academic performance.

8. RESULTS

There are a number of points worth noting from the findings of the data analysis. Two major themes in connection to learning science were found from the iterative analysis of students' online discourses and interviews of teachers and students. Then, results focus on aspects of student perceptions and student participation arising from the online discourse are presented.

Broadening the Basis for Learning and Teaching Science

First of all, we observed that the online experience broadened the basis for learning science in a wired world. Both teachers and students perceived searching information on the web or books was crucial in building science knowledge. This can be illustrated by the following teacher interview and student discussion.

"That's students explored into, or searched for the most abundant information from web sources, carried out analysis, might sum up, get new things done, and subsequently a project came out. That meant self-extraction of knowledge from the public webs including KF. This was what we mean by knowledge building" (Extract from teacher interviews). "Student A: Why do you think coal is from the land? [...] Student B: Because I found it from my science book. ... " (Extract from student discussions).

Students found that searching information and learning science are closely linked. Thus, they realized the online discussion provided a new learning experience for their science learning, as a student said: "We learn about computers when using KF. We also learn how to search information, unlike the past case of doing projects. Now we have to search information from the Internet or library. Throughout the search process, we learn more knowledge and thereby we gain a lot" (Extract from student interviews).

Secondly, we found that the online experience broadened teachers' view on teaching science, as teachers sensed that they are not the only knowledge source for student learning: "In fact, our role is being changed. We don't dominate learning. Knowledge sources are no longer from us or textbook, but we've played a very important role" (Extract from teacher interviews).

Furthermore, some teachers realized their roles have been changed from knowledge provider to providing guidance and directions for students in the discussion, as illustrated in the following interview: "I've done more things. For instance, give them guidelines. So they've got directions for discussion. Before, the teacher's role was that teachers asked questions. But now when learning science through KF, students actively learn to ask questions whilst teachers need give them valuable help especially finding relevant web contents for them" (Extract from teacher interviews).

Scientific Knowledge Building

Four elements were identified in building scientific knowledge through online discussion, namely, question-and-response, cognitive conflict, cooperation, and conceptual improvement.

In the process of online discussion, students posed questions or responses in the threaded discussion. Using questions as catalyst, students initiated the building of scientific knowledge, as illustrated by the following student discussion and interview.

"Student C: How can we know the population in the well-planed city? Student D: We can use the census to get the answer." (Extract from student discussions). "Without linking others' answers with mine on KF, we posted questions to wait for others to answer" (Extract from student interviews). "What we learn from KF is more impressive, especially the structure of learning and questioning" (Extract from student interviews).

In the knowledge building process, students some time played a "critical friend" and challenged the "mistakes" made by peers. Such cognitive conflict is clearly shown in the following student discussion and interview. "Student E: I think animals have no twins. ... Student F: I think you are wrong. Animals have twins. ... Student G: Animals have twins, but not common" (Extract from student discussions). "We'll find out correct answers and show others where they made mistakes. KF provides chances of communicating with others. It is because the better the communications means, the more frequent they would ask you how you acquire knowledge. It is possible to encounter different viewpoints with other school partners. We'd like to investigate how we obtain knowledge mutually" (Extract from student interviews).

"This is why we create new notes, as we can judge which are right and wrong things on KF through discussion. Others will pose new notes, informing me of such things. Consequently, we mutually know that new answers are correct", said by a student. Cooperative development of shared knowledge is a focus of building scientific knowledge in the online discussion. Students tested knowledge and learned from each other through cooperation. Examples of student discussion and interview are given below.

"Student H: I think the oil and coal are from the dead animals and plants. Student I: How do you know? Student H: I found it from the book. Student I: No, the oil and coal are not from animals and plants. Student J: Oil is from animal and coal from plant." (Extract from student discussions). "We pose notes, mutually complementary to each other on KF" (Extract from student interviews). "Yes, exactly. Others teach me, I teach others. This is what we learn from each other on KF" (Extract from student interviews). "Without co-operations, I can't know why I have made mistakes and never know the answers" (Extract from student interviews).

In the online knowledge building process, understanding is perceived as conceptual improvement of certain problems through sharing, collaboration, and communication. This is demonstrated by the following student interview: "The more you pose KF notes, the more you address other problems, construct other aspects of knowledge, and find out other related answers to the same studying problems with better understanding. This is what we mean by knowledge building" (Extract from student interviews).

"In communicating with others on KF, I can figure out wrong things", said by a student. In such peer co-construction process, students perceived the product of collaborative learning and scientific knowledge building through online discussion is a growing and improving process, as a student expressed: "The product of our collaborative learning looks like a baby. At the start, we know nothing, like its innocence. In the ongoing process of posing KF notes, the baby starts to grow up. The more we build up knowledge, the more knowledgeable it becomes and more relationships we find [...] Knowledge grows in this way" (Extract from student interviews).

9.   STUDENT PERCEPTIONS

To explore the factor structure of the 13 items in the questionnaire, the principal component analysis with varimax rotation (Kaiser normalization) was used. The factor analysis of the post-test data generated four constructs: (1) SP1-4, (2) SP5-6, (3) SP7-9, and (4) SP10-13, which were labeled as inquiry-based learning (IL), conventional learning (CL), science knowledge (SK), and communal discussion (CD) respectively, and total variance explained was 45%. Table 4 shows the factor loading and reliability of the four constructs. Furthermore, the 4-construct model on student perceptions was tested using LISREL with both pre-test and post-test data, whereas LISREL is a software product designed to estimate and test structural equation models, that is, statistical models of linear relationships among latent (unobserved) and manifest (observed) variables. This software is also used to carry out both exploratory and confirmatory factor analysis, as well as path analysis. It is found that the pre-test and post-test data fits the model satisfactorily (value of Chi-square, RMSA, CFI, and NNFI was 435, .08, .92, and .91 respectively).

Table 4. Factor loading and reliability of the four constructs

Measurement items	Factor loading	Cronbach's alpha
SP1	0.718	.721
SP2	0.658	
SP3	0.574	
SP4	0.592	
SP5	0.852	.780
SP6	0.861	
SP7	0.490	.552
SP8	0.775	
SP9	0.677	
SP10	0.593	.728
SP11	0.642	
SP12	0.662	
SP13	0.537	

It is found that there are correlations among the four perceptions in the pre and post project data. Table 5 shows the correlation coefficients and their significance, in which the upper-left and lower-right corner shows the correlations within the post and pre perceptions, and the lower-left corner shows the correlations across the post and pre perceptions.

Table 5. Correlations of student perceptions

	1	2	3	4	5	6	7	8
Post-IL	1	-	-	-	-	-	-	-
Post-CL	.097**	1	-	-	-	-	-	-
Post-CD	.584**	.158**	1	-	-	-	-	-
Post-SK	.400**	.030	.456**	1	-	-	-	-
Pre-IL	.314**	-.055	.206**	.163**	1	-	-	-
Pre-CL	-.030	.363**	-.016	-.016	-.038	1	-	-
Pre-CD	.259**	.030	.285**	.211**	.415**	.006	1	-
Pre-SK	.135**	.024	.108**	.197**	.308**	.043	.305**	1

$*p < .05; **p < .01$

Obviously, the pre-test and post-test perceptions are positively correlated (ref. the diagonal of the lower-left corner). It is found that the perceptions on inquiry learning, communal discussion, and science knowledge are significantly correlated to each other within pre and post as well as across pre and post activity. The correlation between perception on conventional learning and other perceptions is not noticeable.

10. PATTERNS OF ONLINE PARTICIPATION

In view of students' activities in the usage of KF, eight participation elements, which are listed in Table 2, were used for the classification of student participation. Cluster analysis (Bailey, 1994) was applied to the codes of eight participation elements in order to obtain patterns of online participation. A cluster analysis is a quantitative method of classification. Unlike factor analysis, variance is not partitioned among clusters. We performed k-means cluster analysis specifying 2 through 6 clusters. The best solution depends on a qualitative assessment of resulting models. Two dimensions (read and write) were used to construct the classification. These dimensions are dichotomized as low and high. Eventually, a 4-cluster model was emerged from the analysis, and the final cluster centre (means of each variable) of the model is described in Table 6.

As a whole, the means of cluster 1 tended to be smaller than other clusters. For the students belonging to this group, they read, created and edited fewer notes in KF, that is, both dimensions are low. Thus, we name this cluster as "All Low". On the contrary, students in cluster 2 tended to read, create and edit more notes. We label this cluster as "All High". For cluster 3, students tended to read but write fewer notes. This cluster is labeled as "Read More". Finally, students in cluster 4 tended to write more but read few notes. We then label this cluster as "Write More".

Table 6. Four clusters of student participation

	Cluster 1	Cluster 2	Cluster 3	Cluster 4
		Clusters		
PE1	1.17	6.18	4.14	4.67
PE2	.18	1.33	.80	.60
PE3	1.10	10.23	5.79	3.76
PE4	.55	5.21	2.22	4.11
PE5	1.14	9.20	4.37	3.75
PE6	.55	5.00	4.07	.93
PE7	.24	5.25	1.69	3.10
PE8	.06	1.73	.89	.27

However, when observing the means of clusters 3 and 4, we could find that their differences were not as significant as other two clusters. In general, the number of editing (PE2) and the number of new built-on across different school (PE8) were particularly low among all clusters. From Table 7, we could find that the group All Low consists of about 50% of the sample students. All High has the least number of students. The group size of Write More is a slightly larger than Read More.

Table 7. Distribution of different participation patterns

Cluster	Number of students
All Low	388
All High	101
Read More	120
Write More	177
Valid Total	786
Missing	7

Table 8 shows the frequency distribution of the four clusters among schools. In each school, it also displays the distribution across genders (M for male and F for female).

In the inspection of the frequencies among schools, the Pearson Chi-square value is 168.01 (df = 15, p<0.001), indicating that School E and F tend to have higher frequencies of "All High" than expected, and School A tends to have higher frequencies of "All Low" than expected. The Chi-square test for genders is not significant (Chi-square value = 2.07, df = 3).

Table 8. Distribution of different participation patterns among schools

Cluster	School A		School B		School C		School D		School E		School F	
	M	F	M	F	M	F	M	F	M	F	M	F
All Low	75	35	117	0	46	5	100	0	4	0	4	2
All High	6	3	16	0	5	2	35	0	9	0	18	7
Read More	4	4	22	0	24	4	36	0	17	0	5	4
Write More	16	7	61	0	18	1	55	0	7	0	7	5
Total	101	49	216	0	93	12	226	0	37	0	34	18

11. ONLINE PARTICIPATION PATTERNS AND ACADEMIC PERFORMANCE

Analysis of variance (ANOVA) was applied to compare the academic performance of the four participation patterns in the pre-test and post-test data, and it was found that the F-ratios were statistically significant (Table 9).

Table 9. Summary for ANOVA of academic performance

Online Interaction Patterns		N	Mean	S.D.	F
Pre	All High	101	.327	.736	
	Write More	177	.136	.936	7.92 ***
	Read More	120	.020	1.02	
	All Low	388	-.152	1.05	
Post	All High	101	.346	.821	
	Read More	120	.102	.907	7.84 ***
	Write More	177	.068	.891	
	All Low	388	-.151	1.09	

*** $p < 0.001$

The post hoc test for pre-test academic performance showed that (1) All High and Write More were significantly higher than All Low, and (2) All High was significantly higher than Read More. The post hoc test for post-test academic performance showed that (1) All High, Read More and Write More were significantly higher than All Low, and (2) All High was significantly higher than Write More.

12.   THE CHANGE OF STUDENT PERCEPTIONS

In order to explore the change of perceptions, t-test was applied to compare the mean scores of student perceptions between pre-test and post-test in 5 groups: all students and students grouped under the four clusters. Significant results were found only in the clusters of All Low and Read More (Table 10).

Table 10. Summary of mean comparison

		N	Mean	S.D.	t
All Low	Post IL	388	3.201	.643	-.523
	Pre IL	388	3.218	.500	
	Post CL	388	2.097	.995	1.086
	Pre CL	388	2.039	.870	
	Post CD	385	3.198	.637	-2.033*
	Pre CD	385	3.271	.533	
	Post SK	386	3.339	.614	.338
	Pre SK	386	3.326	.528	
Read More	Post IL	120	3.210	.565	-1.635
	Pre IL	120	3.309	.441	
	Post CL	120	1.833	.924	-2.281*
	Pre CL	120	2.058	.917	
	Post CD	120	3.231	.661	-.967
	Pre CD	120	3.290	.517	
	Post SK	120	3.351	.588	.250
	Pre SK	120	3.335	.579	

*p<.05

From the above table, the mean score of the perception of communal discussion in the post-test is significantly lower than the pre-test in the All Low cluster, indicating students in the All Low group had a less positive perception towards communal discussion after the online discourse exposure. For the Read More cluster, the mean score of the perception of conventional learning in the post-test is significantly lower than the pre-test, indicating students in the Read More group had a less conventional perception towards learning after the online discourse exposure.

13.   CONCLUSION

The experience of teachers and students reported in the current study demonstrates a case that learning science through online discourse can broaden the basis for learning and teaching science and help in advancing knowledge in different ways which are consistent to the demands of the knowledge age. However, the experience of such pedagogical innovation brings about implications for pedagogical change. How should science be learned in primary schools? Learning is perceived as the result of individual rather than group, which is a key assumption about teaching and learning in conventional pedagogy (Krechevsky & Stork, 2000). Conventional science instructional activities discourage the sharing of knowledge, and the goal is to transmit the textbook's or teacher's knowledge to students (Bielaczyc & Collins, 1999). The notion of learning communities and knowledge construction is opposed to such assumption. It is argued that learning science is to develop bases for shared understanding (Bereiter et al., 1997). Through the process of building online learning communities, we found that students' perception on science knowledge, inquiry-based learning, and communal discussion are closely related to each other, indicating the importance of such online discourse in learning science. Nevertheless, the pedagogical challenge is how teachers can change their deep-rooted conventional belief and learn to be a facilitator for student discourse and to provide meaningful environments for collaboration. The theory improvement view of science and learning through discourse leads to implication for pedagogical change, which needs further attention in the implementation of science curriculum.

In most online discussion forums, passive recipients of messages (lurkers) are the majority and a small number of active participants provide a large portion of message contributions. This paper attempts to investigate the participation patterns arising from asynchronous online discourse among 793 primary students. Further to the distinction between passive and active participants, four clusters were clearly identified based on eight participation elements. This classification provides a conceptual differentiation of active or passive participation in terms of "read" and "write" engagement. Students can be active or passive in "read", "write", or even both. Similarly, we found the majority (about 50%) of students is passive in both "read" and "write" and only 13% of students are active in this regard. Apart from these active and passive groups, two other forms of engagement were found, namely, Read More and Write More. It is found that the patterns of participation are related to the academic performance, in particular noticeable improvement of academic performance through the online discourse experience is found among the Read More students. This reflects reading in online discourse cannot be assumed to be passive rather it can be perceived as another form of active engagement. However, the questions of participation patterns in connection to various learning issues raised in this study warrant further investigation.

It is evident that ICT tools can help establish a collaborative learning network. In general, CMC tools can help achieve the work of community and facilitate communication (Gilbert & Driscoll, 2002). The KF is not only a CMC tool fostering knowledge construction and collaborative community building but shifting the focus of classroom instruction to a communal approach to learning and providing an environment to engage students in online threaded discourse. Does such online engagement work for primary students? The change of perceptions arising from the online discourse experience was unclear, however, we found that negative change in the perception of communal discussion and positive change in the perception towards conventional learning among All Low students and Read More students respectively. This raises the question whether learning through online discourse is suitable for all students. The results seem to indicate student participation patterns need to be accounted. However, apart from participation patterns, other pedagogical factors affecting student online discourse require further examination.

It is believed that the practice of learning community and knowledge discourse for science curriculum helps students in dealing with new situations and reason critically as emphasized in the science curriculum (CDC, 2001; NSES, 1996). The current study aims to investigate the participation patterns in online threaded discourse and to explore their relationship to student perceptions on aspects of learning science. However, there are limitations in the study. Firstly, students used their second language in the online discourse and they could only manage to write very brief notes in the discussion. This is an obvious obstacle for the quality of discourse. Secondly, the absence of a control group in the study indicated possible concerns for sources of research design validity. Thus, this study does not claim to be able to provide a comprehensive investigation of the issues in learning through online discourse, but rather it raises observations from the experience of a group of primary students with the hope to stimulate discussion in the research area.

To help inform future development of building collaborative learning communities and foster online threaded discourse in science pedagogy, further examination in the following issues would be summarized based on the experience of the current study: (a) how the engagement of online threaded discourse can help and advance students' learning of science, (b) how online discourse and learning communities can integrate with the other subjects to make science curriculum accessible to students, (c) what are the roles for students, teachers, and technology, and (d) how teacher facilitation or other pedagogical approaches can advance the online threaded discourse among students, and (e) how social processes can improve collaboration, online discourse, knowledge construction, and community building.

REFERENCES

Barab, S.A., Makinster, J.G., Moore, J.A., & Cunningham, D.J. (2001). Designing and Building an Online Community: The Struggle to Support Sociability in the Inquiry Learning Forum, *Educational Technology Research & Development*, 49(4), 71-96.

Bailey, K.D. (1994). *Typologies and Taxonomies: An Introduction to Classification Techniques*, London: Sage.

Bereiter, C. (2002). *Education and Mind in the Knowledge Age*, Lawrence Erlbaum Associates, NJ, Mahwah.

Bereiter, C., Cassells, C. & Hewitt, J. (1997). Postmodernism, Knowledge Building, and Elementary Science, *The Elementary School Journal*, 97(4), 329-340.

Bielaczyc, K. and Collins, A. (1999). Learning communities in classroom: Advancing knowledge for a lifetime. *NASSP Bulletin*, Feb. 1999, 4-10.

Bigum, C. (1998). Boundaries, barriers and borders: Teaching science in a wired world, *Australian Science Teachers' Journal*, 44(1), 13-24.

Brown, M. E. (1999). Beyond the first wave: A framework for online learning, *Journal of Online Learning*, 11(1), 15-21.

Campbell, D.T. & Stanley, J.C. (1963). *Experimental and Quasi-experimental Designs for Research*, Boston: Houghton Mifflin Company.

Carswell, L., Thomas, P., Petre, M., Price, B., & Richards, M. (2000). Distance education via the Internet: the student experience, *British Journal of Educational Technology*, 31(1), 29-46.

Caverly, D.C. & MacDonald, L. (2002). Online Learning Communities, *Journal of Developmental Education*, 25(3), 36-37.

CDC (2001). *Learning to Learn: The Way Forward in Curriculum Development*, Curriculum Development Council, Hong Kong SAR Government.

Drucker, F. P. (1999). Knowledge worker productivity: The biggest challenge. *California Management Review*, 41(2), 79-94.

Fishman, B.J. (1999). Characteristics of Students Related to Computer-Mediated Communications Activities, *Journal of Research on Computing in Education*, 32(1), 73-97.

Gilbert, N. J. and Driscoll, M. P. (2002). Collaborative knowledge building: A case study. *Educational Technology Research and Development*, 50(1), 59-79.

Glaser, R. E. and Poole, M. J. (1999). Organic chemistry online: Building collaborative learning communities through electronic communication tools. *Journal of Chemical Education*, 76(5), 699-703.

Harasim, L., Hiltz, S.R., Teles, L. & Turoff, M. (1996). *Learning Networks*, Cambridge, Mass: MIT Press.

Howard, A. & England-Kennedy, E.S. (2001). Transgressing Boundaries Through Learning Communities, *Journal of Cooperative Education*, 36(1), 76-82.

Jonassen, D. H., Peck, K. L. and Wilson, B. G. (1999). *Learning with Technology: A Constructivist Perspective*. Prentice Hall, Upper Saddle River, New Jersey.

Krechevsky, M. and Stork, J. (2000). Challenging educational assumptions: Lessons from an Italian-American collaboration. *Cambridge Journal of Education*, 30 (1), 57-74.

Law, N., Yuen, H.K., Ki, W.W., Li, S.C., Lee, Y. & Chow, Y. (2000). (Eds.) *Changing Classrooms & Changing Schools: A Study of Good Practices in Using ICT in Hong Kong Schools*, Hong Kong: Centre for Information Technology in Education, The University of Hong Kong.

NSES (1996). *National Science Education Standards*, Washington, DC: National Academy Press.

Pelgrum, W.J. & Anderson, R.E. (1999). *ICT and the Emerging Paradigm for Life Long Learning*, Armsterdam: International Association for the Evaluation of Educational Achievement.

Poole, D.M. (2000). Student Participation in a Discussion-Oriented Online Course: A Case Study, *Journal of Research on Computing in Education*, 33(2), 162-177.

Romiszowski, A. & Mason, R. (2004). Computer-mediated Communication, In D.H. Jonassen (ed.) *Handbook of Research on Educational Communications and Technology*, 2nd Ed., NJ: Lawrence Erlbaum Associates, Publishers.

Roschelle, J.M., Pea, R.D., Hoadley, C.M., Gordin, D.N. & Means, B.M. (2000). Changing how and what children learn in school with computer-based technologies, *The Future of Children*, 10(2), 76-101.

Rose, S. and Winterfeldt, H.F. (1998). Waking the Sleeping Giant: A Learning Community in Social Studies Methods and Technology, *Social Education*, 62(3), 151-152.

Scardamalia, M. (2000). Can schools enter a knowledge society? In M. Slinger & J. Wynn (Eds.), *Educational technology and the impact on teaching and learning*, Abingdon, RM, 6-10.

Scardamalia, M. and Bereiter, C. (1991) Higher levels of agency for children in knowledge building: A challenge for the design of new knowledge media. *The Journal of the Learning Sciences*, 1(1), 37-68.

Scardamalia, M. and Bereiter, C. (1996). Student communities for the advancement of knowledge. *Communications of the ACM*, 39(1), 36-37.

Scardamalia, M. and Bereiter, C. (1999). Schools as knowledge building organizations, In D. Keating & C. Hertzman (Eds.), *Today's children, tomorrow's society: The development health and wealth of nations*, NY: Guilford, 274-289.

Scardamalia, M. and Bereiter, C. (2002). Knowledge Building. In J.W. Guthrie (Ed.), *Encyclopedia of Education*, 2nd Ed., NY: Macmillan Reference.

Slevin, J. (2000) *The Internet and Society*. Blackwell Publishers Ltd., Malden, USA.

Swan, K. (2001). Virtual interaction: Design factors affecting student satisfaction and perceived learning in asynchronous online course, *Distance Education*, 22(2), 306-331.

Wellman, B. (1999). The Network Community: An Introduction, In B. Wellman (ed.) *Networks in the Global Village: Life in Contemporary Communities*, Oxford: Westview Press.

Yuen, H.K., Law, N. & Wong, K.C. (2003). ICT Implementation and School Leadership: Case Studies of ICT Integration in Teaching and Learning, *Journal of Educational Administration*, 41(2), 158-170.

Yuen, H.K. (2003). Fostering Learning Communities in Classrooms: A Case Study of Hong Kong Schools, *Educational Media International*, 40(1/2), 153-162.

Chapter 8

ENGAGE, EMPOWER, ENABLE: DEVELOPING A SHARED VISION FOR TECHNOLOGY IN EDUCATION

Dr Geoff Romeo
Monash University, Australia

Abstract: After more than two decades of computers in education in Australian schools there is still confusion at all levels about why technology matters and widespread reluctance to move beyond the tokenistic use of computers in classrooms. Why? The reasons are probably many and varied but this chapter proffers the notion that the confusion and reluctance stems from the lack of a shared vision, at the school and classroom level, and the lack of pragmatic teaching frameworks that take into account the realities of teaching in the 21st century. In this chapter *scenario planning* will be applied to the conundrum that is, Information and Communication Technologies in Education (ICTE). The focal point selected will be how ICT's impact on teaching and learning. The organizational mental models that exist range from, the use of ICT underpinned by constructivist theory, to the behaviorist view, that technology makes learning faster, easier and cheaper. Colliding forces and trends include; outcomes based curriculum, rapidly changing technology, and increasing accountability. Two themes are chosen. The first theme, not surprisingly, is the technology itself. We can choose to saturate teaching and learning with technology or not. The second theme is teaching and learning theory. The two themes are placed on a continuum, intersected, and positioned on a matrix. From the matrix scenarios are extracted and presented as vignettes. It will be argued that the scenario planning stages of establishing a focal point, identifying organizational mental models, and conducting an environmental scan can greatly assist schools in developing a shared vision, and that the teasing out of narratives can greatly assist in the development of realistic teaching methods.

Keywords: technology, education, computers, scenario planning, teaching, learning, theory, practice, vision

D. Hung and M.S. Khine (eds.), Engaged Learning with Emerging Technologies, 149-175.

1.   INTRODUCTION

After more than two decades of computers in education in Australian schools there is still confusion, at all levels, about why technology matters, and widespread reluctance to move beyond the tokenistic use of computers in classrooms. Why? The reasons are probably many and varied but this chapter presents the notion that the confusion and reluctance stems from the lack of a *shared vision*, at the school and classroom level, about why the technology matters and why it should be integrated across the curriculum.

So what should that *shared vision* be, how should it be developed, and how do you assist staff to make the vision a reality? How do you develop practical teaching methods that integrate information and communication technologies in meaningful ways? How do you convince teachers that the technology matters? The journey begins, not by focusing on the technology, but by assisting teachers to understand what is now known about how people learn, the design of effective learning environments, and the impact that technology can have on these environments. This provides a theoretical framework that can then be used to explore likely educational technology futures in a systematic way. The exploration of these futures helps teachers to explore the issues, acknowledge the realities, and reach a consensus about how technology will be organised and for what purposes. Developing the shared vision and cultivating loyalty and commitment to it is the first vital element in establishing an effective, technology rich, learning environment.

2.   HOW PEOPLE LEARN

Humans *are designed to be flexible learners and active agents in acquiring knowledge and skills; learning is a basic, adaptive function of humans;* and, *much of what people learn occurs without formal instruction* (Brown, Bransford et al. 1999). A pertinent example of this is the mobile (cell) phone phenomenon. Most, especially teenagers, have no problems learning the intricacies of making a call, sending a text message or installing a ringtone from the internet. Formal courses in *mobile telephony* are not needed, most people learn what is required for their immediate needs and the community of learners ensure that new knowledge, not only about the complexity of the handset but also about the practices of the mobile phone companies is passed on. However when it comes to systematic and highly organised information systems such as reading, mathematics, science, literature and history; formal training, usually in schools, is required. This involves the design of learning environments that should be, but are often not, premised on the accumulated understanding of what it is we think we know about how people learn (Brown, Bransford et al. 1999).

In the last three decades much new information about learning has been generated. There is currently an extraordinary out pouring of scientific work on the mind and the brain, on the processes of thinking and learning, and on the development of competence. The work of cognitive psychologists, educationalists, anthropologists, neuroscientists and others, using a variety of approaches and techniques, is beginning to converge and give a much clearer picture of how people learn.

What is perhaps currently most striking is the variety of research approaches and techniques that have been developed and ways in which evidence from many different branches of science are beginning to converge. The story we can now tell about learning is far richer than ever before ...(Brown, Bransford et al. 1999).

Research on memory and the structure of knowledge, the analysis of problem solving and reasoning, the significance of early foundations, the importance of metacognitive processes and self regulatory capabilities, and the value of cultural experience and community participation, has focussed attention on learning with understanding, the role of pre-existing knowledge, and the importance of active learning. A review of literature by Brown, Bransford et al. (1999) highlights some key findings and conclusions regarding *how people learn.* The findings and conclusion focus on the differences between novices and experts, understanding how learners transfer knowledge, children as learners, and the effects of learning on the brain.

Developing expertise is not simply about memory, general ability, or generic strategies. Experts

...have acquired extensive knowledge that affects what they notice and how they organize, represent, and interpret information in their environment. This, in turn, affects their abilities to remember, reason, and solve problems (Brown, Bransford et al. 1999).

Experts notice features and meaningful patterns that others do not, they organise their vast store of content knowledge to reflect a deep understanding, they are able to select knowledge that is relevant to a particular problem, they retrieve important aspects of their knowledge with little effort, they know their topic thoroughly and they are flexible in applying their expertise to new situations. This is not to suggest that all students should become experts; the point is that the study of expertise demonstrates what effective learning looks like and suggests that learning environments should be designed to assist learners to develop meaningful patterns of information, to organise and contextualise their knowledge, and to fluently retrieve and adapt that knowledge.

Understanding how learners transfer what has been learned in one situation to new situations is important for educators. The school system is predicated on this transfer being carried out successfully from year to year and from one course to the next. There are several factors that influence successful transfer including; the extent of mastery of the initial subject matter; the degree to which learners learn with understanding, the amount of time learners are apportioned to learn complex subject matter, the quality of the feedback learners receive, and the learner's level of motivation. When considering motivation, educators need to take into account the power of intrinsic reward and the need to design appropriate challenges. Other factors that impact a learner's ability to transfer knowledge include; overly contextualising knowledge, the adoption of an active, metacognitive, approach rather than a passive approach to learning, the importance of understanding conceptual change and building on pre-existing knowledge, including pre-existing cultural knowledge.

Learners of all ages have many things in common but in many ways children differ from adult learners. There is a massive body of research, which has dramatically increased in the last three decades, on how children learn. Many of the theorists are familiar - Bruner, Dewey, Gagne, Gardner, Piaget, Rogoff, Skinner, Vygotsky. Brown, Bransford et al. (1999) classify much of the research done in the last 30 years into four major domains. First children have a strong predisposition to learn rapidly and readily by actively making sense of their world. However, there is evidence that young children have an early predisposition to learn about some things and not others. These *privileged* domains include physical and biological concepts, casuality, number and language. Second, contrary to earlier thinking, young children do have strategic and metacognitive competence; they do have knowledge about their own learning and can learn to learn intentionally. It is therefore important for teachers to assist children to develop strategies for learning.

Third, young children lack knowledge and experience but they can reason effectively with the knowledge they have. As they mature they develop theories of what it means to learn and understand. The theories they develop influence their learning and their lack of knowledge and experience can lead to misconceptions and misinformation. Finally children are problem solvers and problem generators who are self motivated and self directed in their learning. Others, including teachers, parents, coaches, and other children, play a major role as guides in cultivating their learning, assisting them to make connections, and supporting their curiosity and persistence by structuring and supporting learning attempts. Crucial to that support is ensuring children have appropriately challenging and novel problems to solve and opportunities to pose their own problems. Books, television, videos, and technology can also serve as guides and support for learning, and technology can be especially useful in assisting teachers to present interesting and novel problems.

Advances in neuroscience are also shedding light on learning and its impact on the brain. Learning actually changes the physical structure of the brain and reorganises it, and different parts of the brain may be ready to learn at different times. These findings are significant for educators because they indicate that the development of the brain is an active process that feeds on vital information gained from experience, and that the brain depends on and benefits positively from learning. Neuroscience is also providing some indications that sensitive periods exist where some experiences, such as language learning, have the most powerful effect, and for other experiences the time of exposure is less critical (Brown, Bransford et al. 1999).

3. DESIGNING FOR EFFECTIVE LEARNING

According to Brown, Bransford et al (1999) designing an effective learning environment that considers what we now think we know about learning, requires a rethink about what is taught, how it is taught and how it is assessed. However the theory does not always provide a simple recipe for practice, at most, it offers some basic principles that should be taken in to account when teaching for effective learning. These basic principles can be scaffolded around four interrelated and interconnected perspectives – *learner-centered, knowledge-centered, assessment-centered* and *community-centered* environments.

Learner-centered environments pay careful attention to the knowledge, skills, attitudes, and beliefs that learners bring to the educational setting. In learner-centered environments learners use their current knowledge to construct new knowledge and teachers recognise the importance of building on the concepts and the pre-existing knowledge that they bring with them. Learners are encouraged to take charge of their own learning and provided with opportunities for reflection and self-regulation. There is a balance between the processes involved in, and the content of, learning; self esteem, motivation and commitment to learning are nurtured. Activities are designed to stimulate learners intellectually and creatively, and learners are viewed as explorers, cognitive apprentices and producers of knowledge rather than consumers. The aim is to excite students about learning and develop a passion for life long learning. The role of the teacher in the learner-centered environment is as facilitator, guide, co-learner and co-investigator.

Knowledge-centered environments *help students acquire the knowledge and skills necessary to function effectively in society.* In knowledge-centered environments learners are assisted in developing meaningful patterns of information, making connections, organising and contextualising their knowledge, and fluently retrieving and adapting knowledge. This is achieved by, adopting a variety of instructional models (including multidisciplinary and integration approaches to curriculum organisation), by utilizing presentations and materials aimed at cultivating high level thinking skills and, by developing learning and problem solving strategies. Within this perspective it is also important to consider the changing goals of education and schooling. Educational goals in the *Digital Age* of the 21st century are very different to the educational goals of the 20th century;

In the early part of the twentieth century, education focused on the acquisition of literacy skills: simple reading, writing, and calculating. It was not the general rule for educational systems to train people to think and read critically, to express themselves clearly and persuasively, to solve complex problems in science and mathematics. Now ... these aspects of high literacy are required of almost everyone in order to successfully negotiate the complexities of contemporary life. The skill demands for work have increased dramatically, as has the need for organizations and workers to change in response to competitive workplace pressures. Thoughtful participation in the democratic process has also become increasingly complicated as the locus of attention has shifted from local to national and global concerns (Brown, Bransford et al. 1999).

Assessment-centered environments provide opportunities for feedback and revision, and assessment activities that reflect the learning goals. They promote formative, relevant, and authentic assessment, encourage risk taking, learning from errors, cooperative learning, self evaluation and taking responsibility for one's learning. Community-centered environments encourage learning from one another, foster a sense of community within the classroom and the school, and *connect students, teachers, and administers to the larger community of homes, businesses, states, the nation, and even the world.* Community-centered environments encourage shared ownership of learning and recognise that students learn a lot from each other, from other adults and from cultural artefacts. They develop a sense of a collaborative learning community that uses the strength of its members to build knowledge. This is achieved by promoting the use of heterogeneous, flexible and equitable groupings to facilitate learning and by catering for a variety of learning styles and individual differences, including cultural differences. The premise is that all students should have the opportunity to learn and develop to their full potential.

Much has been said about learners and effective learning but the role of the teacher in these four perspectives is also important. Effective teachers in *learner- centered, knowledge-centered, assessment-centered* and *community-centered* environments are able to weave the concepts and enquiry methods of their disciplines into clever instructional designs that make it easy for learners to understand complex ideas. Expert teachers have knowledge of their discipline/s and knowledge of pedagogy. The ability of the teacher to use her understanding of teaching and learning, and her knowledge of the structure of her discipline to generate effective learning environments is what distinguishes the novice from the expert (Brown, Bransford et al. 1999).

4. THE ROLE OF INFORMATION AND COMMUNICATION TECHNOLOGIES IN EDUCATION

What should the role of technology be in these *learner/knowledge/assessment/community-centered* environments? There is great interest in technology. Much is written about how it is changing our lives, there is considerable curiosity about its future, and there is great expectation that it will transform the way we learn, however just how this is to happen is still a mystery to many. Ever since the pioneering efforts of Atkinson and Suppes (Atkinson 1968; Suppes and Morningstar 1968) a massive amount has been written about how technology will transform teaching and learning. A great deal of the literature focuses on the dichotomy between *computer education* and *computers in education*, although the word computer is now often replaced with the more inclusive term - *information and communication technologies* (ICT). The explanation of, the now generally accepted dichotomy, is that learning *about* computers is the substance of computer education and information technology courses where the focus is on computer literacy and awareness. Computers *in* education, or learning *with* computers, is about the use of the technology to build powerful learning environments where computers and other technologies are used as intelligent tutors, supportive mindtools (Jonassen 1996; Jonassen 2000) and challenging tutees (Taylor 1980) across the curriculum, to engage, enhance and enable learners. This latter perspective focuses attention on the intersection between pedagogy and technology, and the resulting effect on psychology, epistemology and teaching praxis.

It is important to note that within the *computers in education* perspective differing views on learning *with* technology exist. Many of these views focus on developing, emerging and yet to be invented technologies and sometimes the focus is on the fanciful. The Sci-Fi perspective, for example, is often reinforced by popular culture where a simplistic view of human learning is often depicted. In science fiction cinema, for example, humans can be programmed like a computer. In Star

Trek after a cataclysmic event that destroys his memory Captain Kirk relearns his life via a computer program that magically reprograms his brain. In the Matrix, Trinity needs to learn how to fly a helicopter to rescue Neo. This is a simple matter of finding the right computer program that can be uploaded to Trinity's brain via a convenient parallel port that she has in the back of her head. In fact they all have it.

Closely linked to this view is the techno-romantic view. In the techno-romantic perspective the teaching and learning environment becomes more engaging when, yet to be invented or improved versions of current technologies are introduced. By the sheer presence of technology in the classroom, education will be renovated, learning will become easier, teaching will be more dynamic, and curriculum more engaging. In this idealistic perspective all that seems to be required is to get the wires, boxes and screens in place and educational reform will be a reality. Some believe, of course, that the yet to be invented gadgets won't make a jot of difference. Pausch (2002) for example, states that when virtual reality finally arrives, we won't use it. Technology will eventually allow children to access the world's experts on any given topic, but the experts won't have time to respond, and that telepresence won't take over, children will still physically go to school – *touch and general proximity will still matter*, and that children won't learn to reason, make better judgments, become better citizens because of the technology - they will still need good adult role models (Pausch 2002).

Perhaps it is also possible to include some views about network technologies under the umbrella of techno-romantic. For Spender and Stewart (2002), network technologies will shift teaching and learning online and the notion of anywhere and at anytime learning will become a reality. Anywhere/anytime learning will be characterized by student-centered, project-based learning with the role of the teacher and the learner redefined. The future will belong to the *eteacher* and the *elearner*. The eteacher will no longer be the talking head at the front of the class, s/he will be as adept with technology as s/he is with books and s/he will use new technologies to empower and engage learners. In the digital networked classroom, technology will be infused with the learning process to create knowledge products, the one size fits all curricula will be banished, and digital repositories and learning objects will be the new tools of the teaching profession (Romeo, 2003).

One of the problems with these perspectives is that the complex and protracted nature of human learning is often not considered, and unrealistic expectations are generated. For many teachers, the promised synergy between technology and learning is proving as elusive as ever even with the astonishing array of new technologies that are now available. There is

Table 1 (*Continued*)

A variety of instructional models - including multidisciplinary and integration approaches to curriculum organisation, presentations and materials aimed at cultivating high level thinking skills and, learning and problem solving strategies are adopted	Traditional instructional models are used. These models encourage convergence on the right answer
Assessment-centered environment	
Provide opportunities for feedback and revision, and assessment activities that reflect the learning goals	Assessment is used as a tool to rank students
Formative, relevant, and authentic assessment is promoted and risk taking, learning from errors, cooperative learning, self evaluation and taking responsibility for one's learning are encouraged	Assessment is summative and designed to divide, sort and classify
Community-centered environment	
Encourage learning from one another, foster a sense of community within the classroom and the school, and connect students, teachers, and administrators to the larger community of homes, businesses, states, the nation, and even the world	The environment is individualistic, competitive and not connected
Encourage shared ownership of learning and recognise that students learn a lot from each other, from other adults and from cultural artefacts	Learning from others is discouraged. There is minimal contact with adults. Virtual learning agents are meant to scaffold learning but act as watchdogs
Develop a sense of a collaborative learning community that uses the strength of its members to build knowledge	Test scores are valued not the diverse strengths that learners might bring to the classroom
This is achieved by promoting the use of heterogeneous, flexible and equitable groupings to facilitate learning and by catering for a variety of learning styles and individual differences, including cultural differences	Learners are streamed, sorted and classified. The objective is to find the cream of the crop
The premise is that all students should have the opportunity to learn and develop to their full potential.	Elitist, selective, discriminatory

At Highville little attention is paid to the knowledge, skills, attitudes, and beliefs that Jess and Kim bring to the educational setting. The content of the curriculum is determined by the producers of AchieveHigh2 and there is little time for Jess and Kim to use their current knowledge to construct new knowledge. Most of the knowledge construction that does happen is associated with *hscworkarounds*. Jess and Kim are not encouraged to take charge of their own learning and there is little opportunity for reflection and self-regulation; regulation is Peedy's job. Self esteem, motivation and commitment to learning and, taking responsibility for one's learning are not nurtured. In fact learning and behaviour are strictly monitored; technologies are used to track and police. Activities within AchievHigh2 are designed to stimulate learners intellectually and creatively but, even with the glitz and glamour of interactive multimedia, they somehow full short, with learners quickly becoming bored and disengaged. At Highville Jess and Kim are not viewed as explorers, cognitive apprentices or producers of knowledge; they are seen as empty vessels ripe for knowledge transfer. They are not excited about learning and it is doubtful whether they will develop a passion for learning and or be the slightest bit interested in life-long learning unless perhaps it is connected to earning.

Perhaps the strength of Highville lies in its claim to help students acquire the knowledge and skills necessary to function effectively in society. After all AchieveHigh2, through its interactive content, developed in partnership with some of the world's best mathematicians, historians and scientists, claims to be serious about making students knowledgeable, and it contains some serious content. But Jess and Kim have difficulty in developing meaningful patterns, making connections, organising and contextualising their knowledge, and fluently retrieving and adapting that knowledge. This is even more problematic when the content of the curriculum focuses on the *Three Rs* and *Back to the Basics* rather than contemporary skills for the 21st century.

Assessment at Highville is mostly summative, it is not authentic, nor relevant; there is little opportunity for quality feedback and revision. Jess and Kim are not, encouraged to take risks, to learn from errors, to self evaluate or take responsibility. Assessment is not about helping the learners to learn, it is about attainment, competition and economic reward; he who has the best ENTER score (university entrance score) wins! Jess and Kim are not encouraged learn to from one another; chatting is frowned upon and an idle computer screen is seen as a call for help. There is no sense of community in classrooms at Highville - students, teachers and outside communities don't connect; they compete. There is no shared ownership of the curriculum or a sense of collaboration; learning is a competition where individual difference is about attaining the best test scores and homogeneous, inflexible groupings is a way of ranking learners.

The role of the teacher at Highville is not as facilitator, guide, co-learner and co-investigator; it is as supervisor, custodian, and gatekeeper. The magic is not in being able to weave the concepts and enquiry methods of disciplines into clever instructional designs that make it easy for learners to understand complex ideas, but in getting the server up and running after it crashes for the third time in a week. Technical skills, technological innovation and the ability to author learning objects is what will get you a job at Highville.

Scenario one is meant to be extreme, harsh and unsympathetic so as to highlight the inconsistencies between recent learning theory and some of the things done in schools in the name of good teaching and learning, especially some of the things that are done with technology. For many teachers it is absurd to think that Highville, or any school, would operate in this way, but on the other hand, with a little bit political interference, and a good dose of economic rationalism, it could happen.

Scenario 2 – e-ngage, e-mpower, e-nable

Jessica and Kimberley have arrived early. They know Ms Mancuso will be in her room and will allow them to come in and do some work. They want to work on their project. Jess and Kim are in Year 9 at Plainville High School and their home teacher is Michelle Mancuso. Ms Mancuso is also their English and Social Studies teacher. The girls love Ms Mancuso and they love coming to school. At Plainville High they have some cool technology – super-fast computers, with super-fast network and Internet connections in every room, and students have easy access to digital cameras, handheld computers, laptop machines, scanners and other peripherals. The girls are very adept at pushing data around the Internet and the network and they also have their personal digital communicators and assistants (PDCA). In the old days people carried a palm pilot, a mobile phone *and* a laptop computer– Jess and Kim giggle at the thought and think how clumsy all of that must have been. These days high speed wireless networks make the handling of data and communications through a PDCA so seamless that even Jess's little brother can do it and he's an idiot.

"You buy a PCDA like you used to buy a mobile phone," Jess tells Kim. "At least that's what my Dad says, but what would he know?"

But the cool technology is not why Jess and Kim love coming to school. School is a social event - chatting to Ms Mancuso, the canteen, watching the Year 12 boys play football at lunch time, the debating club, the house athletics, swimming, netball, writing a story for the school magazine, deciding what to do on the weekend, art classes, learning to speak Chinese, school excursions, the debutante ball in year 11, wood working, community service.

"You know what is the coolest thing about this school?" Jess says to Kim.

"The Year 12 boys?" ventures Kim. "The new eighty centimetre plasma screens?"

"The coolest thing is that we get to have a say about what it is we want to learn and how we learn. You know how Ms Mancuso does all that brainstorming with us, how what we do in Maths, Science and other subjects is all connected to the topic we are studying and how we get a chance to select the topic and the sort of activities we want to do and all that stuff - that's cool," says Jess.

As the girls approach the room their PCDAs vibrate and they read the message. Ms Mancuso has gone to the staff room to get a cup of tea she will be back in five minutes. The message was not specifically sent to the girls by Ms Mancuso, she did not know they were coming, but the smart technology incorporated into the building allows messages like this to be received as people approach the door. This sort of technology is now available in many buildings throughout the city, last week the girls went to the new museum, as they passed exhibits they could access, download, send and store information via their PCDAs, as well as interact with the many exhibits. The girls also use their PCDAs to pay for movie tickets, public transport; they can even use them to buy a can of coke from a vending machine.

Ms Mancuso returns, she greets the girls and they all enter the classroom. A student from the 1990s would find difficulty in calling this a classroom, some things are familiar but others are straight out of Star Trek. There are pods of several small flat LCD screens as well as two large plasma screens, projectors, cameras, printers, and all sorts of other devices. There are some very comfortable looking sofas, office type chairs, an area for formal instruction, tables arranged for small group work, whiteboards, and displays of students' work. A closer examination of the whiteboards and the notice boards and it is easy to determine that the students are investigating the topic *Australian Discovery and Exploration.* There are lots of concept maps, questions and ideas displayed all over the place. On one noticeboard several sub topics and focus questions have been written, and projects assigned.

Some other students enter the room and pleasantries are exchanged. Without direction from Michelle screens flicker and digital images illuminate the room. Matthew and Kate want to show the others what they have been working on. They are investigating the expeditions of Matthew

Flinders and Nicholas Baudin. Through their PCDAs and the wireless network they have downloaded their latest work onto the school network and have it displayed on one of the large plasma screens. Using some very clever programming they have created a very interactive piece of multimedia that helps to answer several questions that the class has about the rivalry between Flinders and Baudin and the significance of their expeditions. It starts by tracing the voyages of the explorers on a map of the world and as the ships reach certain points on the map the user is invited to explore what happened at these locations. Kim, Jessica and Michelle watch fascinated. The pair has used primary historical documents available online at French and British museums to build their project. The paintings done by artists and scientists on the Baudin exhibition are stunning and the sea charts of the Australian coast made by Baudin are exquisite.

The love letters written by Flinders to the new bride he left behind for 10 years are interesting. Michelle thinks about how she can use them to help the students understand the notions of *duty, honour, and glory for queen and country* and whether these things are still relevant today. It seems that Matthew has become very curious about the French and is talking about doing some research on some guy called Napoleon. Other teachers might reflect on the power of the technology and its impact on Matthew but Sue reflects on the power of *curiosity*. It drove Baudin, Flinders, generations of historians and scientists and academics and now it is driving Matthew. Curiosity may have killed the cat but the lust for *wanting to know* is probably one of the greatest gifts a teacher can nurture in her students. Michelle thinks about how she can weave this thought into the students' learning.

Jessica and Kim have been investigating the First Fleet and are ready to show what they have done. Through the brainstorming done at the beginning of the topic they became very interested in what it was like to be a teenager on the First Fleet and as part of the First Settlement. They have decided to do this by presenting a series of two narratives – a female convict and a male convict. Their research has led them to primary documents available online, to several databases about the First Fleet, to an old Alan Ladd movie, which they were able to download from the net, and hundreds of web sites about the topic. They have decided that they will present the narratives to the class as a multimedia slideshow, similar to the television show they watched last year about the American Civil War.

The writing of the narratives will need to be spot on – crisp, accurate and entertaining. Michelle is pleased with their choice as it gives her an opportunity to talk to the class about writing genres and writing for an audience. There choice of graphics and images for the slideshow, and how these are matched to the narrative will also be important. Kim and Jessica have the first narrative displayed on the screen. Kim gets Peedy, a virtual agent, to read the narrative and looks to the others for some feedback.

"That's horrible," states Matthew. "I would have just jumped overboard."

"Why don't you use some images from the movie to show how awful it was," suggests Kate.

"You will need to be careful about copyright," cautions Michelle.

Michelle makes a few suggestions; Peedy makes some suggestions about spelling and grammar in the 18th century. Jessica dictates the changes and the computer obliges. Jessica and Kim begin discussing the second narrative.

As the rest of the class start to arrive Michelle takes a couple of minutes to reflect on the impact technology has made to the teaching and learning environment. If she chooses she can access a range of virtual learning objects on every topic and concept under the sun. She sometimes uses them to fill gaps in her own knowledge and sometimes to help her explain specific concepts to groups of children. She rarely uses them to assemble a *course* because she wants the students to have some control and ownership of the curriculum. Other teachers tell Michelle that all the brainstorming, integration of subjects and a multidisciplinary approach to the investigation of topics is messy.

She looks across at Jess, Kim, Matthew, Kate, and the others entering the room and thinks about the commitment these kids make to their own learning – yes it is messy but it is worth it. With the technology Michelle can bring the outside world to the classroom and take the classroom to the outside world. Recent breakthroughs in wireless networks, data compression and bandwidth make synchronous video communication cheap and real. Later today the class will link to the British Museum to look at Captain Cook's journal and when John comes in later for a Maths class they will link to the maritime museum at Plymouth in the United Kingdom to analyse the mathematics of ship building in the 18th century (Romeo 2003).

7.   DISCUSSION (II)

The Plainville High scenario is also extreme in that it is idealistic, romantic, perhaps even naïve; after all everybody knows that getting Year 9 students to work in this manner is virtually impossible. However the learning environment portrayed in this scenario is cognisant with what we know about good teaching and learning (see Table 2).

Table 2.   Linking Scenario 2 to Brown, Bransford et al's (1999) ideas on
              effective learning

Effective Learning	Scenario 2
Learner-centered environment	
Careful attention is paid to the knowledge, skills, attitudes, and beliefs that learners bring to the educational setting	This is an important part of the instructional design. Teacher uses many techniques to explore what is known and what is not known
Learners use their current knowledge to construct new knowledge	Learners are encouraged to build new understandings
Learners are encouraged to take charge of their own learning and provided with opportunities for reflection and self-regulation	Learning is cooperative and collaborative. Learners are encouraged to deviate and pursue their own interests
There is a balance between the processes involved in and the content of learning	A balance between content and process is sought
Self esteem, motivation and commitment to learning are nurtured	This is nurtured through collaboration, cooperation and intrinsic reward
Activities are designed to stimulate learners intellectually and creatively	Learners are engaged, curiosity is stimulated and challenges are appropriate
Learners are viewed as explorers, cognitive apprentices and producers of knowledge rather than consumers	There is a shared ownership of the curriculum, generative assessments and a sense of a journey of discovery
The aim is to excite students about learning and develop a passion for life long learning	Learners are switched on to learning and their curiosity is nurtured
The role of the teacher is as facilitator, guide, co-learner and co-investigator	Teacher is facilitator, guide, co-learner, co-investigator, mentor
Knowledge-centered environment	
Help students acquire the knowledge and skills necessary to function effectively in society	Helping students to become knowledgeable for the 21st century with an emphasis on multiple literacies
Learners are assisted in developing meaningful patterns of information, making connections, organising and contextualising their knowledge, and fluently retrieving and adapting knowledge	Use of flow charts, concept mapping, and schematic diagrams as well as clever instructional designs assists learners to make connections, retrieve and adapt knowledge.
A variety of instructional models - including multidisciplinary and integration approaches to curriculum organisation, presentations and materials aimed at cultivating high level thinking skills and, learning and problem solving strategies are adopted	Integration and multidisciplinary instructional models are adopted. Divergence, curiosity, multiple perspectives are encouraged

Table 2 *(continued)*

Assessment-centered environment	
Provide opportunities for feedback and revision, and assessment activities that reflect the learning goals	Assessment is used to feedback to the learner. It is an integral part of the learning process.
Formative, relevant, and authentic assessment is promoted and risk taking, learning from errors, cooperative learning, self evaluation and taking responsibility for one's learning are encouraged	Assessment is formative and designed to provide learner with feedback
Community-centered environment	
Encourage learning from one another, foster a sense of community within the classroom and the school, and connect students, teachers, and administrators to the larger community of homes, businesses, states, the nation, and even the world	Learners are members of a learning community where collaboration and cooperation are valued as is a connection between learners, teachers and the outside world.
Encourage shared ownership of learning and recognise that students learn a lot from each other, from other adults and from cultural artefacts	Explicit strategies are implemented to encourage learning from others, from other adults and from cultural artifacts
Develop a sense of a collaborative learning community that uses the strength of its members to build knowledge	All learners are valued and encouraged to contribute to the collective construction of knowledge
This is achieved by promoting the use of heterogeneous, flexible and equitable groupings to facilitate learning and by catering for a variety of learning styles and individual differences, including cultural differences	Learners are grouped to facilitate collaborative and cooperative activity
The premise is that all students should have the opportunity to learn and develop to their full potential.	Opportunity for all to develop to their full potential

At Plainville careful attention is paid to the knowledge, skills, attitudes, and beliefs that learners bring to the educational setting. Jess and Kim use their current knowledge to construct new knowledge. They are encouraged to take charge of their own learning and are provided with opportunities for reflection and self-regulation. Motivation and commitment to learning are promoted and nurtured. Learners are intellectually and creatively challenged, and are viewed as cognitive apprentices and knowledge explorers who are excited and passionate about learning.

Learners are also encouraged to be knowledgeable. For Ms Mancuso, being knowledgeable, *is* knowing about the voyages of Flinders and Baudin and about the First Fleet and the First Settlement. But it is also about knowing how a historian analyses a primary document, about how mathematicians develop a theory or how a scientist collects evidence. At Plainville, Jess and Kim and Matthew and Kate construct knowledge so they can solve problems and are assisted in developing meaningful patterns, to make connections, to organise and contextualise their knowledge, and to retrieve and adapt that knowledge. High level thinking skills and problem solving strategies are developed, and there is a focus on developing, tolerance, persistence, determination, excellence and inquiry.

Assessment at Plainville is mostly formative, generative and authentic. Jess and Kim are encouraged to take risks, learn from their mistakes, to self evaluate and take responsibility. There is plenty of opportunity for collaboration, cooperation, reflection and revision. There is a sense of community at Plainville; students, teachers and the outside world connect. Shared ownership of the curriculum is encouraged and scholarship is seen as a social event where there is much to learn and much to learn from each other. Ms Mancuso's role at Plainville is as co learner, co investigator, facilitator, and guide. But not always, sometimes, when the occasion warrants, she is tutor, lecturer and instructor. Her ability to weave her understanding of pedagogy and her in-depth knowledge of her disciplines into an effective learning environment is astonishing. Equally astonishing is how she employs technology to bring exciting, real-world problems into the classroom, to provide scaffolds and tools to enhance learning, to connect to global communities, and to expand her own learning. Plainville is idealistic and romantic. It is also messy, expensive and requires the most able to be employed as teachers but maybe it is worth it.

8.   CONCLUSION

The purpose of this chapter has been to scaffold teachers' learning about why the technology matters and to help them to develop a practical, enduring, mutual vision about technology in education. It could be argued that the process employed to do so, with its focus on educational technology futures where clever web cams, smart cards and virtual agents exist, is a little strange considering the objective was pragmatism. But, if all that can be seen in the vignettes is clever, futuristic, technologies then the point has been missed, as the focus should not be on the technology but on how people learn and how we can design environments where learners can learn effectively. The technology can make a significant difference and having learners engage critically with the technology is important but what matters more is good teaching and good teachers.

REFERENCES

Atkinson, R. (1968). Computerized instruction and the learning process. *American Psychologist.* 23, 225-239.

Brown, A. L., J. Bransford, et al. (1999). *How people learn: brain, mind, experience, and school.* Washington, D.C: National Academy Press.

College of Marin (2002). Scenario Planning, College of Marin 835 College Ave Kentfield California. Accessed on 17.10.2002 at http://www.marin. cc.ca.us/scenario/what_exactly_is.htm.

Dede, C. (2002). Vignettes about the Future of Learning Technologies. *Visions 2020.* U.S. Department of Commerce. Washington DC: Technology Administration Office of Public Affairs.

Edwards, S. and G. Romeo (2003). Interlearn: an online teaching and learning system developed at Monash University. Paper presented at the E-Learn 2003 World Conference of E-Learning in corporate, government, healthcare & higher education, Arizona, USA.

Helfgott, D. and M. Westhaver (2003). Inspiration, Inspiration Software Inc.

Jonassen, D. H. (1996). *Computers in the classroom: mindtools for critical thinking.* Englewood Cliffs, N.J: Merrill.

Jonassen, D. H. (2000). *Computers as mindtools for schools: engaging critical thinking.* Upper Saddle River, N.J: Merrill.

NCREL (2002). Engauge, North Central Regional Educational Laboratory. Accessed on 17.10.2002 at http://www.ncrel.org/engauge/.

NCREL, N. C. R. E. L. and G. Metiri (2003). enGauge 21st Century Skills for 21st Century Learners: Literacy in the Digital Age. Naperville, Illinois: 85.

Papert, S. (1980). *Mindstorms: children, computers, and powerful ideas.* Brighton: Harvester.

Papert, S. (1992). *The children's machine: Rethinking school in the age of the computer.* New York: Basic Books.

Pausch, R. (2002). A Curmudgeon's Vision for Technology in Education. *Visions 2020.* U.S. Department of Commerce. Washington DC: Technology Administration Office of Public Affairs.

Romeo, G. I. (2003). *Technology matters but good teaching matters more.* In Information and communication technology and the teacher of the future: IFIP TC3/WG3.1 & WG3.3 Working Conference on ICT and the Teacher of the Future, January 27-31, 2003, Melbourne, Australia. International Federation for Information Processing; 131. C. Dowling and K.-W. Lai. Boston, Kluwer Academic Publishers: 191-202.

Schwartz, P. and Australian Business Network. (1996). *The Art of the Long View: Paths to Strategic Insight for Yourself and Your Company.* St. Leonards, N.S.W: Australian Business Network.

Spender, D. and F. Stewart (2002). Embracing e-learning in Australian Schools. Melbourne, Commonwealth Bank. Accessed on 17.10.2002 at http://about.commbank.com.au/GAC_File_Metafile/0,1687,2003%255F e%252Dlearning%255Freport,00.pdf.

Suppes, P. and M. Morningstar (1968). Computer-assisted instruction. *Science, 166*, 343-350.

Taylor, R. (1980). *The Computer in the school: tutor, tool, tutee.* New York: Teachers College Press.

learn most creatively, and quite possibly most effectively. There is anecdotal, as well as research based evidence that, for some people the level of concentration and engagement generated by the use of certain computer applications is very high. These factors seem to come into play with computer games, as well as other computer based activities. It is also of interest to those attempting to sell.

As long ago as 1993 (and in fact prior to this) the Impact Report (Watson, 1993) noted some "positive effects of using IT such as increased concentration and motivation." Impact2 (McFarlane et al, 2000) seven years later, also reports increased motivation and concentration resulting from computer use. A group of teachers working with academic colleagues reported that computer use led to "…improved presentation and increased concentration." (Preston 2000.)

Against the backdrop of increasing use of electronic sources of information – the Internet in particular, we can consider ideas of flow and engagement in the context of computer mediated information handling, that is, finding things out from the Internet.

King (2003) sets out a list of factors which he says will enable flow when making use of websites. His work is aimed at those who produce websites for commercial customers, but much of what he includes can be seen as having possibilities in web-based educational settings. He says that, "Users can experience flow only if their trips through cyberspace feel seamless, with fast response, immediate feedback, and few distractions." (King 2003, online) A summary of King's points is included below since they are of potential interest when considering how to work towards generating some measure of flow and raising the potential for effective learning when using web-based materials.

- Speed—Interactive speed is a significant factor in all models of user satisfaction. Sluggish responses put people off.
- Feedback—Provide fast, unambiguous feedback for user input and other actions.
- Clear navigation—signposts and site maps help users to find their way so they can easily form a mental model of a site and understand it more fully.
- Match challenges to skills—an adaptable/adjustable interface that gives users control over the environment's complexity that is appropriate to skill level.
- Simplicity—An uncluttered layout with minimal features reduces the user's attention load.

- Design for fun and utility—Offer a rich yet responsive experience, plus tools to help users accomplish goals quickly and easily.
- Avoid cutting-edge technology—Cutting-edge technology gets in the way of user goals. Research shows that users don't want it; they just want to get their information.
- Minimize animation—It distracts users, who often have limited attention.

(King 2003, online)

With King's last point in mind, it could be argued that in Early Years settings, and indeed other school contexts, animation is possibly more important and useful than it might be in commercial settings, since children are interested in, used to and often engaged by animated characters, at least, to a greater degree than many adults.

With another of King's points in mind – putting a certain amount of control in the hands of the user (learner), the notion of the "locus of control" (Rotter, 1975; Weiner, 1978) which, in contexts considered to be good for learning in computer mediated situations, should rest with the learner, is a justification for this point. When learners are "out of control" of the ways and means of their learning lack of motivation becomes apparent, and less effective learning is likely to be the outcome.

Reid et al (1989) propose a model for learning which places "engagement" at the start of the process:

- Engagement
- Exploration
- Transformation
- Presentation
- Reflection

(Reid et al 1989 p.28)

Engagement is described as "the time during which students acquire information and engage in an experience that provides the basis for, or content of, their ensuing learning..." (ibid p.28) This is not an identical description of engagement in the terms that others might offer, but it is a stage in the process where learners begin to become involved with material in question, and to develop an initial familiarity with the content and the context for the learning. The next stage in the model – exploration is closely related to the stage of engagement. This stage can be an open ended process, where exploratory learners follow their instincts. A more profitable approach might be the setting of short tasks by the teacher, which develop both engagement and exploration. These tasks would be designed to give the child an overview of what is contained in the information under consideration and may take many forms.

Transformation is the stage in which information with which the child has engaged, and has explored, might be re-configured into a form which allows for presentation (the next stage), but importantly, transformed into a format which will, from the teacher's point of view, enable learning objectives to be met. From the point of view of the child, certain questions will now be able to be answered. Transformation and the resultant presentation is not the end of the process. Time to reflect upon what has been undertaken, the process and the content, gives the opportunity for internalisation, and for a deeper level of understanding to be developed. Reflection can also take many forms. One common approach is to ask children to give a short presentation/explanation of what they have been doing and what they have learned. This too can take a variety of different formats, prepared for a variety of different audiences – a poster to display, a newspaper front page, a multimedia presentation, and so on.

This model is based upon constructivist and socio-constructivist views. (Reid, Forrestal and Cook, 1989) They suggest that effective learning is most likely to take place when the intention to learn has been established. This, they suggest, is most likely to occur when learners

"…

- have a clear sense of direction and purpose,
- can build upon what they know already, and
- are actively participating, using their own language and cultural images to help them to understand" (ibid p.10)

The model above, and the comments of Reid et al concerning the prerequisite's for learning are based firmly in the realm of constructivist learning theory. In particular, the idea that learners need to build upon what they already know, and indeed, what they already understand. This can be traced back to schema theory. A schema is a mental model which can be used to help us to understand the way in which knowledge and understanding develops. We are told that: "Human beings understand the world by constructing models of it in their minds." (Johnson-Laird, 1983)

Schemas

Mental models form the basis of schema theory, and have been described and examined over many years by many psychologists (Piaget – 1920s onwards, Bartlett – 1930s, Schank – 1970s, Rumelhart – 1980s, to mention but a few), and, are widely considered as a clear and descriptive way of looking at human memory and learning. Johnson-Laird also tells us that mental models are the basic structure of cognition: "It is now plausible to suppose that mental models play a central and unifying role in representing objects, states of affairs, sequences of events, the way the world is, and the social and psychological actions of daily life." (Johnson-Laird, 1983) Holland and associates state clearly that "... mental models are the basis for all reasoning processes. "(Holland, et al., 1986)

A schema can be described as a theoretical multi-dimensional storehouse for a very large number of items of knowledge. A schema is a framework with numerous nodes and even more numerous connections between nodes. At each node there is a single piece of information or an idea, which might be in any of a range of different formats – picture, sound, smell, feeling and so on. Each node is connected to many others. The connections are formed when some sort of link between the connected items exists. The links are personal, and identical items in the schemas of two different people will most likely have very different links constructed for different reasons. It is the gradual addition of items to schemas and their subsequent connection other items that constitutes constructivist learning. The more connections which exist within and between schemas, the more construction has taken place, this allows us to say that more knowledge and understanding has been gained.

Some of the characteristics of schemas (mental models, scripts) are:

- they are based on our general world knowledge and experiences;
- they are generalised knowledge about situations, objects, events, feelings and actions;
- they are incomplete and constantly evolving;
- they are personal;
- they are not, in almost all cases, wholly accurate representations of a phenomenon;
- they typically contain inaccuracies and contradictions;
- they provide simplified explanations of complex phenomena;
- they contain uncertainty but are used even if flaws are present;
- they guide our understanding of new information by providing explanations of what is happening, what it means and what is likely to result.

Prior knowledge has a crucial part to play in constructivist learning. An existing schema represents an individual's current state of knowledge and understanding of a particular topic, event, action, and so on. New learning concerned with the particular topic will involve the processes incorporating new items into an existing schema, and forming new links. In Piaget's terms, accommodation and assimilation. For this reason it is very important that a schema which is to be the focus of these processes in the introduction of a new area of work in school, is activated. In simple terms, if new learning is to take place it is sensible to review what is already known about the topic in question. The starting point of what is already known and understood is very important if any new learning is to be effective. Schema activation is a process which can be encouraged in classroom situations, and teachers frequently make use of this idea in their work.

3.   SOCIAL CONSTRUCTIVISM

The origins of the constructivist view of learning have their roots in the work of Piaget. Piaget's view of the growing child was what he called a 'lone scientist'. This description gives an image of a child alone, exploring the immediate environment and drawing conclusions about the nature and structure of the world. Social constructivism adds a very important dimension to the theory. Emphasis is given to interaction between the learner and others. The other can come in many forms, it is the dimension of social interaction which is crucial to the social constructivists. The main proponents of this branch of constructivism are Vygotsky, a Russian whose work was carried out towards the start of the twentieth century, but not available in the west until many years later, and Bruner, an American publishing his work in the second half of the twentieth century.

Social constructivism gives a high priority to language in the process of intellectual development. Dialogue becomes the vehicle by which ideas are considered, shared and developed. Dialogue is often with a more knowledgeable other, but his need not always be the case. Dialogue with peers can be of equal value. Out of dialogue it is possible to develop what has become known as "shared understanding". This is a level of understanding that would not have been achieved without the possibilities provided by dialogue, including, perhaps, disagreement and even conflict. Prior knowledge has a part to play. It is an individual's prior and current knowledge which forms the basis of any contribution to a dialogue and it is with reference to existing knowledge and understanding that new ideas and understanding can be constructed in the course of dialogue. More knowledgeable need not imply older, or position of responsibility for learning. It is very often the case that learning will take place in very different environments. Most learning does not take place in school. Any social interaction with anybody at all may well lead to learning. The building and exchange which takes place in the course of a discussion, in any context at all, is likely for at least one of the participants, and often for both or all of them, to lead to a greater understanding of the topic of the conversation.

The role of the more knowledgeable other in formal learning situations is usually taken by a teacher. The teacher has the role of stimulating dialogue and maintaining its momentum. In a very real way, the teacher engages groups and individuals in dialogue and supports the development of understanding. The undertaking of this role, in a planned way, has a particular name and is known as scaffolding. To fully understand the concept of scaffolding we need to first look at another aspect of Vygotsky's work, which is the notion of a zone of proximal development.

The zone of proximal development is a refreshingly simple description of something which many teachers and other adults understand and work with. The zone of proximal development is a theoretical space of understanding which is just above the level of understanding of a given individual. It is the area of understanding which a learner will move into next. In the zone of proximal development a learner is able to work effectively, but only with support. Sewell (1990) explains it as "a point at which a child has partly mastered a skill but can act more effectively with the assistance of a more skilled adult or peer."

Passing through the zone of proximal development is a process which can be aided by the intervention of another. A teacher can fulfill this role, and so can a range of other people. In planning work for children a teacher needs to take into account the current state of the understanding of the children in question. It has been suggested that a computer based teaching situation can act as the more knowledgeable other in some well designed situations. (Sewell, 1990)

Scaffolding is the process of giving support to learners at the appropriate time and at the appropriate level of sophistication to meet the needs of the individual. Scaffolding can be presented in many ways. It can be through discussion, through the provision of materials, or by designing tasks which match and give help appropriate to the individual .

Working collaboratively, in pairs or small groups, is an obvious socially constructive approach to learning. The converse of this would be working in a silent classroom, where contact with others is discouraged. There are times when quiet individual working is useful and important, there are times when a children should be encouraged and required to work alone and quietly. As a mainstay approach to teaching and learning this would totally ignore all that we know about socially constructed knowledge and understanding.

4.   SITUATED LEARNING

The situatedness of learning is another important constructivist idea. Situated learning refers to the fact that all learning takes place in a context.

The context may, or may not be familiar to the learner. If the context is unfamiliar to the learner, the learning will not necessarily proceed smoothly.

Situated learning (Lave and Wenger 1991), in part, suggests that skills, knowledge and understanding which are learned, and even mastered, in one context may not necessarily be transferred successfully to another. Another aspect of situated learning which is more relevant here, is the notion that learning can be situated in social and cultural settings, and that if a learning activity falls beyond the cultural understanding of the learner then learning is likely, at best, to be less successful than if had it been situated in a more familiar setting. For example giving children the task of investigating the pros and cons of, for example, the arranged marriages which take place in some religious traditions when their cultural setting is far away, both in geographical, and intellectual terms. In order to introduce the children to the ideas of making a case, and arguing for particular points of view, it would be far more reasonable to invite them to consider something within their cultural domain – fox hunting in the area of rural England where they live perhaps.

There is a link between the idea of learning being situated, and the need for authentic learning tasks. Much has been written on this matter. (See for example, McFarlane, 1997.) Authentic tasks are ... "tasks which pupils can relate to their own experience inside and outside of school; tasks which an experienced practitioner would undertake." (Selinger, 2001) When learning is made up of authentic tasks there is a greater probability of engagement with the task and also with the information and ideas involved. Authentic tasks are likely to hold the attention and interest of the children and lead to a deeper level of engagement than with another similar but "non-authentic" or at least, less authentic, task. This links closely with the ideas put forward by the socio-cultural learning theorists. Bruner (1996), Brown Collins and Duguid (1989) and others support the need for culturally linked and authentic learning tasks, this has the desirable effect of making the difference between school learning and "out of school learning" less well defined.

5.   METACOGNITION

Metacognitive knowledge is the knowledge that an individual has about their own cognition, and which can be used to consider and to control their cognitive processes. To work metacognitively is to consider, and take active control of the processes involved in learning and thinking, as they are happening.

Metacognition as an areas of study is associated with the psychologist John Flavell, (1976, 1977). He tells us that metacognition consists of metacognitive knowledge and metacognitive experiences or regulation. Metacognitive knowledge is knowledge about cognitive processes, which an individual has come to understand, and can be used to control mental processes. "Metacognition refers to one's knowledge concerning one's cognitive processes and products or anything related to them .. metacognition refers, among other things, to the active monitoring ... regulation and orchestration of these processes." (Flavell 1976) Brown (1987) offers a simpler version of this when he says that "Metacognition refers loosely to one's knowledge and control of [one's] own cognitive system".

When we are metacognitively aware, we are able to consider the ways and means of our own learning. These ways and means are usually very personal and at times idiosyncratic. Many of us have particular ways of learning for tests and exams, and we know that they are effective for us. In some respects this has connections with Gardener's multiple intelligence theory (Gardner 1993) which proposes the idea that we all have various levels of intelligence across a range of intellectual areas. There are also links with learning style, which can affect approaches which an individual favour and make use of in learning situations. We actually learn in different ways to each other and we often choose to use our preferred learning style. If a particular approach to learning is encouraged by a teacher, it can lead to a situation where some pupils might well work and learn less effectively than others in the class.

Gardner's theory of multiple intelligences comes, in part, out of a concern that when intelligence is measured the most commonly used devices (standard verbal and non-verbal reasoning tests) often don't allow those tested to demonstrate what they are really good at, or where their intelligence lies. Gardener gives us a set of different *intelligences* which as individuals we display to greater or lesser degrees, according to our particular intellectual make up. An individual's particular strengths and preferences in intelligences have a direct bearing upon the way in which learning takes place. Some with interpersonal strengths would be most likely to learn effectively in a social situation where relating ideas and knowledge to others can be encouraged. The opposite might be true for an individual with low interpersonal intelligence and a strength in intrapersonal intelligence.

To be aware of multiple intelligence strengths and our preferred or most effective learning approach is to be thinking metacognitively.

There are two examples from the United Kingdom which illustrate an understanding of the power of metacognitive thought. It has become accepted practice in UK Primary schools, during lessons dealing with Literacy and Numeracy in particular (both covered by the introduction of

that his first bike was a Penny Farthing, but I don't believe that because he was born in 1968."

The purpose of this rule is similar to the purpose of the first. It is an attempt to encourage children to engage with the text. This rule also encourages the child to think more broadly about the extract and to give it a context.

3.   Say where the information came from:

This rule is to encourage honesty about where ideas and information have come from, and to encourage clarity about the difference between the work of the children themselves and the work of others. It is hoped that the application of this rule will lead to good habits, and help to avoid unintentional plagiarism.

The children's comments made it clear that the Internet can be a highly motivating resource. When the children were told that they were going to be using the Internet there were clear signs of delight and excitement. During all of the lessons, the children were interested, involved generally well motivated. For a variety of reasons, the end products were a little disappointing in this particular project, lack of time being a notable problem. However many of the requirements for effective learning were in place and with more experience and directive reminders it seems that the quality of the product would also be indicative of effective learning.

Apart from the general atmosphere detected in the room, it was also clear from speaking with some of the children at a later date, that the work had been enjoyable:

Researcher: Did you enjoy the work?
Child A: I <u>definitely</u> enjoyed it. It wasn't easy, but it wasn't the hardest thing ... I really got into it.

Researcher: Did you enjoy the work that we did on the computer?
Child B: Yes I did, I thought it was fun, I enjoyed it. ... I enjoyed doing it ... So it was fun yes.

Researcher: Was it enjoyable?
Child C   : Yes ...fun. It was fun, but complicated.

Researcher: So did you enjoy the work?
Child D: Oh yes, it was great a real ... it was a challenge and I love that sort of challenge ... and the Internet too ... makes me work harder.

The comments from the participants are in line with the findings of other research (Hammond and Mumtaz 2001, BECTa, 2001) which links the use of the Internet, and ICT in general, to high levels of pupil motivation.

9.   CONCLUSION

We have seen that the work of the cognitive psychologists has the potential for helping us to understand how to encourage effective learning in many situations. This is particularly the case when making attempts to use large sources of information, which is often electronically mediated in these days of high speed Internet connections and encyclopedic subject based CD-ROMs. It seems that to spend a little time revisiting what is known already by a group, and "group" is stressed here, can lead to benefits in the longer term. The activation of prior knowledge is recognised by the theorists as important and this importance is reinforced by those closer to practice who have direct experience of working with children in this way. (Wray and Lewis, 1997; Kumpulainen and Wray, 2002; Pritchard and Cartwright, 2004)

Models of different approaches to dealing with the problems of using information successfully stress, in different ways, the same important elements of effective learning. Learning is seen, time and again, through the medium of a recommended and successful approach as a constructive, collaborative, well situated and often authentic activity which it is beneficial to approach in open and metacognitive ways. Children working alone, without the support of either peers or a sound preparation and clear focus are not likely to reach their potential for either learning, or enjoyment of the process of learning. We can see from the evidence presented here, and from many other sources not used directly that learning is:

- a process of building links between what is known and what is to be learned;
- a social, and often collaborative, process;
- a situated process; and
- a metacognitive process.

It is with this firmly in mind, and with due consideration to the knowledge, concepts and skills which we consider important, that we should be planning work and designing approaches for children to use in order to gain the utmost from the opportunities that a twenty-first century engaged education can offer.

REFERENCES

BECTA. (2001). *Primary Schools of the Future: Achieving Today. Report to DFEE.* Coventry: BECTA.

Bloom, B. S., Englehart, M.D., Furst, E. J., Hill, W. H. and Krathwohl, D. R. (Eds.) (1956). *Taxonomy of Educational Objectives I: Cognitive Domain* New York: McKay.

Biggs, J. B. and Moore, P. J. (1993). *The Process of Learning.* New York: Prentice Hall.

Brown, A. (1987). Metacognition, executive control, self-regulation, and other more mysterious mechanisms. In F. E. Weinert & R. H. Kluwe (Eds.), *Metacognition, motivation, and understanding* (pp. 65-116). Hillsdale, New Jersey: Lawrence Erlbaum Associates.

Brown, J. S., Collins, A. and Duguid, P. (1989). Situated Cognition and the Culture of Learning. *Educational Researcher, 18*(1), 32-42.

Bruner, J. (1996). *The Culture of Education.* Cambridge: Harvard University Press.

Csikszentmihalyi, M. (1996). *Creativity: flow and the Psychology of Discovery and Invention.* New York: Harper Perennial.

Csikszentmihalyi, M. (1975). *Beyond Boredom and Anxiety.* San Francisco: Jossey-Bass.

DFEE (Department for Education and Employment). (1998). *The National Literacy Strategy (NLS).* London: DFEE.

DFEE (Department for Education and Employment). (1999). *The National Numeracy Strategy (NNS).* London: DFEE.

Flavell, J. H. (1976). Metacognitive Aspects of Problem Solving. In Resnick (Ed.). *The Nature of Intelligence.* (pp. 231-235). New Jersey: Lawrence Erlbaum Associates.

Gardner, H. (1993). *Multiple Intelligences: The Theory in Practice.* New York: Basic Books.

Hammond, M. and Mumtaz, S. (2001). How trainee teachers of ICT approach teaching their subject. *Journal of Computer Assisted Learning, 17*(2), 166 – 176.

HMI/DES (1985). *Curriculum Matters 2: The Curriculum from 5 – 16* London: HMSO.

Holland, J. H., Holyoak, K. J., Nisbett, R. E., Thagard, P. R. (1986). *Induction: Processes of Inference, Learning and Discovery.* Cambridge: MIT Press.

Johnson-Laird, P. (1983). *Mental Models: Towards a Cognitive Science of Language, Inference, and Consciousness.* Cambridge: Harvard University Press.

Jones, B. F., Valdez, G., Nowakowski, J. and Rasmussen, C. (1995) What is effective learning and how can it be measured? (North Central Regional

Educational   Laboratory   –   NCREL)   Online   at: www.ncrel.org/sdrs/edtalk/newtimes.htm accessed 21.3.04.

Kumpulainen, K. and Wray, D. (2002). *Classroom Interaction and Social Learning.* London: Routledge Falmer.

Lave, J. and Wenger, E. (1991). *Situated Learning.* Cambridge: Cambridge University Press.

Means, B. and Olson, K. (1995). *Restructuring schools with technology: Challenges and strategies.* Menlo Park, CA: SRI International.

King, A. (2003) Enabling Flow in Web Design (Chapter Two in: *Speed Up Your Site: Web Site Optimization* New Riders, Indianapolis) Online at: http://www.websiteoptimization.com/speed/2/2opt.pdf (Accessed 26.3. 04).

McFarlane, A. (Ed.) (1997). *Information Technology and Authentic Learning: Realising the Potential of Computers in the Primary Classroom.* London: Routledge.

McFarlane, A. et al (2000). *ImpacT2 Project Preliminary Study 1: Establishing the Relationship between Networked Technology and Attainment.* Coventry: BECTA.

NCET. (1995). *Making Sense of Information.* Coventry: NCET.

NSIN (The National School Improvement Network). (2002). *Bulletin No. 1.* London: Institute of Education, University of London.

Ogle, D. M. (1989). The Know, Want to Know, Learn Strategy. In K. D. Muth (Ed.) *Children's Comprehension of Text.* Newark, Delaware: International Reading Association.

Preston, C. (2000). *Teachers as Learning Innovators.* The Keynote Speech at BETT 2000.

Pritchard, A. and Cartwright, V. (2004). Transforming what they read: helping eleven year olds engage with Internet Information. *Literacy, 38*(1), 26-31.

Reid, J., Forrestal, P., and Cook, J. (1989). *Small Group Learning in the Classroom.* Chalkface Press, Scarborough (Australia). London: English and Media Centre.

Rotter, J. (1975). Some Problems and Misconceptions Related to the Construct of Internal Versus External Control of Reinforcement. *Journal of Consulting and Clinical Psychology.*

Selinger, M. (2001). *Setting Authentic Tasks Using the Internet.* In Leask, M. (Ed.) *Issues in Teaching Using ICT.* London: Routledge Falmer.

Sewell, D. (1990). *New Tools for New Minds.* Wheatsheaf, London: Harvester.

Watson, D. (1993). *The Impact Report: An Evaluation of the Impact of Information Technology on Children's Achievements in Primary and Secondary Schools--a comprehensive study.* London: Kings College/DfEE.

Weiner, B. (1978). *Human Motivation.* New York: Holt, Rinehart and Winston.

Wray, D. and Lewis, M. (Eds.) (2000). *Literacy in the Secondary School.* London: David Fulton.

Wray, D. and Lewis, M. (1997). *Extending Literacy.* London: Routledge.

Chapter 10

CREATING ICT-ENRICHED LEARNER-CENTRED ENVIRONMENTS: MYTHS, GAPS AND CHALLENGES

Kar Tin Lee
Department of Information and Applied Technology, Hong Kong Institute of Education, Hong Kong

Abstract: Creating ICT-enriched learner-centred environments requires a holistic approach that calls for changes at three levels – teacher, schooling environment and learning activities. Fundamentally, however, it is teachers who, with support from parents, administrators and policy makers, can optimise the benefits of ICT-enriched environments to make learner-centred learning a reality. This chapter therefore pays due attention to the salient issues confronted by teachers in the creation of ICT-enriched learner-centred environments, by using Hong Kong as an example to highlight the myths, gaps and challenges. Reviewed in the chapter are three myths that many educators in Hong Kong subscribe to, including ICT having limited values, ICT being a panacea to learning problems and technical knowledge of ICT being paramount. Highlighted are the gaps that can be observed in the field, of which include gaps in perception; the theory and practice of teaching every student; team-building; and the desire to use ICT. The challenges discussed include teachers encouraging students to become active participants; teachers assisting students to understand their weaknesses and strengths; changing classroom dynamics; leadership in existence; and teachers having an individual sense of how they are able to successfully influence student learning. In the discussion, literature is reviewed and practical solutions are offered.

Keywords: assessment, ICT-enriched learning, leadership, school cultural change, student-centred learning, teaching strategies

D. Hung and M.S. Khine (eds.), Engaged Learning with Emerging Technologies, 203-223.

1.   INTRODUCTION

Education reform is often a disappointing business (Carpenter, 2000; Wagner, 2003). In the case of information and communication technologies (ICT) in education, various countries have made massive injection of funds in the education sector, trying to enhance a new generation of ICT-literate capable of rapidly applying ICT for enhancing economic competitiveness and quality of life (see, e.g., Cheah & Koh, 2001; Fujitani, Bhattacharya, & Akahori, 2003). Yet, similar critics continue to emerge and highlight, on the one hand, the absence of evidence to show that reform efforts to make education ICT-driven have induced any significant impact (Hinostroza, Guzman, & Isaacs, 2002) and, on the other hand, most students are still educated in the same way as their parents were – that is, text-book based learning and teacher-centred teaching (Peters, 2000).

In the case of Hong Kong, while some researchers (e.g., Law, Lee, & Chow, 2002) have found pieces of evidence that ICT does make a difference in school education, many teachers, school principals and policy makers are still prone to point out that there is a lack of evidence to demonstrate the desirable results that stakeholders have anticipated from the introduction of ICT into Hong Kong classrooms since the late 1990s. Nevertheless, basing on the author's frequent in-depth interactions and discussions with many teachers in Hong Kong, in particular, and in the Asia-Pacific generally, it has been noted that some progress has been made. It is also fair to say that expert teachers and educational researchers are now more inclined to report that the government and education stakeholders do have the critical tools and are available to support and reinforce an ICT-enriched learner-centred environment in ways never thought possible before.

More importantly, it needs to be recognised that for teachers today, who function in the ICT-enriched learner-centred environment, they now have much greater capacity than before to make a difference in student-centred learning. However, concomitant with this occurrence though is that full-scale and wide scope evaluation and assessment have yet to be fully developed and/or deployed. All interested parties need explicit evidence to demonstrate that learning gains have been made in schools from these huge investments. To a great extent, what is needed is a better understanding of the problems and issues of enhancing teaching and learning with the support of ICT – or what I called the myths, gaps and challenges. Such an understanding, blended with postmodernist elements, is essential in helping teachers realise the benefits of ICT-driven learner-centred education. The purpose of this chapter then is to use Hong Kong as an example to highlight the myths, gaps and challenges in the creation of ICT-enriched learner-centred environment.

2. EVIDENCE OF SUCCESS

In the recently published consultation document "Information Technology in Education – Way Forward" (Education and Manpower Bureau [EMB], 2004), it is recognised that the necessary infrastructure had been laid, teachers had been provided with the basic training on the use of IT and a rich repository of digital education resources had been collected (EMB, 2004, p.1). The document also reports that "(R)egional centres of IT excellence have emerged, innovative pedagogies and practices have surfaced, and students' generic IT skills have improved" (*ibid.*).

In the same document in relation to curriculum matters, the EMB continued to highlight that "the Basic Education Curriculum Guide - Building on Strengths" published by the Curriculum Development Council (CDC) in 2002 provides, among others, "guidance to schools on fostering an appropriate environment for interactive learning with IT, and making appropriate use of IT in teaching various subjects" (EMB, 2004, p. 2).

With regard to actual implementation in schools, Fung and Pun (2001) reviewed the use of ICT in Hong Kong's school education, giving a detailed account of the government's ICT in education policy and of ICT implementation in relation to access and connectivity, teacher enablement and curriculum development. From computers as a teaching subject which was introduced in secondary school education in the 1980s to the investments of millions of dollars since 1997 to make ICT a critical component of schooling, Fung and Pun (2001) reported that substantial improvements have been made in Hong Kong, particularly since Hong Kong became a Special Administrative Region (SAR) of China on 1 July 1997 when the Chief Executive, the Honourable Tung Chee-hwa, announced that education would be a top priority of the Hong Kong SAR.

Despite the fact that Hong Kong has had a very short history of integrating ICT in the classroom, there is already some evidence that several schools have tapped into the vast capacity of ICT-enhanced classrooms and have successfully generated new learner-centred environments (Law, Yuen, Ki, Lee & Chow, 2000; Law, Lee, & Chow, 2002; Lee, 2002a). Given time, these environments will impact on every aspect of education and will lead to a new definition of where and how learning occurs, meeting the high expectation of the education reforms orchestrated by the government and educators and setting direction for reformers to further strive for more meaningful teaching and learning in the globalised, knowledge-driven and ICT-intensive community. From the teachers' perspective though, this remains a daunting task as many of them have yet to fully acquire the needed skills to effectively frame the pedagogy of the ICT-enriched learner-centred classroom and to garner up sufficient courage to convince the stakeholders of its eventual benefits.

The lack of teacher skills to frame pedagogy is congruent with the views of the aforementioned EMB consultation document that highlights the major obstacles affecting the use of IT in learning and teaching. The consultation document states that "while all teachers have been provided with basic training in the use of IT, many are still not familiar with the application of IT to enhance the effectiveness of learning and teaching" [EMB, 2004, Section 14(e), p.5]. It also goes further to highlight the fact that "some training courses provided have been skewed towards training in IT skills, not the application of IT to enhance learning and teaching".

On a more positive note, it is evident in Hong Kong that after intensive professional development and up-skilling over the last few years, a small percentage of teachers are no longer asking how will the use of ICT affect their work; instead, they are now asking how as educators they can use ICT to affect their student's learning (Lee, 2002b), and how a variety of technologies can be used to create efficiency and effectiveness in learning and to encourage students to take more responsibility for their own education? Without doubt, the introduction of new technologies into classrooms has already challenged many teachers to rethink their professional practice as educators and has opened up opportunities for teachers to approach their vision for teaching in new, optimal ways. The "Information Technology in Education – Way Forward" consultation document (EMB, 2004) rightly points out that "increased use of IT in teaching requires the re-engineering of classroom management and routines, as teachers need to tackle the interaction between machines and students while striving for results" [(Section 14(f)).

From an analysis of the results of some of the completed and ongoing projects in Hong Kong (see, e.g., Lee, 2004), it is found that teachers in the project schools where ICT have been purposely used have been able to push beyond the four walls and have been successful in shaping students to become lifelong learners, in catering for the different individual learning styles of students and in achieving different levels and dimensions of impact on student attainment. It is further found that teachers in these project schools have been able to reflect and to ask what good can come from using technology in the classroom in ways that support student learning. Functioning in the ICT-enriched learner-centred environment, they have been challenged to think of smarter ways to use ICT, represented not by a focus on the technologies but on the intent of the learning activities and on the ways in which the learner-centred environment is conceived and constructed. Yet, the projects also reveal that there are still major barriers to effective use of ICT. The first perhaps most difficult job that needs to be accomplished is dispelling myths in Hong Kong schools.

3.   DISPEL THE MYTHS FIRST!

There are various myths that many educators in Hong Kong subscribe to, including (1) ICT is of limited value, (2) ICT is a panacea to learning problems and (3) technical knowledge of ICT is paramount. These myths help frustrate efforts to maximise the return on investment in ICT in schooling. Regarding the first myth, the author's interviews with Hong Kong teachers and school administrators conducted over the past five years reveal that many educators still consider that ICT merely supports their students' preparing for public examinations and that fundamentally the key is that of individual students' efforts, intelligence and devotion that get them good or passing grades. These educators are hardly those who are ignorant in the ICT era, or the so-called information-deprived (Tiene, 2002). They are well aware of current research findings such as those of Lesley Parker (2000), who has established that many students might have access to the Internet, but are only using it mostly for entertainment and games.

Research, however, has documented that ICT can be of great value in various ways. First, even under the conventional mode of examination-driven education, the use of ICT in education can generally help improve students' memory retention, increase their motivation and deepen their understanding of materials learned (Wheeler, 2001). Second, in a study (that involves 28 countries) on analysing the pedagogical practices of teachers and learners, as well as the role of ICT played in these practices, Kozma and Anderson (2002) have found that ICT-contextualised innovative pedagogical practices are observable in the 28 participating countries (see, e.g., Law, et al., [1999] for Hong Kong schools as it was included as one of these countries), promoting effective learning. Third, while "Leading-edge ICT pushes education by expanding where and when learning can take place" (Anderson, 2002, p. 381), "… the most significant outcome of innovative learning activities involving ICT was empowerment, particularly of students" (p. 383). With empowerment, students and teachers are better prepared for learning to learn from a variety of others and learning to create and to contribute to a learning community (Anderson, 2002). Fourth, with ICT, schools can promote a cooperative and collaborative learning environment (Schultz-Zander, Buchter, & Dalmer, 2002), changing teachers' and students' roles in learning, and can devise unconventional classroom pedagogies to enhance not only cognitive learning outcomes (Mioduser, Nachmias, Tubin, & Forkosh-Baruch, 2002) but as well as affective and socio-cognitive learning outcomes, which are important to the preparation for lifelong learning (Law, Lee, & Chow, 2002). And fifth, ICT can be used to help students in problem solving, creative cognition and social interaction (Wheeler, Waite, & Bromfield, 2002).

In light of these findings, it is obvious the power of ICT in education being under-utilised is not the same thing as ICT power being limited, and that the key is how educators can realise the real and potential values of ICT in education - an issue to be discussed in the following section. As such, what educators need to do is to dispel this myth and to shift their focus on how teaching and learning in the ICT-intensive era can be enhanced.

Regarding the second myth that ICT is a panacea to learning problems, some teachers and teacher educators in Hong Kong who are fascinated by the power of ICT are prone to argue that ICT in Hong Kong, just as in other countries (Wheelers, 2001; Williams, Coles, Wilson, Richardson, & Tuson, 2000), can bring various benefits to teachers and students: for example, "shared learning resources, shared learning spaces, opening up the classroom, the promotion of collaborative learning, the move towards autonomous learning, teachers' move towards electronic management of learning spaces" (P. 13). Then, believing that ICT would be good for students, many teachers work hard to improve their mastery of ICT as a set of skills or competencies and to use ICT in instructional designs.

In reality, however, while ICT does serve as a vehicle for effective teaching and learning, it cannot provide solutions to all the learning problems. Indeed, researchers have found that ICT does not in itself make people more likely to participate in education (Selwyn & Gorard, 2003) as there are various constraints imposed by sociocultural settings (Lim & Barnes, 2002), that there are various barriers to ICT use in school education (Higgins, 2001), that individual teachers cannot optimise the use of ICT as there are factors at work (for example, access to ICT and effective management of ICT resources, appropriate training in ICT skills, and ongoing support to encourage progression beyond initial teacher education [Goodison, 2002; Williams, Coles, Richardson, Wilson, & Tuson, 2000]) and that often children's learning take place outside school and is thus beyond the control of teachers unless concerted efforts are made to relate students' home use of ICT and with schooling (McNicol, Nankivell, & Ghelani, 2002).

In light of these research findings, it is obvious that dispelling the myth of ICT being panacea to learning problems would help draw educators' due attention to important factors and variables that influence the use of ICT as a tool, as learning support and even as revolutionary agent (McFarlane, 2001). By doing, teachers can be re-oriented towards developing a more supplicated, complex understanding of ICT, not only as technology in education but as a social phenomenon shaped by multi-factors, often in non-linear ways, and interpreted differently by different learners.

Regarding the myth of technical knowledge of ICT being paramount, currently, it is hardly unusual or surprising that a large proportion of school administrators and policy makers in Hong Kong continue to cling onto their past notions and assumptions about ICT and teaching. Many principals and teachers continue to believe that any teacher who has a computer science degree or who has a mathematics or science background will be "*good*" ICT teachers. This belief is of the same essence as other fallacies, such as he who is a master of subject matter knowledge is to be a "good" teacher. What is seriously missing in the assumption is that unless the teachers are willing to dispel their beliefs which are often embedded in traditions of teaching and learning where conventional uses of computer technology are inconsistent with the current reform approaches and current views on teaching and learning, then any interventions by these teachers will not achieve true ICT integration in their classrooms.

Added to the inapt assumption above is the failure of the education reform movement to take into consideration the redesign of schools when implementing ICT. The newly built schools continue to establish computer rooms that take on the look of factory models where computers are lined up in rows and each laboratory accommodates an enormous number of computers. Typically this kind of development continues to support technology being used to deliver teaching rather than shifting the emphasis to a design based on a student-centred approach or an open-ended environment for learning.

In short, this myth is based on conventional understanding of teaching and learning, and must be dispelled in the light of findings from postmodernist studies. Regarding postmodernism, some scholars try to avoid it, because to them "(P)ostmodernism takes an eclectic approach to analysis, taking fragments of social analysis as sufficient unto themselves: critique for the sake of critique..." (Lembcke, 1993, p. 67). Yet, in fact, postmodernism as an intellectual movement is itself vaguely understood. In essence, it has two branches - skeptical and the affirmative. "Skeptical postmodernists deny the possibility of an empirical social science and engage largely in critiquing existing work rather than undertaking new empirical approaches ... (and) emphasize the negative and lack confidence or hope in anything" (Rosanau, 1992, p. 183). In contrast, the affirmative postmodernism challenges the content and form of dominant models of knowledge and focuses on "what is non-obvious, left out, and generally forgotten ... and examined what is unsaid, overlooked, understated, and never overtly recognized" (Kilduff & Mehra, 1997, p. 460). When people recognise that reality is a social construction, their focus inevitably shifts to the nature of "situational context" and to "the discursive processes that shape the construction" (Fischer, 1998, p. 135). In the field of education, scholars have advocated that the postmodern school curriculum should be a "kaleidoscopic phenomenon" (Slattery, 1995, p. 244), compelling teachers and students to ask questions about what the use of ICT means and how it would affect them and why. After all, knowledge is personally constructed and reconstructed in the learning context. These postmodernist propositions challenges the conventional mode of teaching and learning and role of teachers (Wheeler, 2001), which are no longer viable in the current knowledge-based society which compels teachers and learners to actively engage this world and to hold ownership of their own learning rather than be receivers of objectively existed and transmitted knowledge. In the age of postmodernism, students are to be explorer, constructor, researcher, collaborator, judge, reflective practitioner and problem solver (Squires, 2000). There is thus the need for educators to undo the conventional thinking and to collaborate with students to construct knowledge of emerging technology practices that are transforming teaching and learning (Breuleux, 2001).

To undo conventional thinking requires a certain breed of teachers. Riel and Becker (2000, p.1) in their study of 4,000 U.S. teachers concerning their educational background, teaching philosophy and instructional practices both with and without computers found that "teachers who assume a professional orientation to teaching are far more likely to have made high investments in their own education, to have constructivist-compatible philosophical beliefs about education to develop the instructional practices that are related to their beliefs and to integrate computers into their classrooms in ways support meaningful thinking and the sharing of ideas with peer" (p. 34). Riel and Becker called this group the "Teacher Leaders and Professionals". It is precisely this kind of teachers that the schools in Hong Kong currently need. These will be the teachers who would not be subject to the will of administrators and not so easily pressured by parents to demonstrate student learning in terms of higher test scores (Riel & Becker, 2000, p.22). On the other hand, Riel and Becker (2000) have also identified another group of so-called "Private Practice Teachers" who continue to support "direct instruction tied closely to textbook materials with a high value on convergent thinking and view tests as a valuable strategy for assessing this content accumulation" (p.33). It would be reasonable to say that at this juncture a significant portion of Hong Kong teachers would fall into this latter category.

Researchers have happily reported progress in the creation of ICT-enriched learning environment. For example, Parker (2000) reports that Canada already boasts the highly sophisticated electronic classroom, which has a distributed control system that "automatically controls a room's technology (including lights, screen, projector, electronic document camera, VCR and electronic whiteboard) in response to instructor activity" (p. 12).

4.   OPEN UP TO NEW IDEAS AND SKILLS

In order to maximise the potential of ICT-enriched learner-centred environments, teachers, when planning classroom activities, need to consider factors that will enable students with different abilities to participate fully in all aspects of the lesson (Lee, 2002c). They need to create deep and durable learning situations for their students and persist in querying whether their traditional classrooms manifest sound pedagogical practice. It is also the case that teachers need to continually strive to ensure that, when ICT is in fact used, it is promoted on the basis of quality, rather than expediency. Teachers need to be convinced that learning can be qualitatively different and that the process of learning in the classroom can become significantly richer. Four areas need particular attention: gaps in perception; the theory and practice of teaching every student; team-building; and the desire to use ICT. Opportunely in the recent consultation document "Information Technology in Education – Way Forward" (EMB, 2004), adequate attention has been given to this aspect of teacher professional development (see, e.g., Section 19 [Goal 2]). It is just hopeful that policy makers in Hong Kong, as well as those in developing educational systems, would recognize, just as researchers in the US, for example, have noted, that "around 30% of the educational ICT budget needs to be spent on professional development" (Parker, 2000, p. 14).

I. Assessing learning – gaps in perception

It is important for teachers and principals in schools using ICT to arrive at a common understanding on the following aspects regarding assessment for learner-centred learning and to be clear about what they are assessing:

- as schools are currently organised, it is not always possible for each individual student to receive the appropriate educational experiences without more targeted efforts to deal with individual differences;
- equal opportunity in education means that school-based curriculum can be adapted and developed to meet specific needs of each child to reach their optimal potential;
- the demand for tests and examinations, as well as the meeting of teaching schedules, may often inhibit the development of each child in the classroom;

- the excessive demands on teachers may prevent them from taking any risks to explore new ideas and teaching strategies that help promote learner-centred learning;
- children in schools may have varied interests or levels of comprehension of classroom tasks and therefore may have difficulty in conforming to existing practices;
- teachers need to have a comprehensive understanding of student individual differences in order to have more success in educating students better.

Closing the gaps in perception, teachers would then have a common ground to share and/or explore their precious experiences, successful or failing, in assessing learner-centred learning. They too would acquire a fuller and broader understanding of the ramifications of assessment and appropriate means and ways to addressing assessment problems, particularly with reference to ICT in teaching and learning, as suggested in the field (see, e.g., Burger & Burger, 1994; Esteve, 2000; Lin, 2002; McFarlane, 2001).

II. Adopting the notion of teaching every student

If ICT is to be truly integrated into the classroom learner-centred learning, then when using ICT teachers need to be consistently reminded to:

- develop a heightened awareness of the many different approaches in evaluating students;
- understand that their belief about how students learn (or how intelligent they are) influences the way they plan for the educational development of students in their charge;
- aim to provide opportunities for students to express their creativity in a wide range of ways - including intuitive and affective domains – to ensure a safe place for creativity to be expressed and to value its expression;
- establish a learning and teaching environment which responds to individual student needs through the provision of an array of experiences in and out of the classroom to encourage optimal learning;
- develop a clear understanding of school-based curriculum development and curriculum adaptation which incorporates effective design principles in lesson planning (including variations of pace, level and grouping);

integration of ICT in schools, just as it is with the implementation of any innovations in a school. Implementation, however, is not enough: the integration of ICT has to be institutionalised in ways that all teachers would become committed to effective integration and would actively involve to achieve ICT-integration-oriented school improvement. Such an institutionalisation pursuit demands forceful leadership in practice. Thus, the role of the school principal cannot be underestimated. To achieve any level of teacher success with ICT integration, the principal or senior management needs to be, on the one hand, receptive to ICT-enriched schooling and, on the other hand, actively involved in any attempts to integrate ICT into the learner-centred environment, notwithstanding difficulties and even resistance from teachers and students. From the precious experiences so generated over the past few years, school administrators will become keen supporters of ICT-driven learner-centred environments only after they fully understand how ICT can be used to fulfil the demands for school improvement and the achievement of increased student learning.

And fifth, teachers need to gain successful experiences in new learning environments and acquire an individual sense of how they are able to enhance student-centred learning. Teachers' initial reticence to the use of ICT would eventually dissipate if advice and support to teachers on instructional design are given on a timely basis. The provision of the needed reinforcement is a responsibility of educational leadership that must be fulfilled.

While there have been some successes, the constraints of the classroom and the curriculum are still very evident, and the demands made on teachers extremely high. Many issues are being dealt with in the current reform climate; yet, many conflicts between the old and the new are only starting to surface and may not be resolved so quickly. Teachers may have to rationalise the content of their syllabus in their school context and may have to admit that some of the old content will just have to go. Teachers would also need to be more ready to acknowledge that new ideas and methods have proven their worth. All these are becoming pressing tasks that must be handled by more teachers in the current reform context in which fostering an ICT-enriched learner-centred environment is more mandatory than preferential.

In reality, it should be noted, each day teachers are taking professional risks with their exploration in the use of ICT. Thus, a challenge that must be effectively coped with is how educational leaders of the government and schools can readily give teachers some comfort they need and to be reassured that they will be supported when they are being challenged to reflect on the effectiveness of their current teaching practice. In essence, ICT in education must be deployed from a holistic perspective as suggested by researchers (see, e.g., Lim, 2002; Tan, Hu, Wong, & Wettasinghe, 2003; Wellington, 2001; Williams, Coles, Wilson, Richardson, & Tuson, 2000) who have highlighted the very facts that various parts of the educational must give support to the pursuit and that application of ICT triggers chain reactions not only within the classroom but the whole school and the community.

6.   WAY FORWARD

Just as their counterparts do in other developing educational systems, teachers, administrators, politicians and parents in Hong Kong have already gone through the stage of "getting ready to get ready" in making ICT an indispensable component of schooling. Today, they should be more than prepared for a new approach to using ICT. It is hoped that this chapter will offer insights into both the potential and the present dilemmas of and challenges in the use of ICT in schools. For those teachers who are already using ICT, we hope that they will continue to explore further pedagogical approaches that will ultimately benefit both themselves as professional teachers and their students as interdependent learners. For all of us as educators, we need to perpetually strive to become good custodians of teaching and learning. While some of the ways in which ICT can be used have great potential, as teachers we must take time to step back and seriously investigate what we are advocating in the classroom. After all, nothing is a substitute for our own reflective practice, and it is ultimately up to us to reflect on whether our students are indeed learning and whether our approaches are in effect sound.

We must avoid the tendency to assume that if teachers learn how to use common applications or become computer literate, then they will be able to integrate ICT into their lessons. We need to realise that teachers need to go beyond computer literacy to become technologically competent for pedagogical advancement. As Westhaver (2003) pointed out, the current challenge is how teachers and administrators can promote learning to learn - "helping students develop thinking skills, learning skills and, most importantly, a passion for learning" (p. 46) - which will generate long-term and widespread impact on individual students' learning. To meet this challenge is to make available to students appropriate software, methodologies and tools that are critical parts of a leaner-centred learning environment and that help students structure their work, evaluate information, clarify thinking, learn difficult concepts, assimilate information and communicate what they have learned (p. 46). It is only when those software, methodologies and tools are present can teachers then more effectively use their knowledge of student learning and ICT to design, manage and facilitate a student-centred, multidimensional learning environment. More importantly, however, teachers themselves must continuously strive to enhance their capacity in managing ICT-tools and to reflect on their teaching and ways to further improve within the ICT-enriched environment. Unavoidably, all of us need to develop confidence and self-efficacy, along with the recognition that ICT-enhanced leaner-centred environments need a clear and informed vision of what new leaner-centred environment might look like. The question remains: *Are we ready for this change, administratively, professionally and passionately?*

If schools are serious about integrating ICT into the classroom to create leaner-centred learning environments, then all teachers must begin to ask and reflect on the following issues:

- "How would integrating ICT in my classroom compel me to go beyond my daily work and do things differently?"
- "Am I ready to being pushed out of my comfort zone?"
- "Does my usual practice in the classroom fit into the scheme of ICT integration?"
- "What changes do I need to make and am I flexible enough to want to make the change?"
- "How can I enjoy the adventure of upgrading my professional life from mediocrity and superficiality in ICT integration to enchanted integration with which students, myself, the school, parents and other stakeholders will all benefit from the optimisation of school education?"

Finally, we must not succumb to the factory style constraints that limit what we can and cannot do! Fortunately, in Hong Kong, the Internet has become widely accessible and user-friendly, while added to this is the affordability of web servers and the setting up of Intranet at all schools. Therefore, the time is right for all teachers to work in a more progressive manner to grasp the potential of ICT tools for the benefit of their students! Creating ICT-enriched learner-centred environments requires a holistic approach that calls for changes at three levels – teacher, schooling environment and learning activities. Fundamentally, however, it is teachers who, with support from parents, administrators and policy makers, can optimise the benefits of ICT-enriched environments to make learner-centred learning a reality. Hopefully, this chapter does help teachers clarify the various myths, gaps and challenges in creating ICT-enriched learner-centred environment that confront teachers in Hong Kong as well as other developing educational systems.

Acknowledgement: The projects mentioned above have been supported by the Education Department (now the Education and Manpower Bureau) of the Hong Kong SAR and the Quality Education Fund.

REFERENCES

APEC. (2001). *Bridging the Digital Divide e-Educational Leadership in ICT*, APEC Cyber Education Cooperation Project.Accessed on 28 March 2004: http://acec.cite.hku.hk/rationale.asp

Becker, H. J., & Riel, M. M. (2000). Teacher Professional Engagement and Constructivist-Compatible Computer Use. Teaching, Learning, and Computing: 1998 National Survey. Report #7.Available: http://www. crito.uci.edu/tlc/html/findings.html.

Breuleux, A. (2001). Imagining the present, interpreting the possible, cultivating the future: Technology and the renewal of teaching and learning. *Education Canada, 41*(3), 12-15.

Burger, S. E., & Burger, D. L. (1994). Determining the validity of performance-based assessment. *Educational Measurement: Issues and Practice, 13*(1), 9-15.

Carpenter, W. A. (2000). Ten years of silver bullets: Dissenting thoughts on education reform. *Phi Delta Kappan, 81*(5), 383-89.

Cheah, H. M., & Koh, T. S. (2001). Integration of ICT into education in Singapore. *Journal of Southeast Asian Education, 2*(1), 147-64.

Dexter, S., Seashore, K. R., & Anderson, R. E. (2002). Contributions of professional community to exemplary use of ICT. *Journal of Computer Assisted Learning, 18*(4), 489-97.

(2004). *Information Technology in Education – Way Forward*, Government of the Hong Kong SAR.

Esteve, J. M. (2000). Culture in the school: Assessment and the content of education. *European Journal of Teacher Education, 23*(1), 5-18.

Fischer, F. (1998). Beyond empiricism: Policy inquiry in Postpositivist perspective, *Policy Studies Journal, 26*(1), 129-146.

Flecknoe, M. (2002). How can ICT help us to improve education? *Innovations in Education and Teaching International, 39*(4), 271-79.

Fujitani, S., Bhattacharya, M., & Akahori, K. (2003). *ICT* implementation and online learning in Japan. *Educational Technology, 43*(3), 33-37.

Fung, A. C. W., & Pun, S. W. (2001). ICT in Hong Kong education. *Journal of Southeast Asian Education, 2*(1), 165-80.

Goodison, T. (2002). Enhancing learning with ICT at primary level. *British Journal of Educational Technology, 33*(2), 215-28.

Granger, C. A., Morbey, M. L., Lotherington, H., Owston, R. D., & Wideman, H. H. (2002). Factors contributing to teachers' successful implementation of IT. *Journal of Computer Assisted Learning, 18*(4), 480-88.

Harris, S. (2002). Innovative pedagogical practices using ICT in schools in England. *Journal of Computer Assisted Learning, 18*(4), 449-58.

Higgins, S. (2001). ICT and teaching for understanding. *Evaluation and Research in Education, 15*(3), 164-71.

Hinostroza, J. E., Guzman, A., & Isaacs, S. (2002). Innovative uses of ICT in Chilean schools. *Journal of Computer Assisted Learning, 18*(4), 459-69.

Kilduff, M. & Mehra, A. (1997), Postmodernism and organizational research, *Academy of Management Review, 22*(2), 453-81.

Law, N., Lee, Y., & Chow, A. (2002). Practice characteristics that lead to 21st Century learning outcomes. *Journal of Computer Assisted Learning, 18*(4), 415-26.

Law, N., Yuen, H, K., Ki, W. W., Li, S. C., & Lee, Y. (1999). Second International Information Technology in Education Study: Hong Kong SAR Report. Hong Kong, Centre for Information Technology in School and Teacher Education, The University of Hong Kong. Also accessible at: http://sitesdatabase.cite.hku.hk/online/index_eng.asp

Law, N., Yuen, H, K., Ki, W.W., Li, S. C., Lee, Y. & Chow, Y., (2000). *Changing Classrooms & Changing Schools: A Study of Good practices in Using ICT in Hong Kong Schools*, Hong Kong, Centre for Information Technology in School and Teacher Education, The University of Hong Kong.

Lee, K. T. (2002a). Effective teaching in the information era: Fostering an ICT-based integrated learning environment in schools. *Asia-Pacific Journal of Teacher Education & Development, 5*(1), 21-45.

Lee, K. T. (2002b). Using information technology (IT) as a catalyst for altering the constraints of conventional classrooms to cater for individual differences (ID). *Journal of Quality School Education, 2,* 5-25.

Lee, K. T. (2002c). Enhancing teaching and learning in schools through facilitation of online learning: Issues of implementation in Hong Kong schools. In J. Mason (Ed.), *Connecting the Future, Proceedings of the Global Summit of Online Knowledge Networks* (123-29), March 4-5, Adelaide, Australia.

Lee, K. T., Lam, Y. S., Li, K. M. (2004). *Use of information technology to cater for individual differences: 2000-2003, Final report,* Research and development project commissioned by the Education Department of the Hong Kong SAR, Hong Kong. (Submitted to the EMB in February, 2004)

Lembcke, J, L. (1993). Classical theory, Postmodernism, and the sociology liberal arts curriculum. *American Sociologist, 24*(3-4), 55-68.

Lim, C. P. (2002). A theoretical framework for the study of ICT in schools: A proposal. *British Journal of Educational Technology, 33*(4), 411-21.

Lim, C. P., & Barnes, S. (2002). Those who can, teach - The pivotal role of the teacher in the information and communication technologies (ICT) learning environment. *Journal of Educational Media, 27*(1-2), 19-40.

Lin, Q. Y. (2002). Beyond standardization: Testing and assessment in standards-based reform. *Action in Teacher Education, 23*(4), 43-49.

McFarlane, A. (2001). Perspectives on the relationships between ICT and assessment. *Journal of Computer Assisted Learning, 17*(3), 227-34.

McNicol, S., Nankivell, C., & Ghelani, T. (2002). ICT and resource-based learning: Implications for the future. *British Journal of Educational Technology, 33*(4), 393-401.

Mioduser, D., Nachmias, R., Tubin, D., & Forkosh-Baruch, A. (2002). Models of pedagogical implementation of ICT in Israeli schools. *Journal of Computer Assisted Learning, 18*(4), 405-14.

Parker, L. (2000). Learning technologies and their impact on science education: Delivering the promise. *Australian Science Teachers Journal, 46*(3), 9-18.

Peters, L. (2000). Bridging the new digital divide: Lessons from across the Atlantic. *TECHNOS, 9*(2), 26-29. Available: http://www.technos.net/tq_09/2peters.htm.

Reynolds, D., Treharne, D., &Tripp, H. (2003). ICT - The hopes and the reality. *British Journal of Educational Technology, 34*(2), 151-67.

Rosenau, P. M. 1992. *Postmodernism and the social sciences*. Princeton, NJ: Princeton University Press.

Schultz-Zander, R., Buchter, A., & Dalmer, R. (2002). The role of ICT as a promoter of students' cooperation. *Journal of Computer Assisted Learning, 18*(4), 438-48.

Selwyn, N., & Gorard, S. (2003). Reality bytes: Examining the rhetoric of widening educational participation via ICT. *British Journal of Educational Technology, 34*(2), 169-81.

Slattery, P. (1995). *Curriculum development in the postmodern era*. New York: Garland.

Squires, D. (2000). The impact of ICT use on the role of the learner. *Lifelong Learning in Europe, 5*(1), 55-60.

Tan, S. C., Hu, C., Wong, S., K., & Wettasinghe, C. M. (2003). Teacher training on technology-enhanced instruction - a holistic Approach. *Educational Technology & Society, 6*(1), 96-104.

Tiene, D. (2002). Addressing the global digital divide and its impact on educational opportunity. *Educational Media International, 39*(3-4), 211-22.

Wagner, T. (2003). Reinventing America's schools. *Phi Delta Kappan, 84* (9), 665-68.

Wellington, J. (2001). Exploring the Secret Garden: The growing importance of *ICT* in the home. *British Journal of Educational Technology, 32*(2), 233-44.

Westhaver, M. (2003). Learning to learn: The best strategy for overall student achievement *T.H.E. Journal, 30*(2), 46.

Wheeler, S. (2001). Information and communication technologies and the changing role of the teacher. *Journal of Educational Media, 26*(1), 7-17.

Wheeler, S., Waite, S. J., & Bromfield, C. (2002). Promoting creative thinking through the use of ICT. *Journal of Computer Assisted Learning, 18*(3), 367-78.

Williams, D., Coles, L., Richardson, A., Wilson, K., & Tuson, J. (2000). Integrating information and communications technology in professional practice: An analysis of teachers' needs based on a survey of primary and secondary Teachers in Scottish schools. *Journal of Information Technology for Teacher Education, 9*(2), 167-82.

Williams, D., Coles, L., Wilson, K., Richardson, A., & Tuson, J. (2000). Teachers and ICT: Current use and future needs. *British Journal of Educational Technology, 31*(4), 307-20.

Chapter 11

CYBERGOGY FOR ENGAGED LEARNING: A FRAMEWORK FOR CREATING LEARNER ENGAGEMENT THROUGH INFORMATION AND COMMUNICATION TECHNOLOGY

Minjuan Wang[1] and Myunghee Kang[2]

[1]*San Diego State University, USA;* [2]*Ewha Womans University, Korea*

Abstract: The continued and growing need for new learning opportunities, linked with newer information systems and communication technologies, has pushed online learning into the center of the discussion of educational practice. There is a need to establish a framework for generating meaningful and engaging learning experiences for distance students with diverse cultural and linguistic backgrounds. We coin the term "Cybergogy" as a descriptive label for the strategies for creating engaged learning online. Our model of Cybergogy for Engaged Learning (see Figure 1) has three overlapping/intersecting domains: cognitive, emotive, and social. This model is a synthesis of current thinking, concepts, and theoretical frameworks on the extent and nature of the three domains in learner engagement online. The instructors can use this model to profile each learner and then design tactics to engage individuals accordingly, a process we call "customized engagement." As a consequence, learners will not only have the opportunity to accomplish their learning goals, but also will be actively involved in the learning process.

Keywords: cybergogy, engaged learning, online presence, instructional design, online facilitation

1.   CYBERGOGY MODEL AND INDICATORS OF ENGAGEMENT IN ONLINE LEARNING

In any learning environment, truly engaged learners are behaviorally, intellectually, and emotionally involved in their learning tasks (Bangert-Drowns & Pyke, 2001). Engagement is a multidimensional phenomenon that varies from setting to setting: time-on-task, self-regulated learning, intrinsically motivated involvement of integrated cognitive process, learning environment (quality of the dialogue), and production of tangible results (Bangert-Drowns & Pyke, 2002). For K-12 schools that use computer

D. Hung and M.S. Khine (eds.), Engaged Learning with Emerging Technologies, 225-253.

technologies in teaching, Jones and his/her colleagues (1995) identify vision, tasks, assessment, instructional model, learning context, grouping, teacher roles, and student roles as the indicators of engaged learning.

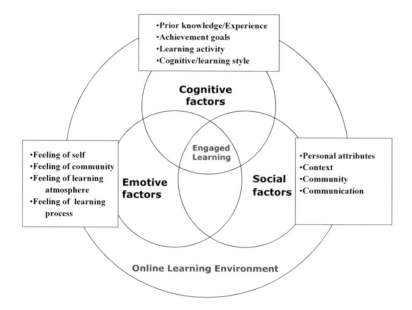

Figure 1. The "MM" Model: Cybergogy for Engaged Learning

Here we regroup indicators discussed in the literature to derive the taxonomy of engagement and assessment strategies in online learning. Table 1 (see appendix A-Taxonomy of Forms of Engagement and Assessment Strategies) displays several forms of engaged learning online, their indicators, and ways to assess each form of engaged learning. The taxonomy qualifies forms of engagement and assessment strategies.

Below we examine each of the three domains and suggest a cybergogy for engaging learners through activating cognitive, emotive, and social factors. For instance, we explore ways that instructors can use to detect learners' emotional cues and cultivate their positive feelings; to increase learners' self-confidence and arouse their curiosity through course design and e-facilitation; to conduct online communication and build a supportive learning environment.

2.   COGNITIVE FACTORS

Cognitive domain points to the factors that initiate an individual's construction of knowledge. It investigates the way an individual optimizes personal relevance and meaning through the knowledge construction process.

Knowledge construction has been researched in cognitive sectors as well as constructivist sectors. Information processing theory, as a part of cognitive psychology, envisions the human mind as being similar to a computer processor and explains psychological events in terms of the input, process, storage, and output of information. Self-regulated learning theory explains learning as a form of cognitive engagement, such as a learner's intellectual involvement in planning and monitoring, when performing tasks in classroom.

According to this theory of cognitive engagement, knowledge construction has three major stages: information acquisition, information transformation, and knowledge construction. In the information acquisition stage, learners review their own knowledge structure, which in turn stimulates their interest in finding useful information and in exploring and transforming external stimuli. In the information transformation stage, learners select appropriate information, organize and integrate it with existing knowledge, and plan for specific activities. The final destination is the knowledge construction stage, where the products of knowledge construction are realized. The knowledge that is constructed is not the type that is the result of rote memorization, but a kind that could be applied in new circumstances, used to solve problems, and used in relationship with other elements in the context. The following factors are thought to affect an individual's knowledge construction during the process: prior knowledge/experience, learning goals, learning activities, locus of control, and assessment style (Hannafin et. al., 2003).

However, constructivists have defined knowledge construction as the extent to which learners are able to construct and confirm meaning through sustained discourse in a critical community of inquiry (Garrison et al., 2003). In their view, knowledge construction is a circular process of conception, experience, perception, and judgment, in which major roles are played by practical inquiry of the stages of resolution, triggering event, exploration, and integration. From this perspective, it is assumed that knowledge construction could be greatly assisted by a tool to assess critical discourse and reflection for the purpose of acquiring intended and worthwhile learning outcomes.

For both approaches, interrelated factors relating to cognitive processes and outcomes are considered to be important in cognitive domain. Learners' prior knowledge, their goals and learning tasks, and their cognitive styles are important factors. Therefore, learning designers should enhance their abilities to consider these factors as a means of making the learning most relevant to students. In addition, instructors could also use this knowledge to set course goals, design activities, select the methods of delivery, and generate appropriate assessment.

3.   PRIOR KNOWLEDGE/EXPERIENCE

Included in the model's cognitive domain, prior knowledge is important when enhancing the learning experience. A large body of findings shows that learning proceeds primarily from prior knowledge, and only secondarily from the presented materials. Moreover, when a new curriculum is related to existing knowledge and skills, learners are usually more interested. Learning is promoted when existing knowledge is activated as a foundation for new knowledge (Merrill, 2002). Learning takes place when students process new information. Several factors, such as students' prior knowledge, values, expectations, and the learning environment, heavily influence their learning process (Newmann et al. in Brown, 1997).

Ironically, to effectively integrate prior knowledge into a teaching plan, an instructor must address defects in existing knowledge that may interfere with learning new concepts. Research has shown that a learner's prior knowledge often confounds an educator's best efforts to deliver ideas accurately. Learners will distort presented material if it is at odds with their prior knowledge. Neglect of prior knowledge can result in the audience learning things opposed to the educator's intentions, no matter how well those intentions are executed in an exhibit, book, or lecture.

4.   ACHIEVEMENT GOALS

Allowing students to set their learning goals could boost motivation and thus encourage their immersion in the learning process. Once expectations and goals are clearly set, the instructor can then select the best methods of delivery and the type of assessment to evaluate performance. Any type of course assessment can be used as long as they align with and are consistent with both the instructional methods used and the student learning objectives (SLOs) for the course.

Dweck and Leggett (1988) identify two types of achievement goals-performance and learning - that affect students' academic performance. Performance goals are associated with the desire to achieve favorable grades and social approval. Performance-oriented students are typically concerned with the outcome rather than with the actual process of learning and are more likely to subscribe to an entity theory of intelligence, believing that intelligence is a fixed attribute. Students with performance goals tend to perform well on easier tasks for which a positive evaluation can be achieved, but they often become discouraged and give up easily when faced with a difficult task, attributing their failure to a lack of ability. In contrast, learning-oriented students are interested in new material and they tend to subscribe to the incremental theory that intelligence is malleable. These students display "mastery-oriented" behavior, showing more persistence on difficult tasks, using alternative strategies, and attributing failure to a need to work harder rather than to a lack of ability (Heyman & Dweck, 1992).

Dweck introduces the idea of learning and performance goals as a unidimensional variable (Dweck & Leggett, 1998). Roedel and his colleagues, (1994), however, suggest that learning and performance goals seem to be independent of one another. Thus, a person may be high in both learning and performance goals, low in both of the goals, or high in one and low in the other. Eppler and Harju (1997), using Roedel's scale, divide college students into four categories of goal patterns: low on both learning and performance goals; high on both learning and performance goals; high on performance goals while low on learning; and high on learning goals while low on performance. In their study, students who endorsed learning goals only or who endorsed both learning and performance goals had significantly higher GPAs than the group with low levels of goal orientation. This study therefore supports Dweck's hypothesis about goal orientation being predictive of academic success.

Goal orientation does not seem to influence student performance in low-stress conditions. However, when faced with stress, such as failing to pass an exam, learning-goal dominant students can persevere and adopt more successful learning strategies. By contrast, performance-goal dominant students can perform more poorly or engage in irrational behavior, such as giving up but not dropping the class. Hoyert and O'Dell report that these results often occur when students perceive learning and performance goals as competitive factors, rather than as continuous or independent factors.

5.   LEARNING ACTIVITY (TASK AND ASSESSMENT)

To stimulate engaged learning, tasks need to be challenging, authentic, and multidisciplinary. Such tasks are typically complex and involve sustained amounts of time. They are authentic in that they correspond to the tasks in the home and workplaces of today and tomorrow. Collaboration around authentic tasks often takes place with peers and mentors within school as well as with family members and others in the real world outside of school. These tasks often require integrated instruction that incorporates problem-based learning and curriculum by project.

Assessment of engaged learning involves presenting students with an authentic task, project, or investigation, and then observing, interviewing, and examining their presentations and artifacts to assess what they actually know and can do. This assessment, often called performance-based assessment, is generative in that it involves students in generating their own performance criteria and playing a key role in the overall design, evaluation, and reporting of their assessment. The best performance-based assessment has a seamless connection to curriculum and instruction so that it is ongoing. Assessment should represent all meaningful aspects of performance and should have equitable standards that apply to all students.

6.   COGNITIVE AND LEARNING STYLE

In an extensive overview of the work on learning and cognitive styles over the past 30 years, Riding and Rayner (1998) attempt to classify and integrate much of the earlier work. They argue that many of the different labels used to categorize cognitive styles and learning styles were "different conceptions of the same dimension". After comparing and contrasting a range of classifications, they identify two major cognitive style dimensions:

- **Verbal-Imagery** - an individual's position on this dimension determines whether that person tends to use images or verbal representation to represent information when thinking.
- **Wholist-Analytic** - an individual's position on this dimension determines whether that person processes information in parts or as a whole (Riding & Rayner, 1998).

Kolb (1984) proposes a theory of experiential learning that involves four principal stages: concrete experiences (CE), reflective observation (RO), abstract conceptualization (AC), and active experimentation (AE). The CE/AC and AE/RO dimensions are polar opposites as far as learning styles are concerned, and Kolb postulates four types of learners, depending upon their position on these two dimensions: According to Kolb (1984), the four basic learning modes, correspond to four basic learning styles: pragmatist, reflector, theorist, and activist. These learning styles display the following characteristics: (1) Pragmatist. The pragmatist learning style depends mainly on the dominant learning capacities of active experimentation and abstract conceptualization. (2) Reflector. This style depends mainly on concrete experience and reflective observation; it has great advantages in imaginative abilities and awareness of meaning and values. (3) Theorist. The theorist learning style depends mainly on abstract conceptualization and reflective observation. This style has great advantages in inductive reasoning, creating theoretical models, and assimilating different observations into an integrative entity. (4) Activist. This style depends mainly on active experimentation and concrete experience; it has great advantages in doing things, implementing plans, and engaging in new tasks (Thorne, 2003).

7.   EMOTIVE FACTORS

It is commonly known that teaching and learning work best in a classroom atmosphere of mutual affection and respect, rather than in one of fear and intimidation. However, the western scientific community tends to dichotomize cognition and emotion (McLeod, 1991). In adult education, for instance, theory and practice often marginalize emotions and elevate rationality; the ability to reason has always superseded emotions (Dirkx, 2001). Teaching and learning are often framed as largely rational and cognitive; emotions are perceived as either impediments to learning or only motivators of it (Dirkx).

Recently, a growing body of literature (e.g., Currin, 2003; Dirkx; Hara & Kling, 2000; O'Regan; Kort, Reilly & Picard, 2003; Weiss, 2000) has begun to espouse the central role of emotion to any learning endeavor and outcomes, especially in e- or online learning. Dirkx argues for the power of feelings (emotion and imagination) in adults' meaning-construction. Once considered "baggage" or "barriers" to learning, emotions and imagination are now perceived as integral to the process of adult learning (Dirkx, p. 67).

Continuous and increasing exploration of the complex set of parameters surrounding online learning reveals the importance of the emotional states of learners and especially the relationship between emotions and effective learning (e.g., Kort, Reilly & Picard; O'Regan). Kort and his colleagues (2001) find that in a technology-based environment, learners commonly experience emotional changes during their learning journey. From frustration to excitement, from boredom to fascination; the emotive dimensions of learning could contribute to a positive educational experience or attribute to a negative one. The efficiency and effectiveness of learners' information processing can be affected by the range of emotions emerging from the learning process.

A few have also attempted to create models connecting emotions with either social factors or cognitive process. For instance, Martinez devises a model of online learning orientations, which recognizes a dominant influence of emotions, intentions and social factors on how individuals learn differently" (in O'Regan, p. 3). Kort and his colleagues propose a model relating the cognitive dynamics of the learning process to the range of various emotional states (see Figure 2).

Our Cybergogy for Engaged learning is unique in its synthesis of constructs from the existing model and in its interweaving the factors in the affective domain (primarily emotions and feelings) with both cognitive and social dynamics of the learning process. Thus, this model provides a more systematic and holistic view of factors that cultivate engaged learning.

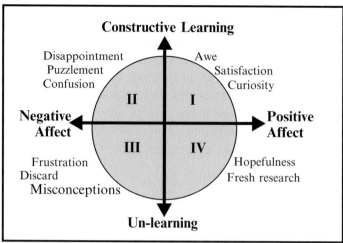

Figure 2. Proposed model relating phases of learning to
emotions (reprinted with the authors' permission)

The understanding of emotions is diverse and multifaceted, from Darwin to behaviorist representation, from physiological to psychological terms. Here emotions are defined from the social-cultural perspectives as "social acts involving interactions with self and interactions with others" (Denzin in O'Regan, p. 7). In essence, emotion is "a transitory social role" that exists in both an interpersonal and a socio-cultural context (Averill, p. 7). To address emotions more clearly and expansively, we identify four kinds of feelings that might affect learner engagement: a) feelings of self, b) feeling of interpersonal connection/community, c) feelings of learning atmosphere, and d) feelings emerging from the learning process.

8.   FEELINGS OF SELF (CONFIDENCE, COMPETENCE, EFFICACY *(with online communication and technological tools)*

Dirkx (2001) concludes from empirical data that "emotions and feelings play a critical role in our sense of self and in processes of adult learning. . . . Emotions always refer to the self, providing us with a means for developing self-knowledge" (p. 64-65).

Feelings of self affect learner engagement through motivation. Ample research (Bandura & Cervone, 1986; Locke, Frederick, Lee, & Bobko, 1984; Schunk, 1990) has revealed that learners' perceived self-efficacy, self-confidence, and competence with the learning tasks directly affect their goal-setting and thus their motivation to engage in the learning process. Some (e.g., Lumpe & Chambers, 2001) find that learners' self-efficacy beliefs can be significant predictors of their performance of a task; they argue that a learner can actively engage in the learning process, only if the learner feels that a task is achievable and manageable.

Feelings of self-confidence and efficacy can help students adapt to online learning, which provides them with more opportunities to be engaged in self-paced learning (Katz, 2002). As a result, they might be able to overcome the desire for face-to-face interaction, a habit of learning that is carried over from the traditional classroom learning.

The effect of self-confidence on learner engagement is supported by Keller's ARCS model with which he identifies four key learning motivation: attention, relevance, confidence, and satisfaction. Among them, confidence is essential because "people have a desire to feel competent and in control of key aspects of their lives" (Keller, n.d., p. 381). A perception of control decreases stress and leads to healthier, happier behavior.

9. FEELINGS OF INTERPERSONAL CONNECTIONS AND COMMUNITY

Besides feeling good about themselves, learners also need to feel positively about the broader social world. Engagement requires a sense of "fitting-in" the larger learning environment. The feeling of belonging to a community contributes to students' motivation, involvement, and satisfaction with the learning process (Chan & Rapman, 1999; Wegerif, 1998 in Oren, Mioduser, and Nachmias, 2003).

Socialization, the establishment of a social network and the building of learning communities, has been considered essential for a fun and successful learning experience in technology-mediated learning situations (Rovai, 2001; Preece, 2000). Online communities are social aggregations that emerge from the web when enough people carry on public, lengthy discussions, with sufficient human feeling, to form webs of personal relationships (Rheingold, 2000). The burgeoning literature on online learning communities has generated conclusive findings about the importance and impact of communities on students' engagement, satisfaction, and learning outcomes. In a study of social dimensions of asynchronous learning networks, Wegerif (2003) concludes that "individual success or failure on the course depended upon the extent to which students were able to cross a threshold from feeling like outsiders to feeling like insiders" (p. 34). Although a few studies (e.g., Beaudoin, 2002; Fritsch, 1997) have found that witness learners or "lurkers" who refrain from visible interactivity still meet learning objectives, nearly all of the literature indicates that socializing is essential for a fun and successful learning experience in technology-mediated learning situations.

Our Engaged Learning Model predicts that feelings of community or isolation can be the consequence of activities or lack of activities in the social domain. Strategies to help students enter the learning community and to sustain learning communities are further discussed in the social dimension section.

10.   FEELING OF LEARNING ATMOSPHERE *(safe and positive versus fearful; open negotiation versus domination)*

Engagement in classroom settings is closely tied to the larger learning environment, such as the quality of interaction and the culture of the college campus (Bangert-Drowns & Pyke). This aspect of engagement, we believe, can be more important in online settings. "People who feel unsafe, unconnected, and disrespected are unlikely to be motivated to learn" (Wlodkowski & Ginsberg, 1995, p. 2). Building a supportive learning environment, increasing students' awareness of diversity, and facilitating student-student communication are strategies conducive to success (Wlodkowski & Ginsberg).

Quality interaction among students and instructor are conducive to a positive learning atmosphere, one that is marked by socializing, rapport, connections, debates, and open negotiation. This emphasis for interaction is rooted in social constructivism (Vygotsky, 1986), which holds that shared knowledge develops through joint communication and activity. Communication among online participants facilitates building a community of learners that shares understanding and adopts a common knowledge base (Wang, 2001).

Besides, an instructor must attend to many cognitive factors to develop a positive and supportive learning atmosphere. For instance, the instructor must treat students as individuals by modeling respect for individual differences and by taking into account the expectations and experience of students with different needs (Wlodkowski & Ginsberg, 1995). Learning opportunities need to be created to suit students' different learning styles; presentation styles and assignment requirements must be varied to accommodate students' different talents and learning styles (Hutchines, 2003).

11.   FEELINGS EMERGING FROM THE LEARNING PROCESS

Students often experience a range of emotions while learning online such as interest/curiosity, confusion/anxiety/frustration, fascination or boredom, pride, and satisfaction or dissatisfaction. The most common feelings --

frustration, isolation, anxiety, and confusion -- are often caused by the online environment itself, including communication breakdowns and technical difficulties (Hara & Kling, 2000). Other factors in the cognitive and social domain, such as technological and pedagogical problems, information overload, and social isolation, can also contribute to this frustration. Therefore, effective facilitation in the cognitive and social domains can help reduce negative emotions and cultivate positive ones. In particular, a feeling of satisfaction is essential to the student learning process. In their meta-analysis of studies about student satisfaction in on-line courses, Hill and his/her colleagues (1996) find that students who felt most satisfied (or had the highest level of "perceived learning") interacted with online classmates at a deeper level and participated more actively in their online sessions.

Kort and his colleagues describe learners' emotional changes during the learning journey as taking place in several zones: the zone of curiosity, the zone of anxiety, the zone of flow, and finally the zone to a productive path. Based on their model of emotion-learning (see Figure 2), they hope to devise a computer-based system that has the artificial intelligence of expert teachers who "are adept at recognizing the emotional state of learners and take appropriate action that positively influences learning" (Kort et. al. 2001, p. 1). Before this system becomes a reality, however, the human teacher will need to take actions to keep students engaged. Following we address strategies that instructors can use to emotionally engage students in learning.

12.   SOCIAL FACTORS

Social dimensions are the social acts involving interactions with self and others. Because social domain is so broad and affects learners so profoundly, it holds an important position in our Engagement model. The social factors in our Engagement Model fall into the following categories:

a. Personal attributes: age and gender, language, culture, and media literacy abilities
b. Learner's social-cultural context: goals, motives, expectations, and value (overlapping cognitive)
c. Community-building: establishing group identity, trust, interaction, and construction of shared knowledge
d. Communication: group size, discussion content, requisite software, and group moderation (team building, team maintenance, performing a team)

13.   PERSONAL ATTRIBUTES

Personal traits and learner expectations must be accounted for. Four sets of opposing values help explain differences in social expectations: individualism versus collectivism, achievement versus relationship orientation, loose versus tight structure, egalitarian structure versus hierarchy (Weech, 20001). Instructors need to recognize expectation differences and take actions to align them with learning materials and activities.

14.   SOCIAL CONTEXT

In the social domain, the most critical factor contributing to learning and outcomes is the social context. The learner's social context affects his personal attributes, access to group discussions, and the community within which he is engaged. Every learner possesses a background and distinct culture that the learner will unavoidably bring to every learning endeavor. For this reason, consideration of the social-cultural context is of supreme importance. Often times, the method of online course delivery needs to be shifted to better fit the socio-cultural contexts of the learner involved.

15.   COMMUNITY BUILDING

Although the term "online community" is subject to a variety of definitions, all seem to agree that a social connection is critical to online learning. Ample studies have reiterated that individuals are embedded in their societies and that social and cognitive skills can be enhanced by enhancing social presence. Therefore, the sense of community is essential in online learning for two reasons: a) working together can help students clarify similar confusions; and b) social group can also help maintain student interest and keep them attending to the course (Currin, 2003).

Research on learning processes in face-to-face groups indicates that development of social climate is important to make students feel like insiders in the learning environment, thus contributing to students' motivation, involvement, and contentment (Chan & Rapman, 1999; Wegerif, 1998). Although early studies dealing with computer mediated relationships led to the conclusion that the network does not contribute to the creation of a social climate (Oren et al., 2002), more recent studies show that effectively designed and monitored online environments can create non-alienating social environments.

The Internet clearly transcends time and space and supports the evolution of a dense and multifaceted social life online (Oren et al.). Social interactions in virtual learning groups can be strongly intertwined with learning interactions, and can evolve to respond to functional needs as the groups' work proceeds (Oren et al., Discussion, ¶ 5). Several contextual factors, such as course design, characteristics of the technological media used, and the use of moderators, could help learners enter a learning community (Wegerif, 1998).

16. COMMUNICATION

Some other contextual factors include communication tools and group moderation. The use of email, online conferencing, web databases, groupware, and audio/videoconferencing significantly increases the extent and ease of interaction among all course participants, as well as access to information (Kearsley & Shneiderman, 1999).

17. CYBERGOGY FOR CUSTOMIZED LEARNER ENGAGEMENT

Below we suggest tactics for creating these "customized engagements", mainly through increasing learners' cognitive, emotive, and social presence during the learning process (see Figure 3). Sample strategies discussed include: detecting learners' cognitive-emotive states online, recognizing and detecting their emotional signals, selecting a course of action to respond properly to these signals, structuring teamwork, bridging the cultural divide, and supporting both individual and collaborative learning.

18. DESIGNING ENGAGING INSTRUCTION

Engaged learning should start from design, with instructors designing course materials with the learners in mind, materials that are inherently engaging. Historically, instructional designs are channeled in the direction of leanness, clarity, and alignment of learning objectives with activities and assessment. Most instructional design literature prescribes sequences that proceed smoothly from the familiar to the strange, and do it so gradually and

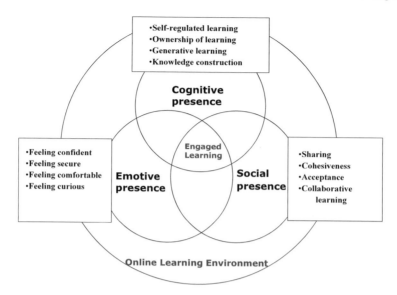

Figure 3. Cybergogy for Engaged Learning: Increasing the Level of
        Presence

systematically that the yet-to-be-learned is never seen as the unknown. Thus
we offer suggestions for designing more engaging activities, by using
mystery, curiosity, and appropriate activities to enhance cognitive, emotive
and social presence (see Figure 3).

19.   CREATING A SENSE OF SURPRISE AND MYSTERY IN TEACHING

The field of instructional design has failed to fully recognize the power
of mystery in the learning process. When used appropriately, mystery can
enhance learning, both cognitively and affectively. Research (Weiss, 2000)
has shown that surprise and mystery can foster emotional connections that
make a direct biochemical link with memory. Also, surprise and mystery can
help grab students' attention, an increasing challenge for students of the 21st
century. Known as Generation X, these students have short attention spans
(Snell, 2000) and require autonomy and flexibility of their own learning
(Brown, 1997).

To effectively engage Generation X, learning must be active and
interactive, including the use of brainstorming, concept mapping,
visualization software, and simulations that enable learners to experiment
with modeling complex ideas and concepts (Driscoll, 2002). Mystery-
embedded simulations will satisfy students' craving for stimulation and for

immediate answers and feedback (Brown, 1997). Good teachers know this well, and intentionally craft situations in which uncertainty is created and resolved.

Keller's ARCS (Attention, Relevance, Confidence, & Satisfaction) model highlights the importance of curiosity in motivating learners (Keller & Suzuki, 1998). The model encourages designers to increase perceptual arousal by presenting information that is incongruous or uncertain. For instance, to create a sense of mystery by partially revealing knowledge in a problem-solving environment. Other tactics include encouraging learners to generate and test hypotheses, modeling curiosity, and using giving learner opportunities to explore their own interests (Arnone, 2003).

Incorporating hidden information into instruction and giving word-guessing games are some other ways to increase uncertainty (Malone & Lepper, 1987). Creating an environment conducive to inquiry further ensures that learning will occur in the presence of mystery. Designers can integrate creative assessment tools into instruction as well for concrete confirmation that learning has transpired.

To summarize, we should value affective learning as highly as cognitive learning, and see the two as interwoven. Likewise, current educational systems must value the learner over the curriculum, and must tolerate learning outcomes that may be less predictable but highly worthwhile.

20.   MESSAGE DESIGN: AROUSING POSITIVE EMOTIONS

Instructors' messages should build emotional connection to learning. For example, an instructor can use messages and images that are intended to be emotionally arousing. In particular, images can be used to represent feelings and emotions in adult learning (Dirkx; Hillman, 1975). Dirkx proposed the imaginal method as an alternative to "the rational and reflective process of meaning-making" (p. 63). The essence of this method is to encourage learners to actively engage and initiate a dialogue with their emotions through imagination (Clark, 1997).

Using socio-culturally appropriate images could stimulate learners' imagination and cultivate their imaginative connection with the self and the broader social world. "Emotionally charged images, evoked through the contexts of adult learning, provide the opportunity for a more profound access to the world by inviting a deeper understanding of ourselves in relationship with it" (Dirkx, p. 64).

Message design must also take learners' cultural contexts into consideration. People from low-context cultures assign less meaning to context but focus on the message itself. Thus, low-context cultures use language with great precision and economy; high-context cultures use language lavishly because words have relatively less value. High-context cultures might involve implicit context; whereas low-context cultures need explicit context (Hall & Hall, 1990).

21.   ACTIVITY DESIGN: INTERACTIVE, COLLABORATIVE OR SOLO AND COMPETITIVE

Activity design should accommodate learners' needs and learning styles. The ultimate goal is to help learners bond and thus build a network in which they can work comfortably. Activities could come in various formats: interactive, cooperative and collaborative, or solo and competitive.

Collaborative learning increases student satisfaction with the learning process (Jung, Choi, Lim, & Leem, 2002). Ample research has shown that the collaborative group experienced heightened satisfaction, which is a precursor for continued student involvement with any given delivery method.

Technological advances are making collaborative online learning more feasible. Along with a greater focus on increasing social presence, this enhanced feasibility in turn increases the ease of building online communities. Collaborative learning, when used wisely, could facilitate learning to a greater extent than individual learning. Exemplary wise uses include:

a. Structured group assignments requiring project outcomes that incorporate e-mail, chat, conferencing, and message boards appropriate to the degree of concurrency in the learning environment.

b. Structured study assignments for pairs of learners that use various communication tools such as chat and e-mail.

c. Knowledge management facilities that extend learning through discussion boards or social software (Clark & Mayer, 2003).

On the other hand, certain constraints could potentially limit the effectiveness of collaborative learning. For example, an over-sized team, mechanically assigning students to a group but failing to provide guidance, and assessing students individually when they are engaged in teamwork.

In addition, despite the great benefits of collaboration in online learning, some learners work best solo or competitively. Thus, instructors should encourage collaborative learning but also allow students to choose the mode of work and learning that suits their learning style.

Effective instruction requires the instructor to step outside the realm of personal experiences and into the world of the learner, who must be engaged for learning to occur (Brown, 197). In addition, learning must be individually constructed to be meaningful (Newmann et al. in Brown, 1997). By varying course delivery methods and providing students with a range of options, the instructor gives students autonomy and flexibility in their own learning (Brown).

22. CULTIVATING A BETTER SENSE OF SELF

This first thing an instructor needs to do is to increase learners' self-confidence, competence, efficacy with technology tools. To help students build a positive sense of an online self, instructors should always start with what students already know and show them the continuity of learning. Instructors should also encourage students to act upon growing their self-efficacy (Kiger, 2001), with not only the learning tasks but online communications and technological tools.

23. DETECTING STUDENTS' EMOTIONAL CUES ONLINE

Accurately identifying a learner's cognitive-emotive state greatly enhances an instructor's ability to help learners take pleasure in the learning process (Kort et al.). In online communication, emotional cues are solely represented in texts on screens. Because of the lack of facial expressions, body language, and the content and tone of speech, instructors need to remain more alert during synchronous interactions such as live chat. Do a few students dominate the conversation? Do other students log on but refrain from participation, playing the role of "lurkers"? What emoticons are students using? Although some discourage using emoticons in professional email communications, the wide array of emoticons could vividly convey students' feelings and emotions in online discussions.

Emoticons are pictographs of facial expressions made by a certain series of keystrokes. Following are the most commonly used ones in online learning situations (http://www.computeruser.com/resources/dictionary/emoticons.html):

: (Sad
:)   Smile
: [Bored, sad
#:-o Shocked
%-(Confused
%-) Dazed or silly
%-6 Brain-dead
%-{ Ironic

%-| Worked all night
%-} Humorous or ironic
>>:-<< Furious
>:-< Angry
(:-\ Very sad
/\/\/\ Laughter
12x@>--->--- A dozen roses
:-| Indifferent, bored or disgusted

Instructors could distribute an emoticon sheet at the beginning and ask students to use it to candidly express their emotions. However, learner emotions are more reflected in their non-emoticon interactions. Thus, instructors should also analyze the content of the online discussions to detect the emerging emotions. Although systematic content analysis (Fraenkel & Wallen, 2003) can be a complex process, instructors could build a transcript analysis scheme (see Table 2 as follows) and use a fast coding approach (Chappel, 2002) to quickly determine the interaction patterns. Table 2 below tabulates the emotions commonly felt by students in online learning.

Table 2. A sample transcript analysis scheme (adapted from Kort et al.)

Anxiety-Confidence	Anxiety	Worry	Discomfort	Comfort	Hopeful	Confident
Boredom-Fascination	Ennui	Boredom	Indifference	Interest	Curiosity	Intrigue
Frustration-Euphoria	Frustration	Puzzled	Confusion	Insight	Enlightened	Ephipany
Dispirited-Encouraged	Dispirited	Disappointed	Dissatisfied	Satisfied	Thrilled	Enthusiastic
Fear-Enchanted	Apprehension	Embarrassment	Frustration	Calm	Anticipatory	Excited

The fast coding approach that Chappel and her colleagues suggest can be used to characterize contextualized online learning behaviors as an interpretative aid for tutors and instructors working in online learning environments. In fast coding, coders pre-determine the elements, such as the categories in a coding scheme, and purposively look for these elements in communication evidence. Accordingly, instructors could use a customized

Transcript Analysis Scheme and fast coding approach to identify the aforementioned emotions revealed in online discussions.

24. FACILITATING ONLINE COMMUNICATION

Communication skills for effective online teaching are twofold: the ability to transmit messages clearly and accurately, and the ability to maintain positive interpersonal relationships (White & Weight, 1999). Ineffective communication has been found to be the major cause of the fragmentation of a learning community, which then leads to feelings of isolation and confusion. The National Teaching and Learning Forum Newsletter suggests guidelines to foster online discussion and collaborative learning, including the following:

a. clearly state the purpose of online discussion
b. help students be metacognitively aware of their learning styles and approaches
c. establish a style of writing and convention
d. link online discussion to assessment
e. use concise and clear language; keeping the posts short and right to the point
f. provide feedback to all participants to summarize the discussion, refer students to further reading, and to evaluate the quality of their contribution to the session.

White and Weight suggest the following methods to successfully build and maintain the positive learning environment. First, an instructor needs to be warm, responsive, inquisitive, tentative, and empathetic when communicating with students. This can be achieved by using appropriate tones (firm, fair, flexible, & fun) and nonjudgmental, non-dogmatic phrases like "it seems that... it appears that... I think"). Second, an instructor needs to model communication netiquette, such as to enhance class visibility by sending public messages, to keep posts brief and to the point, to keep the discussions on topic, and to cite relevant messages while responding. Third, an instructor should also model constructive reactions to technical difficulties. Finally, an instructor should provide appropriate feedback to students' work—to give feedback and grades on a timely and regular schedule and to treat students as unique individuals.

25.   BUILDING LEARNING COMMUNITIES

Meaningful interaction and collaborative teamwork are the natural ways of building online communities. Various types of online interaction include acknowledgement, agreement, apology, self-criticism, questions, humor, invitation, and referential statement; however, debates, open negotiation, and constructive argumentation are the most effective means of strengthening social ties among a group of learners and thus contribute most strongly to building the community (Wang, Folger, & Sierra, 2003). In addition, argumentation and consensus-reaching are the venues for constructing shared knowledge or a knowledge artifact; this artifact can then be continuously referred to and used to support other arguments (Stahl, 1999).

Online relationships can be more intimate and intense than those maintained in face-to-face settings (Anderson & Park, 1994). The lack of physical appearance in online communication in fact facilitates self-disclosure without taking risks. This anonymous mode of communication "serves as a springboard for formation of intensive, pleasurable, deep, and rich interpersonal connections. In addition, it offers the possibility to enter into simultaneous relationships with a number of people" (Schnarch in Oren et al., Introduction, ¶ 5).

Therefore, online instructors should intentionally encourage candid and uninhibited communication, so as to build a foundation for meaningful negotiation. They should establish a netiquette from the beginning of the course, encouraging students to freely express opinions and thoughts that differ from those of others including those of the instructor. Instructors must also attend to individuals who have trouble crossing the "threshold" of a community (Wegerif). In addition, communication will flow freely in these communities only if information is free of personal agendas, power struggles, and hidden prejudices (Stahl). If these negative elements can be avoided and true sharing of ideas becomes the norm, then new knowledge can be created.

Small-team collaboration monitored by an instructor is necessary for an online class to establish social relationships and the sense of community. Collaborative learning strategies help to maintain the sense of community and are crucial for creating positive learning outcomes for students (Hiltz, 1998; Wang, Sierra, & Folger, 2003). Online course design should maintain a good balance between independent and team tasks. The learning tasks should allow individuals to extend their creativity and should use teamwork as a safety net to prevent individuals from suffering "crash-and-burn." The goal is one of creating a balance between community-building and legitimate peripheral learning, where students participate at a distance and eventually become part of a community (Wegerif).

On the other hand, instructors must also respect individual differences and allow witness learners to develop. Some adults take online courses in part because the "socialization" aspect of the experience is secondary to the grade/qualification received (Wang & Aurilio, 2003). In particular, older adults with families might have firmly established their social network and thus have less desire to form a "cyber" network. In these cases, instructors should take the initiative to reach out to witness learners to ensure that they are still engaged in the learning tasks even though remaining outside the community or as "witness learners".

Instructors should tactfully encourage social discussions but then lead the discussions toward course content. Following are some strategies that would increase social interaction in an online community:

    a. Support a healthy group dynamic: encourage collaborative team-work as a powerful configuration for the accomplishment of learning tasks.

    b. Moderate group work in a way that enables students to interact, for example by creating a group space in online course management system;

    c. Encourage participants to abide by the netiquette

    d. Use supportive feedback to enhance the social atmosphere

    e. Create a social forum as a designated place for social integration of the learning group. (Oren et al., Implications, ¶ 3)

How do we know if community is built? Although community is specific to setting (Rovai, 2001), online communities share common attributes such as spirit (feeling of group identity), trust (feeling of safety and support), interaction (dynamics), and learning (construction of shared knowledge) (Wang & Poole, 2004).

26.   USING SOCIAL SOFTWARE TO DEEPEN THE SHARING OF PERSONAL CONCERNS AND EMOTIONS

A variety of online tools can be used to facilitate online communication and community-building: asynchronous discussion groups and conferences, synchronous chats, live audio and video webcasts, informal virtual meeting spaces, and social software such as Blog, Wiki, or Moodle.

Social software refers to the several emerging CMC tools and open-source web-authoring tools such as Blogs, Wikis, Moodle, or other collaboration systems, shared spaces, and any virtual world where people interact, as well as related tools and data structure for identity, integration, interchange, and analysis (Social Software Alliance, 2004). Social software supports easy personal publishing on the Internet without knowing authoring codes (html). Thus, it frees people from technical details and allows them to focus on creating and publishing knowledge with a few mouse clicks.

Social software encompasses support for one or more of the following elements: a) conversational interaction between people or groups, b) social feedback, and c) social networks (Boyd in Kaplan-Leiserson, 2003). Also, social software enables people to organize themselves into a network based on their preferences. Its strong support for social networks encourages the establishment of an immediate online community. Thus, social software represents a new form of communication and community-building that eliminates the need for geographic proximity and face-to-face meetings. In addition, authoring tools like Wikis provide a collaborative workspace for collective work.

Social software puts learners at the center of their educational experience and positions them as active stakeholders who are better motivated to learn (Pierce & Kalkman, 2003; Ferdig & Trammell). Knowing that a larger audience is reading her published work could increase a learner's accountability and desire to produce a quality product. The sense of writing to a larger audience in a global medium can be very motivating. Oravec (2002) contends that social software, such as blogs, also empowers all students by making their voices heard online regardless of their performance in face-to-face meetings.

Social software has not been widely used in teaching and learning, and thus research is still limited. Anecdotal evidence has shown that social software has the unique effect of spurring online interaction, which is the foundation for cognitive, teaching, and social presence. The student is cognitively present through frequent interaction with the material, experiences teaching presence through effective interaction with the instructor, and enjoys social presence through interaction with other students (Hutchins, 2003).

27.   ENGAGING STUDENTS OF DIVERSE LINGUISTIC AND CULTURAL BACKGROUNDS

The diverse cultural contexts of online learners have great implications on their engagement in the learning process. Engaging students emotionally is especially critical for learning environments that involve multi-cultural students distributed around the world.

Engagement is positively correlated with motivation, which may be prompted in different ways for culturally different students (Wlodkowski & Ginsberg, 1995). Wlodkowski and Ginsberg consider engagement the visible outcome of motivation. Emotions influence motivation, and emotional

Merrill, D. (2002). First principals of instruction. *Educational Technology Research and Development, 50*(3), 43-59.

O'Regan, K. (September 2003). Emotion and E-learning. *Journal of Asynchronous Learning Networks, 7*(3), 78-92.

Oren, A., Mioduser, D., & Nachmias, R. (April - 2002). *The Development of Social Climate in Virtual Learning Discussion Groups*, from http://www.irrodl.org/content/v3.1/mioduser.html

Reis, R. (2003). *Tomorrow's Professor Msg.#342 Teaching for Engagement*, from http://sll.stanford.edu/projects/tomprof/newtomprof/postings/342.html

Riding, R. J., & Rayner, S. (1998). *Cognitive styles and learning strategies: understanding style differences in learning and behaviour.* London: David Fulton Publishers.

Roedel, T.D., Shraw, G., & Plake, B.S. (1994). Validation of a measure of learning and performance goal orientations. *Educational and Psychological Measurement.* 54, 1013-1021.

Schunk, D. H. (1990). Goal setting and self-efficacy during self-regulated learning. *Educational Psychologist, 25*, 71-86.

Shin, N. (2003). Transactional presence as a critical predictor of success in distance learning. *Distance Education, 24*(1), 69-86.

Simon, G. (2002). *E-tivities: The key to active online learning.* London: Kogan Page Ltd.

Snell, J. C. (2000). Teaching generation X & Y: An essay part 2: Teaching strategies [Electronic version]. *College Student Journal, 34*(4), 482-484.

Social Software Alliance, S. S. (2004). *Alliance Charter*, from http://www.socialtext.net/ssa/index.cgi?Alliance%20Charter

Stahl, G. (1999). *Perspectives on collaborative knowledge-building environment: Toward a cognitive theory of computer support for learning.* Retrieved December 10, 2001 from http://orgwis.gmd.de/~gerry/publications/conferences/1999/csc199/kbd_workshop/kbe_theory 1.pdf

Vygotsky, L. S. (1986). *Thought and language.* Cambridge: MIT Press.

Wang, M. J. (2000). *The Construction Of Shared Knowledge In An Internet-Based Shared Environment For Expeditions (iExpeditions): A Study Of External Factors Implying Knowledge Construction.* Unpublished doctoral dissertation, University of Missouri, Columbia.

Wang, M. J., & Poole, M. (2004). Nurturing a dynamic online learning community among teens. In M. Kalantzis & B. Cope (Eds.), *The International Journal of Learning, 9.* Melbourne, Australia: the University Press/Common Ground. [Online]. Retrieved December 1, 2004 from http://LC2002. Publisher-Site.com/ProductShop/

Wang, M. J. & Aurilio, S. (2004). *Does socializing enhance learning outcomes in online settings?* Paper to be presented at Ed-Media 2004 conference, Lugano, Switzerland, June 21-26, 2004.

Wang, M. J., Sierra C., & Folger, T. (2003). Building a dynamic online learning community among adult learners. *Educational Media International (Special Issue: computer-mediated communication), 40*(1/2), 49-61.

Wegerif, R. (March 1998). The Social Dimension of Asynchronous Learning Networks. *Journal of Asynchronous Learning Networks, 2*(1), ??

Weiss, R. P. (2000, November). Emotion and learning [Electronic version]. *Training and Development, 54*, 44-48. Retrieved February 10, 2004, from EBSCO Host research database.

White, W. & Weight, H. (2000). *Online teaching guide: A handbook of attitudes, strategies, and techniques for the virtual classroom.* Needham Heights, Massachusetts: Allyn & Bacon.

Wlodkowski, R. J. (Summer 2003). Fostering Motivation in Professional Development Programs. *New Directions for Adult and Continuing Education*(98), 39-47. Retrieved from WilsonWeb.

Wlodkowski, R. J., & Ginsberg, M. B. (Sep 1995). A framework for culturally responsive teaching. *Educational Leadership Alexandria, 53*(1), 17-. Retrieved from ProQuest.

Table 1. A Taxonomy of Forms of Engagement and Assessment Strategies

Critical Factors for Engaged Learning	Indicators of Engaged Learning	Methods of Assessment
Cognitive: • Prior knowledge/experience: • familiar, unfamiliar • Achievement goal: • learning, performance • Learning activity: well-structured, • ill-structured • Cognitive/learning style	Cognitive engagement: • Self-regulated learning • Ownership of learning • Generative learning • Knowledge construction	• Discourse analysis • Observation of learning process • Performance analysis • Survey of students' self-perception
Emotive: • Feelings of self: confidence • competence, efficacy • Feelings of community • Feelings of learning atmosphere: safe and positive versus fearful; open negotiation versus domination • Feelings of the learning process: interest/curiosity, confusion/anxiety/frustration, fascination or boredom, pride, satisfaction or dissatisfaction	Emotional engagement: • Feeling confident • Feeling secure • Feeling comfortable • Feeling curious	• Discourse analysis of communication evidence for emotional cues and words • Survey on student perceptions
Social: • Personal attributes: age and gender, language and media literacy abilities • Learner's social-cultural context: goals, motives, expectations, and value, group size, discussion content, necessary software, and group moderation • Community-building, marked by group identity, trust, interaction, and construction of shared knowledge • Communication skill: student, instructor, moderator	Social engagement: • Sharing resources and information • Cohesiveness • Acceptance • Collaborative learning	• Discourse analysis • Observation of live discussions • Community-forming: group identity, trust, interaction, and construction of shared knowledge

Chapter 12

ENGAGING LEARNERS THROUGH CONTINUOUS ONLINE ASSESSMENT

Cathy Gunn
Centre for Professional Development, University of Auckland, New Zealand

Abstract: Assessment has long been recognized as a significant driver of student learning. A simplistic description of its function is to provide learners with a focus for study activity and feedback on progress at given points in time. Deeper analysis of the role of assessment reveals aspects of learning, motivation, learner control and metacognitive skill development. The advent of sophisticated computer based assessment systems in recent years creates valuable opportunities to promote student learning in ways that were becoming unmanageable due to weight of numbers and breadth of diversity in university classes. Although the greatest practical benefits may be found within tertiary education, online assessment has potential to enhance individual learning and learner autonomy across all levels from primary school to post graduate courses. Evidence of this can be found in a growing volume of published research and case studies. Contextual analysis across studies now supports the development of 'best use' scenarios and frameworks.

This chapter begins with a brief review of developments in online assessment practice over a ten year period, identifies further questions for educational research, and proposes a framework for integrating the use of online assessment into courses for maximum educational benefit. The literature shows the use of online multi-choice assessments originating predominantly in medicine, mathematics and the hard sciences. Expansion of the range of assessment types to include digital portfolios, reflective journals, graded discussions and simulated process models extended its use into management, IT, health and social sciences. With recent increases in the development and use of digital learning resources, ubiquitous networked computing across developed countries and widespread information literacy skills, the potential for online assessment to contribute to a desirable shift from teacher to student centred learning is high. The ultimate aim of this chapter is to present an evidence-based framework for its successful implementation.

Keywords: learning design, formative assessment, online learning, assessment strategies

D. Hung and M.S. Khine (eds.), Engaged Learning with Emerging Technologies, 255-273.
© 2006 *Springer. Printed in the Netherlands.*

1. INTRODUCTION: THE ROLE OF ASSESSMENT IN LEARNING

Assessment has long been recognized as a significant driver of student learning. A simplistic description of its function is to provide learners with a focus for study activity, give feedback on progress and measure achievement at given points in time. Deeper analysis of the role of assessment extends into the realms of motivation, learner control, learning psychology and neuroscience. Studies of the impact of assessment on student learning have been ongoing for many years, with the dual aim of fine-tuning the balance between maintenance of common educational quality standards and promotion of effective learning across student populations. The development of sophisticated computer based assessment systems in recent years creates unique opportunities to promote effective and student centred learning in ways that were becoming unmanageable due to the weight of numbers and breadth of diversity in many university classes. Although the greatest *practical* benefits associated with these developments may be found within tertiary education where enrolments of over a thousand in a single class are common, online assessment techniques have potential to enhance learning and learner autonomy across all levels of formal education systems from primary to post graduate. The main reasons are the opportunity to engage every individual in learning activities and the ability to provide immediate feedback. Evidence of this can be found in a growing collection of published research and case studies on the subject. Contextual analysis and common findings across studies now support development of 'best use' scenarios and guidelines for integrated use of online assessment as a driver of student learning. Such guidelines are proposed in this chapter, and their application in different contexts described.

2. CHAPTER OVERVIEW

The chapter begins with a review of developments in online assessment practice over a ten year period from 1994 - 2004. Guidelines for integrating online assessment into courses for maximum educational benefit are proposed, and further questions for educational research identified.

While technical matters are important, they are not a major focus in this instance. The issues are complex and warrant separate treatment in appropriate publications. From an educational perspective, the literature shows that the use of online multi-choice assessments originated mainly in medicine, mathematics and the hard sciences. At a basic level, learning these subjects involves a significant element of knowledge acquisition and application in relatively well-structured domains. Consequently, they lend themselves well to formative and even summative assessment in multi-choice format. Later expansion of the range of assessment types to include digital portfolios, reflective journals, graded discussions and simulated process models extended the use into management, IT, health and social sciences. With recent increases in the development and use of digital learning resources, ubiquitous networked computing across developed countries and widespread information literacy skills, the potential for online assessment to contribute to a desirable shift from teacher to student centred learning is high. The ultimate aim of this chapter is to present an evidence-based framework for its successful implementation.

3.   A DECADE IN REVIEW, 1994-2004

A timeframe of ten years was selected for this review because opportunities for implementing online assessment increased significantly after the appearance of the WWW in 1993. Early literature of the period summarizes the 'state of the art' of online assessment (Bull, 1993 & 1994a & b; National Council for Education Technology (NCET), 1994). The major uses reported at that time were multiple-choice questions, (a much maligned technique that is proving to have far greater value in the online environment than many educators would anticipate, as I shall argue later in the chapter), self-assessment, coursework and examinations. Initial application of these online assessment techniques focused on the hard sciences and medical education where the type of knowledge being tested lent itself well to the 'right and wrong answer' format that was easy to translate into multi-choice format. That is not to suggest that questions were always well written or tests well managed to achieve the desirable outcomes, just that the potential existed and was well exploited in some cases.

In terms of that potential, a positive though perhaps uncritical perspective of contemporary computer based assessment systems was presented by Griffiths, (1994) who considered that public education institutions did themselves and their students disservice by relying on assessment that measured 'learning and churning' capacity rather than skills and competencies or employability. He suggested that computer based assessment provided a means of enhancing established educational methods as well as solutions to some of the problems associated with them through automation of:

- Directly accessible electronic registration, scheduling and administration systems;
- Sophisticated reporting capacity;

- Provision of in depth statistical information on student and test performance;
- On-demand exam delivery;
- Instant marking and comprehensive performance feedback;
- Continuous monitoring of student progress through objective testing.

Technology then available could provide students with the means to learn at their own pace and for tutors to make better assessment of learning needs and the success of different teaching strategies or learning activities through computerized reporting systems. While continuing to require input from teachers on assessment design and analysis of outcomes, automation of these functions could allow more time for teaching since it dispensed with much of the need for manual marking and generation of individual feedback. The latter process having become so slow as to be almost meaningless to students in terms of contributing to their ongoing learning needs.

As is so often the case with new technology, a skeptical view emerged to temper the initial optimism of writers such as Griffiths. Experience of the various computer based assessment techniques grew, bringing a reality check into the picture. While there was clear potential in some respects, the range of assessment types that could be automated and the practicalities of doing so on a large scale emerged as limitations. The initial optimistic assumption that online assessment would completely replace established summative performance measurement methods proved unrealistic. A parallel to this situation may be found in the experience of developers in the related fields of computer-aided learning (CAL) and computer based learning (CBL) where such ideas were already being largely disproved. Perhaps the greatest insight into future developments among writers at the time is represented by Bull (1994b), who posited that online assessment could be most beneficial when it is **fully integrated** with lecturing and other teacher mediated activity. Thus, face to face sessions could be augmented by computerized assessment, or in some instances, it could provide an alternative to them if a directly mediated relationship with computer based learning activities existed. Another perceived opportunity for effective use of computer-based assessment was self or peer assessment by students. This could be achieved through creation of the opportunity for learning independently from teachers with a facility to accurately gauge ones own and peer achievements. As well as offering the potential to provide an integrated approach to learning and assessment, computer based assessment also created the possibility of immediate, effective and sometimes personalized feedback. The same article by Bull pointed to greater potential breadth of computer based assessment activities, identifying a range of uses beyond multiple choice tests, including assessment in laboratory practicals, problem-solving activities, computer-programming skills, examinations in certain subject areas and self-assessment of project work. The author did not, however, go on to offer case studies or specific examples of how these techniques had been implemented.

Another prevailing assumption of the early years, that online assessment offered greater efficiencies in terms of resource commitment, was called into question by the observation that initial investment and ongoing maintenance were resource intensive activities, (Stephens 1994). The need for policy, teaching practice and sometimes curriculum reviews resulting from institutional rather than single subject integration of such new methods was resource intensive if not intrinsically related to the implementation of assessments within specific courses.

The majority voice of academic authors of the 1990s reached a general consensus that information sharing within and across the education sector was crucial, as was institutional investment and policy development in the area of innovative assessment practice. Without the favorable condition of institutional commitment it was not considered possible to fully realize the potential of emerging computer based assessment techniques. Much evidence has since been produced to support this statement in respect of any educational innovation where provision of adequate technology and support systems are two critical success factors, despite the fact that they fall outside the range of intrinsic, instructional design factors. Another parallel with broader applications of technology in education lies in the fact that the practical and contextual challenges experienced at the time did nothing to dispel the collective belief in the considerable educational potential of online assessment. Consequently, investment in further development of software systems and educational methods as well as research to define best pedagogical practice was considered worthwhile.

Research issues then arising included:

- The need to improve and extend the use of computer-based assessment in appropriate situations;
- The need to create or improve alignment between learning objectives and assessment tasks;
- Development of conceptual frameworks for integration of computer based assessment into courses of study;
- Measurement of long term efficiency gains;
- Evaluation of assessment systems;
- Effective use of assessment information by teachers;

- The need to address staff and student development requirements for effective use of the medium.

It is interesting to note that if the words 'computer-based' were removed from the above text, the principles described would still apply. However, the sole intention here is to examine innovative assessment techniques in the online environment. The relevance of the questions is confirmed by recent developments, which demonstrate at least some, and in some cases, considerable progress in all these areas of investigation.

4.   EMERGING OPPORTUNITIES

Technological advances have brought us to a situation where what was previously referred to as computer based assessment has been largely replaced by online equivalents. The increased use of this dynamic medium supports greater flexibility, complexity and interactivity as well as offering easier maintenance and administration in some circumstances. In this respect, some of the optimism of the 1990s proved to be well founded. So, it must be noted, did some of the skepticism. Some of the techniques in current use are quite simply automated versions of established assessment formats, which have proved to offer efficiencies once the initial investment in their development is made. Others have been made possible by the synergy between contemporary pedagogy and emerging technology.

Online assessment is considered by some researchers to be an emerging method with high potential to encourage deep approaches to learning and to sustain student interest and motivation, (e.g. Loewenberger & Bull, 2003). Depending, of course, on how it is conceived, designed and implemented, there are considerable opportunities to go beyond the 'learning and churning' approach that may sometimes be encouraged by the increasing scale and time constraints associated with longer established assessment methods. As well as driving desirable student learning behavior, it is seen as potentially making a practical contribution to student centred learning in large classes, (Gardner & Sheridan 2002). If one of the main learning activities at university is students attending mass lectures, following this with group or individual activities involving online formative assessment and practice exercises will allow them to test their knowledge level and receive immediate feedback on performance. The benefits that can accrue from even the simplest forms of online assessment in this context are considerable. Where step-wise progress through complex processes and constructive feedback with further guidance is offered, the benefits are considerably greater.

Simplicity is far from being the only option on today's online assessment menu though. Current software systems support assessments in many other forms besides multi-choice quizzes, process application tests and 'fill in the gaps' type questions, although systems that support this type of assessment are increasingly sophisticated, with capacity for:

- Random generation of item variables and tests from large item banks;
- Stepwise analysis of student performance and fuzzy logic marking;
- Provision of immediate individual and constructive feedback;
- Dynamic integration with enterprise systems e.g. gradebooks and student records.

Flexibility is another worthwhile addition as some learners need to work backwards from examples, with model answers or in groups to develop their understanding. With online assessment and appropriate orientation into its use, the choice of how to approach learning is their own.

These types of assessment are often criticized for promoting a surface approach to learning. However, findings from studies of the impact of online assessment in specific contexts suggest, as does some recent literature, that the opposite may be true. Some basic principles of learning psychology lend further support to these preliminary findings as the following section will illustrate. In addition to multi-choice type assessments, a range of other assessment opportunities can be used to engage learners in the online environment. These include simulations, engagement with real world situations, multi-modal representations, problem solving, collaborative activities, interaction with micro and virtual worlds, multimedia and hypertext presentations and simulated clinical or laboratory work. The context of application and objectives of learning will always determine which method is appropriate.

5. GUIDELINES FOR INTEGRATED ONLINE ASSESSMENT

The objective of these guidelines is to present a generic picture of how online assessment can be used to drive student learning and activity towards the achievement of quality learning. The precise definition of quality depends on the objectives of the course or program in which the assessment is embedded.

6.   LEARNING OBJECTIVES

The specific learning objectives in a given context will define the scope of the content knowledge and skills that students are expected to master. In most cases there will be many different paths to reach the same goal, and one aim of flexible and online learning design is to offer choices that accommodate a range of learning styles and preferences. In current reality, this is neither easy to achieve nor an available option for many university courses. In most campus-based courses, degrees of flexibility tend to be limited to matters of access to course materials through online learning management systems and libraries, online communication and submission of assignments. These limited degrees of flexibility still offer significant potential for learning enhancement though, as the range of materials and activities can now include interactive multimedia, simulations, direct channels of communication and access to real world situations that can be integrated into learning environments. The types of activity that best serve the learning objectives can be selected from the rich range now available, and students may sometimes be offered the opportunity to make their own choices in this respect. The opportunities to promote effective learning, to motivate, guide and support learners through various forms of continuous assessment within these environments are very much an under-utilized and undervalued phenomenon. The following psychological perspective illustrates this point.

7.   PSYCHOLOGY OF LEARNING

A key challenge to teachers lies in the accepted wisdom that no direct causal relationship exists between the effectiveness of learning and the quality of teaching and educational materials. The most favorable conditions and opportunities may be presented, but ultimately, success depends on the individual's educational goals, level of motivation, prior knowledge, expectations and engagement with teaching and learning activities. Among these key individual factors that influence learning, interest and attention are two aspects of motivation that have a significant impact (Keller, 1987; Schiefele 1991). Although the jury is still out on whether computer supported learning has a positive effect on student motivation across the board, (and some would say this is an ill-defined question anyway) (Reeves, 1995), there is some compelling evidence that it can have such effect when it is well designed and presented for the purpose, (Keller, 1987). Two psychological factors behind this success are the basic ones of interest and attention.

As far back as 1899, eminent Harvard psychologist William James noted that genius is nothing more than a power of sustained attention, but that most people cannot easily sustain such attention. He posed a challenge, that

> *"the education system that can train students to develop their ability for sustained voluntary attention will be the education system par excellence" (William James, Talks to Teachers, 1899)*

By 'sustained voluntary attention', James referred to the ability to attract and sustain the interest, and by implication, full attention of students to a learning activity. He defined two types of interest. One is the natural or spontaneous interest that sparks when a novel situation arises. The other is the sustained interest that keeps the mind on task and stops it from either wandering off in another direction, failing to make important associations or grasping the meaning of what is happening. While he suggested that training in sustained voluntary attention would be beneficial, he also admitted that he did not know how this could be achieved. It is only necessary to observe the high level of focus of any group of students working on computer based assessment problems and cross check this observation with system log data to realize that online formative assessment, when suitably presented as an integral part of a course of study, may begin to rise to James' challenge. While contemporary educational psychology has produced many more sophisticated methods and hypotheses, this basic and long outstanding question may present the problem in as effective a way as any. It also reiterates a key point, that while technology is relatively new in the context of learning, the educational principles it serves are as old as any on record. The possibility that James could not have anticipated is that regardless of class size, every individual student could be given the opportunity to interact in a computer-mediated environment as a means of moving towards his ultimate goal of sustained voluntary attention.

8.   APPROACHES TO LEARNING

Also relevant to this discussion is a brief mention of the concepts of deep and surface learning, (Marton & Saljo 1976 a & b) and the implications of learner behavior on memory. The original studies and subsequent research both provide evidence to the effect that expectations are influenced by teaching strategies and act as significant drivers of student behavior. Wrong expectations can have a detrimental effect on depth of learning. A frequently voiced criticism of the age of mass higher education is that superficial learning is encouraged by heavy workloads, stressful assessments and limited opportunities for prolonged engagement with content in active learning situations. There may well be more than a single grain of truth in such accusations, and the realities of university classes with large, diverse student populations and increasing staff workloads may further aggravate the situation. Erosion of standards is not the only possible outcome, although the positive route implies some redefinition of the teacher and learner roles and requires willingness on both sides to embrace the change. In the context of large classes, lectures may or may not be the most effective activity in terms of learner engagement and interaction with content. It depends on how well they are structured and presented. For the most part though, as a stand-alone activity, they do not easily create the expectation that deep and sustained engagement with content is necessary to pass a course. Psychologists tell us that information that passes once through the brain is easily forgotten. If there is no existing framework to integrate new information, it will not be retained, yet the goal of learning activity is to promote the development of structures that allow new information to become embedded in webs of meaningful associations and knowledge maps.

A more common and useful model is where lectures provide the signposts and basic structure of knowledge, and are presented in conjunction with other tasks, such as various forms of continuous assessment, where students are actively engaged in practice tests, problem solving activities, and application of learned information. In this case lectures can provide excellent opportunities for teachers to introduce topics, fuel enthusiasm and guide students towards preferred ways of engaging with content that will lead to deep processing and understanding of subject material. To refer again to the work of William James:

> *"...the mind is essentially an associating machine...we remember because of our associations and these associations are due to our organized brain paths"* *(James 1899, op cit).*

The process that is triggered by repeated exposure to problems, exercises and questions in online assessment systems not only works on long-term memory, but also reaches the level of altering the learners' brain paths as neuroscience is now coming to understand. The key point here is that activity is repeated many times and perhaps approached from a range of different perspectives. This level of analysis is mentioned only in passing in this chapter, although current literature provides a widely accessible range of further reading on the subject.

9. PEDAGOGICAL MODELS

A more detailed treatment of pedagogy is warranted here, as the key to the case presented is that learners can be productively engaged in online (or indeed, in face to face) environments through assessment tasks designed to provide the focus of sustained attention and be the driver of activity. The scenarios described relate to processes that are far more complex than simple use of multiple-choice tests designed to measure factual recall. However, it must be noted that enduring memory of rote learned arithmetic tables, language vocabulary and grammar rules may be taken as evidence that such simple activities play an important part of learning at some levels and in certain circumstances. This point is worth mentioning because many critics of online assessment can see no further potential in this type of activity. Now, however, research findings are emerging as evidence that there is considerably more to the matter than this simplistic conception of the process. The added bonus is that learners obviously engage with the innovative opportunities presented by the online environment, particularly the receipt of immediate feedback, and teacher time can be devoted to higher-level engagement with the subject.

10. LEARNING FROM LECTURES WITH INTEGRATED ONLINE ASSESSMENT

The pedagogical model that supports the integrated online assessment approach in a lecture-based teaching environment is firmly learner centred. Although its articulation may well involve collaborative activities, it ultimately extends to the level of individual engagement. However social or collaborative the process and activities that trigger it may be, learning is ultimately an individual journey. So the role of the teacher or instructional designer is to guide, facilitate and support that journey as far as possible for each and every individual in the class. The mix may involve many or few teaching and learning activity types from what has come to be known as the 'traditional classroom teaching or face to face' mode. For example, lectures, laboratories, tutorials and seminars are still very much a feature of many university contexts and are likely to remain so to good effect in many cases. However, the activities that go on outside these events are where the shift of focus may most usefully occur. Laboratory and tutorial classes often give more opportunity for interaction and individual attention, though group sizes are increasing and contact hours tending to decrease in the current context. To illustrate the point by way of a simple example, students attend lectures in year one science. The lecture topic is covered in presentation style with full use of multimedia facilities, animations to demonstrate processes, still images projected large to show effects and structures, videos to illustrate live situations and audio to introduce authentic sound effects. Ideally the lecturer is enthusiastic and inspiring. The impact of this lecture will be slightly different for every student in the room, depending on their prior knowledge, level of motivation and degree of attention paid during the presentation, as well as other factors such as where they were sitting in the room, the level of proficiency in the language of delivery and other cultural considerations. In a more 'traditional' pedagogical model, the student may have taken notes, filled in blanks in a workbook or completed a paper based test on the content. If there are a large number of students in the class, it will be some time before they get feedback on their own performance, maybe the lab class a week later will have a model answer on the board and the opportunity to ask questions of the tutor. This process more or less repeats until major assessments are due, and students go back through their notes, revise with books and generally feel stressed because they know they can't remember everything that was said in the lectures six weeks earlier and there were new terms they didn't understand and can't recall. Shift the focus to a model where online assessment is embedded as a key driver of learning. The student attends a lecture, having already worked through a simple online overview and quiz on the topic. The score may not have been very good, but at least there are some associations already formed, so the lecture makes a bit more sense. The lecturer meanwhile checked the overall performance on the test for all the students in the group through the online learning management system log data and knows which areas are less well understood or the subject of common misconceptions. So the focus of the lecture presentation is geared to suit, and the students have some idea of what they individually do and don't know. The opportunity to ask questions is limited, but every little helps. They have also gained a basic understanding of the structure of the topic or domain they are studying, what Ausubel calls the "advance organizer", (Ausubel, 1960). After the lecture, the students take a slightly harder test and hopefully achieve a higher score. The feedback is immediate and higher scores boost confidence. For areas where they are not performing well, there are more tests and activities that help them to approach the task in different ways, deconstruct problems and work out where they are missing the point. There are study groups they can opt into if they choose to do so, where closer attention is paid to particular topics. Not all students need to do this, some of them will have started with more prior knowledge and some picked it up quicker for other reasons. This is what catering to diversity in educational background means in practice. Anyway, the repeated exposure is helpful to all students. It is working behind the scenes to create new associations, access long-term memory and modify the brain. When it is time for the lab class in this case, the students have fewer and better focused questions. They may have discussed or worked collaboratively with their peers to complete the online assessment problems. Anyway, they have had a few choices of how to go about the task and maybe found a way that suits their style better than others do. This is one generic example of a case that could be developed in a variety of ways to suit different educational contexts.

The shift of focus in these scenarios seems minimal in some respects, but the impact of online assessment is significant. It has potentially enhanced learning, increased confidence, promoted collaboration, formed new associations in the mind of the learner and shifted some of the content knowledge from short to long-term memory.

11. CONVERSATION AS A LEARNING ACTIVITY

The 'art' of conversation is a well accepted method of promoting learning in some disciplines, as authors such as Pask (1976) and Toulmin (1958 & 1978) noted some years ago. Moving the process online adds value to the activity as illustrated by Gunn (2001) among others, and a range of tools and methods are available for assessing the content of contributions, (e.g. Hara & Bonk 1998). While there are limitations that cannot be overlooked, such as typing skills, computer access in the broadest sense of the term, (see e.g. Benseman 2000) and unfamiliarity with this type of study activity, experience suggests that most students quickly become accustomed to communicating in the online environment and consider the activity worthwhile in terms of their learning. Initial presentation of tasks to be completed in this way is a critical success factor as it provides the opportunity for realistic expectations to be set and requirement made known. Ground rules for participation, lessons in 'netiquette', instructions on the size, content and nature of contributions and guidelines on how they will be assessed are usually sufficient for this purpose. Once the scene has been set in this way, it is up to the moderator to decide how much monitoring and intervention is appropriate. Salmon (2000) gives a full description of options in this respect. With more mature students, it may be that the teacher chooses to stay out of the discussion until a certain point in order to let students develop their own perspectives on a topic. With less experienced groups, it may be necessary to guide the discussion in a more structured way. These are just two examples from a range of options that can be selected according to what suits the circumstances. As an assessment activity embedded in a student centred learning environment, online discussion offers many benefits, some obvious and some more subtle, though equally powerful.

The more obvious benefits are that all students have a voice and learn to have confidence in expressing their views or understanding. This is quite a different situation from having to be the lone student to ask or answer a question or make a contribution in a class full of peers. The relative absence of others in the sense of physical presence is a great confidence booster, and in the case of some cultural groups, an important factor in being comfortable to contribute. Most students will contribute if they are required to and instructed in the correct way to do so.

A benefit associated with the asynchronous mode of discussion boards, as opposed to the synchronous medium of chat sessions, is that students have the opportunity to consider, research and reflect before they post a contribution. This is an important factor for the large number of people who think of the right thing to say after the opportunity to say it in a face to face meeting has passed. While this may be dismissed as unimportant because the thinker has still come to the realization, it is important that the opportunity to ask the question, discuss the issue further and learn about other perspectives has been missed. If learning results from reflection, then online discussion offers significant opportunities for this to happen.

Online discussion is also a many-to-many channel of communication rather than a predominantly one-to-many transmission from teacher to students. The opportunity to share experience and engage in conversation with a group of peers offers greater access to the multiple perspectives that exist within any cohort of students. While the teacher's perspective is unquestionably valuable, so are those of the other students and through this activity they become known to all members of the group. This is uncommon in face to face classes because of the sheer weight of numbers and the dynamics that inevitably mean that few people share their views while most others only listen. Again, evidence suggests that this is a time consuming approach to assessment but one where the quality of the interaction and outcomes easily justify the investment.

There are no hard and fast rules about when or how often to include online discussions in courses. This depends on many factors. There is a range of useful possibilities, from disciplines such as computer science where one line answers about correct coding protocols may be the focus, to critical analyses in humanities subjects where viewpoints rather than correct and incorrect answers are the objective. Sherry et al (1999) offer a comprehensive summary of research-based practice in the use of online conversations for readers who wish to explore the subject further.

Keller J. (1987), Strategies for Stimulating the Motivation to Learn, *Performance and Instruction, 26* (8).

Kerka, S., Wonacott, M.E., Grossman, C & Wagner, J., (2000), Assessing Learners Online, Retrieved 10th March 2003, from: http://ericacve.org/docs/pfile03.htm

Loewenberger, P. and Bull, J (2003). Cost-effectiveness Analysis of Computer Based Assessment. *Association for Learning Technology Journal (ALT-J). 11*(2), 23-45.

Marton F & Säljö R, (1976a) On Qualitative Differences in Learning: Outcome & Process. *British Journal of Educational Psychology, 46.* (June), 4-11.

Marton F & Säljö R, (1976b) On qualitative differences in learning. 11. Outcome as a function of the learners' conception of the task. *British Journal of Educational Psychology, 46* (June), 115-127.

National Council for Educational Technology (NCET), (1994), *Going forward: using IT for assessment.* Coventry, UK.

Pask, G. (1976). *Conversation Theory: Applications in Education and Epistemology.* Amsterdam: Elsevier.

Reeves, T C. (1995), Questioning the Questions of Instructional Technology Research, Available at http://www.gsu.edu/~wwwitr/docs/dean/index.html

Salmon, G. (2000). *E-Moderating, The Key to Teaching and learning Online.* London: Kogan Page.

Schiefele U, (1991) Interest, Learning & Motivation, *Educational Psychologist, 26,* 3-4.

Sherry, L., Tavalin, F & Billig, S. (1999). Good Online Conversation: Building on Research to Inform Practice, The Web Project 2001. http://www.webproject.org/resources/pdf/oeri.pdf

Stephens, D. (1994). Using Computer-Assisted Assessment: Time Saver or Sophisticated Distraction? Active Learning 1(December): 11-15.

Toulmin, S. (1958). *The Uses of Argument.* Cambridge: Cambridge University Press.

Toulmin, S., Rieke, R & Janik, A (1978). *An Introduction to Reasoning.* 2nd ed. New York: Macmillan.

ABOUT THE CONTRIBUTORS

Prof. dr. Betty Collis is head of the research team "Technology for Strategy, Learning and Change" in the Faculty of Behavioural Sciences at the University of Twente in The Netherlands. In addition, as leader of a five-year collaborative research project with the Learning and Leadership Development Organization of Shell International Exploration and Production (Shell EP-LLD), she is also head of the research team for Shell EP LLD. In both roles she applies, researches, and evaluates the contribution-oriented pedagogy. See http://users.edte.utwente.nl/collis/ for an overview of her work.

Dr. Cathy Gunn is a Senior Lecturer in Academic Development for e-Learning at the University of Auckland in New Zealand. Her role involves a variety of teaching, research, strategic planning, organizational development and educational consultancy activities, all aimed at promoting the integration of technology to enhance learning, teaching and administration across the institution. Cathy is currently serving a two-year term as President of ascilite, (The Australasian Society for Computers in Learning in Tertiary Education) and is recognized internationally as an expert in this emerging discipline.

Professor John Hedberg is Millennium Innovations Chair in ICT and Education & Director of the Macquarie ICT Innovations Centre at Macquarie University, Sydney, Australia. Macquarie ICT Innovations Centre is a learning partnership with the NSW Department of Education and Training to develop innovative programs in technology enhanced learning for students and teachers. He was previously Professor of Learning Sciences and Technologies at Nanyang Technological University in Singapore where he directed several research projects exploring the role of technologies in engaging students in Mathematics, Science, History and Geography classrooms. He is known for the constructivist learning environments he has designed culminating in a British Academy award for an interactive theatre CD-ROM entitled *StageStruck*. He has wide experience in the design of open and distance learning programs delivered on-line and through CD-ROM. He has published on navigation, cognition and multimodality, design and evaluation in interactive multimedia, the most recent book is *Evaluating interactive learning systems* with Thomas Reeves has been recently published by Educational Technology publications, He is also the Editor-in-chief of *Educational Media International.*

Dr. David Hung is an associate professor at the National Institute of Education (NIE), Nanyang Technological University, Singapore. He is currently a contributing editor of *Educational Technology* and an associate editor of the *International Journal of Learning Technology*. Dr. Hung teaches and supervises students of both undergraduate and graduate levels; and serves as a consultant and trainer to various projects involving education and training, initiated by the Ministry of Education and the Ministry of Defense. Besides being involved in research on the cognitive and learning sciences, Dr. Hung has been actively involved in online learning efforts in NIE and in Singapore.

David Jonassen is Distinguished Professor of Education at the University of Missouri where he teaches in the areas of Learning Technologies and Educational Psychology. Since earning his doctorate in educational media and experimental educational psychology from Temple University, Dr. Jonassen has taught at the Pennsylvania State University, University of Colorado, the University of Twente in the Netherlands, the University of North Carolina at Greensboro, and Syracuse University. He has published 28 books and numerous articles, papers, and reports on text design, task analysis, instructional design, computer-based learning, hypermedia, constructivist learning, cognitive tools, and technology in learning. He has consulted with businesses, universities, public schools, and other institutions around the world. His current research focuses on constructing design models and environments for problem solving.

Dr. Myunghee Kang, professor of Educational Technology at Ewha Womans University in Korea, teaches *e-Learning Design and Development Strategies, Knowledge Construction, Learning Community and Virtual Communications and Emerging Technologies in Education.* Her recent research interest is to find an optimum learning solution for adult learners by investigating c-Learning, e-Learning, m-Learning, learning community and knowledge constructing & managing issues. Her numerous research papers have been published in *Educational Technology Research Journal, Training Research Journal* in Korea and *Educational Technology and eLearning Journal* in U.S.

Dr. Koh Thiam Seng is an Associate Professor in Science Education at the National Institute of Education. He has research interests in the use of ICT in science education. He is currently on secondment to the Singapore Ministry of Education as Director of Educational Technology.

Dr. Lee Kar Tin is Principal Lecturer and Head, Department of Information and Applied Technology at the Hong Kong Institute of Education in Hong Kong. Throughout her career, she has provided leadership for numerous university and government funded projects in ICT innovation. Currently she is involved in research and development projects in both the primary and secondary sectors which focus on designing, implementing and evaluating online learning environments. Along with her interest in researching teaching and learning online she continues to actively explore factors influencing teacher's use of emerging technologies in various learning environments. She strongly believes in introducing new educational options to teachers in the field in order to strengthen and transform current educational practice. In January 2006 she will join the Queensland University of Technology, Australia as Professor and Head, School of Mathematics, Science and Technology Education.

Professor Susan E. Metros (M.F.A., 1976, Michigan State University) is Deputy Chief Information Officer and Executive Director for e-Learning at The Ohio State University. She also holds the faculty appointment of Professor of Design Technology. She has more than twenty-five years of university level teaching experience and almost ten years experience in information technology administration. As Deputy CIO, she is responsible for leading the academic community in appropriately using technology-enhanced teaching and learning, both on campus and at a distance. In her role as educator and designer, she teaches within the visual communication curriculum and has served as principal designer on several international award winning interactive multimedia and Web-based projects. She is also active on numerous international and national committees and task forces and has published and presented widely on the role of eLearning in transforming education to be sharable, engaging, interactive and learner-centered.

Prof. dr. Jef Moonen is emeritus professor in the Faculty of Behavioural Sciences at the University of Twente in The Netherlands where he participates in the research team "Technology for Strategy, Learning and Change". Prior to his retirement he served as department chair and dean of the faculty. His current research includes studying digital portfolios as tools for the contribution-oriented pedagogy. In addition, he continues his long-standing research on return on investment of computer-supported learning.

Reinhard Oppermann received his diploma in psychology in 1973 and his Ph.D. in 1975 at the University of Bonn. In 1979, he joined the GMD German National Research Center for Information Technology, since summer 2001 merged with the Fraunhofer Gesellschaft. Currently he is head of the research department Information in Context in the Institute for Applied Information Technology. In 1993, he was appointed to an honorary professorship at the University of Koblenz now working at the Institute for Computational Visualistics. His main research interests include participatory system development, human factors of human-computer interaction, ergonomic evaluation methodology, adaptive and adaptable information systems and user modelling, contextualized learning, and nomadic information systems.

Alan Pritchard is a researcher and lecturer, and member of the Centre for New Technologies Research and Education (CeNTRE), at the Warwick Institute of Education, University of Warwick, UK where he teaches a range of courses for Undergraduate and Postgraduate trainee teachers, as well as teaching on the Institute's higher degree and in-service programmes. Previously he has been a teacher with responsibility for Mathematics, Science, Design and Technology and Information and Communications Technology (ICT), an Advisory Teacher for ICT, and Deputy Head of a Primary School. He has undertaken research and published articles in the academic press on children's learning, with particular reference to the use of new technology, design and technology, initial teacher education, and the links between ICT and other subjects. He writes widely for professional journals and magazines for teachers. His books include *Education.com: an introduction to learning, teaching and ICT* (2000). *Using ICT in Primary Mathematics Teaching* (2002) *Learning on the Net* (2004) and most recently *Ways of Learning* (2005).

Dr. Geoff Romeo a senior lecturer in the Faculty of Education at Monash University, Australia. He has been with the Faculty since 1991. Prior to this he was a teacher with the Education Department of Victoria. In 1989 he was an International Teaching Fellow and taught for 12 months at Galveston Elementary School in Arizona, USA. His research interests include the use of ICT in education, at all levels, to improve teaching and learning, online teaching and learning, the development of primary and middle school curriculum, action research and education in general. Dr Romeo is the immediate past president of ICT in Education Victoria, and a past member of the Australian Council for Computers in Education and the Standards Council of the Teaching Profession. Dr Romeo is active in delivering and organizing Professional Development for schools, organizations and teachers, and has presented at conferences, seminars and workshops in Australia, the United Kingdom, USA, Denmark and Chile.

Marlene Scardamalia is the Presidents' Chair in Education & Knowledge Technologies at OISE/University of Toronto and the Director of the Institute for Knowledge Innovation and Technology, IKIT—a worldwide network of innovators working to advance the frontiers of knowledge building in various sectors. "Knowledge building," a term now widely used in education and knowledge management, originated with the CSILE/Knowledge Building project. Marlene is the inventor of CSILE (Computer Supported Intentional Learning Environments), which was the first networked knowledge building environment for education. The second generation version of this technology, Knowledge Forum®, is in use in 19 countries, in education, health, business, and professional organizations. Knowledge building theories, models, practices and technologies have been developed in partnership with Carl Bereiter and team members, and form the basis of two recent awards: (1) The Canadian Foundation for Innovation and (2) the INE Collaborative Research Initiative awards. From 1996 till 2002, Marlene has been the K-12 theme leader for Canada's TeleLearning Network of Centres of Excellence. Her work has led to several honours and awards, including an Ontario Psychological Foundation Contribution to Knowledge award, a fellowship at the Center for Advanced Study in the Behavioral Sciences, election to the U. S. National Academy of Education (the second Canadian so honoured) and appointment to the Presidents' Chair in Education and Knowledge Technologies for the Ontario Institute for Studies in Education of the University of Toronto. She has done research and published in the areas of cognitive development, psychology of writing, intentional learning, the nature of expertise, and educational uses of computers. She also headed a project on "Cognitive Bases of Educational Reform," out of which grew the "Schools for Thought" program, notable for its synthesis of major educational initiatives.

Marcus Specht received his Diploma in Psychology in 1995 and his Ph.D. from the University of Trier in 1998 on adaptive learning technology. Marcus Specht currently works as a researcher at the GMD German National Research Center for Information Technology, since summer 2001 merged with the Fraunhofer Gesellschaft. He has rich experience in intelligent tutoring systems and the integration of ITS and Web-based tutoring from former projects in the field of adaptive hypermedia and ITS (ELM-ART, InterBook, AST). His main research interests are adaptive learning and training systems, knowledge management, contextualized computing, and intelligent interfaces.

Myint Swe Khine is Associate Professor at the National Institute of Education, Nanyang Technological University, Singapore, where he teaches undergraduate and postgraduate courses in the area of learning sciences and technologies. His research interests include application of emerging technologies in teaching and learning and technology-rich learning environments. He is an Editorial Board Member of the *Educational Media International.*

Johannes Strobel is Assistant Professor in the Educational Technology programme at Concordia University, Montreal, Canada USA. After studying philosophy, religious studies, psychology, and information science in Germany, he finished his PhD (2004) at the School of Information Science and Learning Techonlogies at the University of Missouri-Columbia. He is focusing in his research and teaching on the intersection between learning and technology. He is interested in the use of computers as cognitive tools including concept mapping, expert systems, system modeling, and hypertext systems. Recent projects include research on teachers' use of technology, case-based reasoning, ill-structured problem solving, every-day learning, students' individual setup like epistemological beliefs, domain specific reasoning, historical reasoning and conceptual change/formation.

Dr. Tan Seng Chee completed his Ph.D. in Instructional Systems from the Pennsylvania State University in 2000. He is currently an academic staff in the Learning Sciences and Technologies academic group, National Institute of Education, Singapore. He is holding a concurrent appointment as an Assistant Director, ETD/MOE, leading the Research & Development team. His research interests include using computers as cognitive tools and Computer-Supported Collaborative Learning. As a new scholar in educational technology, he has actively contributed to the research and publications in this field. For instance, he has recently completed a $260,000 Ministry granted research project on "Fostering scientific inquiry through Computer-Supported Collaborative Learning" and has contributed 3 books, 9 book chapters, 20 refereed journal papers, 11 refereed papers in conference proceedings, and 15 other publications to date. He also contributed actively as a professional member in the field of ICT research, serving in the editorial board for the journals *Technology Source* (2001-2003), *Innovate* (since 2004), and the AACE/SITE journals (since 2004). He is currently a professional member of the Educational Research Association (Singapore) and Association for the Advancement of Computers in Education (AACE).

Dr. Minjuan Wang is assistant professor of Educational Technology at San Diego State University. She teaches *Methods of Inquiry, Instructional Design, Technologies for Course Delivery,* and *Technologies for Teaching.* Her research specialties focus on the sociocultural aspects of online learning (e.g., learning communities, gender and cultural differences in online collaboration) and technological interventions in language and literacy education. She has peer-reviewed articles published in *Educational Media International, TechTrend,* and the *International Journal of Educational*

Technology. She has also published several book chapters on engagement in online problem solving, informal learning via the Internet, and effective learning in multicultural and multilingual classrooms. Her paper on *Gender, discourse style, and equal participation in online learning* won an outstanding paper award from E-Learn 2002: world conference on E-learning in corporate, government, healthcare, and higher education.

Allan H.K. Yuen, (Ph.D.) is Head of the Division of Information and Technology Studies, Faculty of Education, University of Hong Kong, Pokfulam Road, Hong Kong (e-mail: hkyuen@hkucc.hku.hk), and Deputy Director of the Centre for Information Technology in Education (CITE) at the University of Hong Kong since its establishment in 1998. He is the vice president of the Hong Kong Association for Educational Communications and Technology. Dr. Yuen has led a number of research and development projects on information technology in education. His research interests include computer supported collaborative learning, information technology leadership and management in education, computer studies education, and teacher education.

INDEX

abstract conceptualization (AC) 230
academic performance 127, 131, 132, 134, 135, 141, 143, 228
achievement goals 226, 228, 253
acquisition model 52, 53
active experimentation (AE) 230
activist 230
activity design 240
activity theory viii, 14
American Association for the Advancement of Science 38
analysis of variance (ANOVA) 141
anchored instruction 44, 45
annotation facilities 75, 80, 81
assessment xv, 30, 31, 49, 50, 58,, 59, 61-64, 77, 92, 97, 99, 119, 139, 154, 155, 159, 160, 164-166, 171-173, 178, 179, 203, 204, 211, 212, 226-230, 239, 243, 247, 253, 255, 256-268, 270, 271
- methods 253
- options 269
- strategies 236, 253, 255
assessment-centered environments 153
attitudes 34, 103, 130, 153, 164, 166, 171, 172, 179, 113, 247
- development 34
authentic experience 29
authentic learning 33, 38, 73, 107, 187
- environments 39-41
- conditions for 40

best-use scenarios 255, 256
black box models 22

capitalism vii
central experts 73
Christianity vii
classical Greece vii
classroom learning 44, 233
clinical reasoning strategies 36
clinically useful knowledge 36
CMC 128, 131
- tools 128, 144, 245

cognition 8, 24, 32, 34, 44, 184, 187, 208, 231
cognitive strategies 34
cognitive structures 16, 17
cognitive styles 227, 230
cognitive tools 1, 43
collaboration xv, 3, 6, 29, 39-45, 50, 60, 64, 76, 95, 97, 130, 137, 143, 144, 159, 166, 171-173, 177, 229, 240, 244, 245, 267
collaborative learning vii, x, xiv, 91, 108, 133, 137, 144, 154, 159, 165, 171, 172, 207, 208, 237, 238, 240, 243, 244, 253
communal discussion (CD) 138, 139, 142-144
communication 42, 45, 52, 55, 62, 63, 76, 119, 120, 123, 127, 129-131, 137, 144, 159, 215, 226, 230, 234, 237, 241-246, 253, 262, 268
- facilities 75, 83
- functionalities 61
- norms 59
- technologies xv, 108, 127, 149, 150, 155, 158, 162, 225
- - role in education 155
- skills 44, 253
- tools 43, 44, 237, 240
community
- building 42, 131, 144, 235, 236, 244-246, 253
- feeling of belonging to 233
- -centered environments 153-155, 164, 165, 172
computer supported learning 262
computer-aided learning (CAL) 258
computer-based learning (CBL) 59, 258
computer-mediated communication 127
- tools 44, 128
computer-programming skills 259
computers ix, x, xiv, 85, 107, 149, 150, 155, 157, 167, 205, 209, 210
- in education perspective 155
Computer-Supported Intentional Learning Environments 35

computer-supported collaborative
  learning (CSCL) xiv, 91, 95
concept map 17, 23, 43, 112-114, 192
conceptual change 1, 5, 24, 152
concrete experiences (CE) 230
consistent visual metaphors 116
constructivism 1, 44, 52, 55, 91, 109,
  177, 185, 234
constructivist epistemology 91, 104
constructivist learning 78, 91, 92, 104,
  184
- activities 38
- environment 43, 44
- tools 45
constructivist learning theories 109,
  183
contemporary educational psychology
  263
context facilities 75
contributing student 49, 54, 55, 58
- approach 50, 55, 57
- - in practice 56
- - pedagogy 50, 54
contribution-oriented
- activities 53, 54, 59-61, 65
- pedagogy 61-63, 65
conventional learning 130, 138, 139,
  142, 144
conversation as learning activity 267
coursework 109, 257
CoVis (Collaborative Visualization)
  project 33
curriculum innovation 127
customized engagements 225, 237
customized learner engagement,
  cybergogy 237
cutting-edge technology 182
cybergogy xv, 225, 226, 237
- for customized learner engagement
  237
- for engaged learning 226, 231, 238,
  247
cycle diagram 192

data analysis 134, 135
data collection 92, 127, 134
deductive simulations 1, 21

Descartes, R. vii
design intentions 108, 109, 123
Dewey, J. viii, 35, 152
dialogue xvi, 32, 36, 44, 60, 116, 177,
  185, 225, 239, 270
digital age 154, 159, 269
disciplinary engagement 38
domain specific knowledge 34
domain specific problem solving 43

education in the knowledge age xiv, 91,
  93
educational process, problems 36
educational technology xiii, 92, 150,
  157, 160
- futures 173
- - scenario planning 160
effective collaboration 130
effective collaborators 36
effective conceptual model 115
effective learning 128, 151, 153, 154,
  164, 171, 177-183, 188, 190, 197,
  198, 207, 231, 256, 262, 269
- designing 153
- environments 150, 153, 155, 160,
  173
- in the electronic age xiv, 177
effective mapping 115
effective self-directed learning strategies
  36
e-learner 156
e-learning xiv, 69, 70, 79, 107-110,
  113, 114, 121-123
electronic age xiv, 177
electronic working tools 70
embedded information cases 39
emotional cues 226, 241, 253
emotion-learning 235
emotive factors 226, 231, 247
engaged learning
- critical factors 253
- environments, implications 39
- framework xiv, 29, 40, 41, 43, 45
- - proposed 40
- indicators 30-32, 253
- model 234, 247
- technologies x, 43, 44

- with emerging technology vii, xv, 158, 159
engagement 107
- with artifacts viii
- with learning viii, ix
- with technology ix
- with the world vii
engaging instruction, designing 237
engaging interface, creation 110
episodic memory 82
epistemological beliefs 24
epistemological knowledge 34
e-teacher 156
examinations 207, 211, 257, 259, 271
- in certain subject areas 258
EXIT model 190, 191
expert systems 1, 9, 12, 13, 19, 20, 22
experts 22, 23, 32, 36, 38-43, 45, 62, 73, 74, 81, 83, 112, 118, 151, 156
exploration 150, 168, 179, 182, 183, 192, 214, 217, 227, 231

facilitators 35, 40, 41, 92, 215
- role 37
feedback 21, 45, 51, 55, 57-64, 77, 97, 102, 115, 117, 128, 152, 154, 157
- systems thinking 14
formative assessment 160, 165, 166, 255, 257, 263, 269-271

Generation X 238
Gestalt principle 122
globalised community 205
graphical user interface (GUI) 107, 108, 114, 123
- design 119
- interactions 114
group cognition viii

health sciences 255
Hegel, G.W.F. viii
Heidegger, M. vii, viii
Heidegger's critique of western assumptions vii
Hong Kong, special administrative region (SAR) 205
human-computer

- interaction 109
- interface designers 109

information and communication technology (ICT) xv, 127, 128, 144, 149, 150, 155, 160, 162, 198, 203-210, 225
- -enhanced classrooms 205
- -enriched learner-centred environments xv, 203-206, 211, 213, 215-217, 219
- -enriched classroom 216
- -enriched learning 203
- in Hong Kong's school education 205
- -intensive community 205, 208
- tools 144, 213, 215, 219
idea map 192
inductive simulation models 1, 21
information and communication technologies in education (ICTE) 149
information design 110
information handling process loop 193
information technology (IT) xiv, 69, 74, 78, 155, 181, 205, 206, 255, 257
- role in education 155, 204
inquiry vii, 38
Inquiry Learning Forum (ILF) 131
inquiry-based learning 138, 143
- literature 50, 271
instruction 2, 29, 31, 49, 50, 53, 65, 69-71, 75, 76, 79, 81, 104, 108, 128, 130, 132, 144, 150, 162, 168, 179, 189, 210, 229, 230, 237, 239, 240
- first principles of 50
instructional design 118, 217, 225, 238, 259
- literature 237
instructional principles 50
integrated online assessment
- guidelines for 261
- learning from lectures 265
interaction design 114, 116
internet 53, 107, 128, 131, 136, 150, 158, 162, 167, 177, 181, 190, 197, 198, 219, 236, 246

interpersonal connections 232, 233, 244

K-12 learners 93
K-12 schools 33, 97, 225
- in Singapore 97
K-12 teachers 92, 98, 279
Keller's ARCS model 233, 239
knowledge age xiv, 91, 93, 104, 128, 129, 143
knowledge building viii, x, xiv, xvi, 49, 93-95, 97-104, 127, 130-134, 136, 137
- classrooms 91
- communities 2, 95, 99, 103, 104, 130
- discourse 95, 129-131
- engagement in 100
- environment 95
- in transition in Singapore schools 97
- process 134, 137
knowledge construction 24, 45, 97, 130, 132, 143, 144, 160, 166, 226, 227, 238, 253
knowledge creation 50, 91, 93, 95, 130
knowledge forum (KF) 91, 127, 132
Knowledge Forum Client version 3.4. 133
knowledge-centered environments 153, 155, 164, 171
knowledge-driven community 205

laboratory practicals, assessments in 259
leadership 15, 54, 203, 216, 217
learner
- as actor 116
- -centered environments 153, 164, 171
- engagement xv, 50, 51, 107, 108, 110, 122, 225, 232, 233, 237, 264, 269
- - framework for creation of 225
- models 69, 77
- teacher role 116
learning
- activity xv, 34, 35, 38, 44, 49, 50, 53-56, 58, 60, 78, 79, 97, 113, 130, 187, 203, 206, 207, 214, 219, 226,

227, 229, 253, 256, 258, 260, 262-265, 267, 271
- - conversation as 267
- and consultation 69
- and relearning 69
- approaches to 144, 152, 178, 186, 188, 189, 258, 260, 261, 263
- atmosphere 234, 247
- - feeling of 226, 232, 234, 247, 253
- authenticity in 33
- community 31, 129
- - building 244
- context 31, 56, 69, 92, 99, 108, 109, 210, 226
- culture 127
- design 49, 59, 227, 255, 262
- motivation 36, 233
- objectives 110, 121, 156, 162, 167, 170, 183, 189, 228, 233, 237, 259, 262, 270
- on demand 69
- on the job 71
- process xiv, 30, 36, 37, 40, 50, 55, 69-71, 75, 79, 80, 92, 118, 127, 156, 172, 177, 214, 215, 225, 226, 228, 231-238, 240, 241, 246, 247, 253
- - feelings emerging from 234
- - finding out 36
- psychology of 262
- role of assessment in 255, 256
- styles 107, 154, 165, 172, 188, 206, 226, 230
- support 69, 72, 73, 75-77, 80, 81, 86, 208
- - contextualization 76
- - technology xiv, 79
- - tools, components 85
- with technology 149, 155, 159, 161
learning-content management systems (LCMSs) 65
LISTEN 78, 79
local experts 73, 74

Marx, K. viii
meaningful learning xiii, 1, 2, 23-25, 43, 54, 104, 158, 160
- characteristics 3

- modeling 1
meaningful problems 39
mental models 1, 4, 6-9, 22-25, 181,
    183
- individual 4
- collaborative group 6
- modeling 7
message design 239
metacognition 24, 35, 42, 177, 187, 188
- literature of 35
metacognitive activities 35, 189
metacognitive knowledge 34, 187, 188
metacognitive skill 34, 37, 157, 255
metacognitive strategies 29, 39
mind map 192
mindtools 1, 43, 45, 155, 157
model construction 7-9, 23, 24, 243
model-based environments 4
model-based learning systems 9, 20, 25
model-based reasoning 1
model-based software 25
modeling xiii, 1, 3, 7, 9-11, 15, 16, 18,
    20, 23-25, 37, 112, 120, 234, 238,
    239
- domain knowledge 7, 9, 18, 25
- problems 7, 10, 25
- semantic structure 7, 16, 18, 25
- systems 1, 7, 13, 15, 25, 269
- thinking 7, 18, 25
- tools 1, 8-13, 18, 21, 23, 24, 43
Model It 15, 21
monitoring 19, 34, 35, 39-43, 45, 55,
    62, 162, 188, 190, 227, 258, 267
- and planning 39
motivation viii, ix, xii, 33, 34, 36, 49,
    50, 77, 100, 109, 110, 152, 153, 164,
    166, 171, 172, 178, 180-182, 198,
    207, 228, 232, 233, 236, 246, 255,
    256, 262, 266
multimedia 58, 83, 86, 107, 111, 157,
    158, 161, 163, 166, 169, 183, 261,
    262, 265, 269
multiple choice 58, 257, 259, 265

NASA ix
National Research Council 34, 38
NCET process 193

network technologies 50, 156-158
North Central Regional Education
    Laboratory (NCREL) 92, 158
- model of engaged learning 95, 98

online assessment xv, 255, 256
- continuous 255, 258-261, 264-267,
    270, 271
- practice xv, 255
- - 1994-2004 256, 257
online communication 226, 232, 241,
    244, 245, 262
- facilitating 241
online community 233, 236, 240,
    244-246
online discourse xiv, 127, 129, 131,
    132, 135, 142-144
online facilitation 225
online help support 72
online learning xv, 225, 226, 231, 233,
    236, 240-242, 247, 255, 262, 266,
    270
- communities 128, 143, 233
- environment 226, 238, 242
online multi-choice assessments 255,
    256
online participation 121, 134, 137, 139,
    234
- patterns 139, 141
online presence 225
ownership 24, 40-43, 45, 91, 94, 100,
    154, 165, 166, 170-173, 210, 238,
    253

participation model 52, 53
PBL
- active learning strategies 38
- metacognitive learning strategies 38
pedagogical models 49, 50, 52, 54, 265,
    266
pedagogy 35, 49, 54, 56, 61-65, 98, 99,
    101, 127, 130, 143, 144, 155, 173,
    205, 206, 260, 265
perceived learning 131, 235
personal attributes 226, 235, 236, 253
personal digital communicators and
    assistants (PDCA) 167

Piaget, J. 152, 183-185
planning xiv, 34, 39, 44, 61, 63, 113,
     149, 159-161, 186, 198, 211, 212,
     227
Plato vii
postmodernism 209, 210
PowerSim 15, 21
practice-oriented tools 34
pragmatism 173
pragmatist 230
- learning style 230
- viewpoint vii
presentation 43, 53, 76, 78, 79, 85, 118,
     119, 181-183, 234, 265-267
primary education 127
prior knowledge 72, 177, 184, 185,
     190, 191, 196, 198, 226-228, 247,
     262, 266, 271
prior knowledge/experience 228, 253
problem solving 1, 6, 11, 19, 36, 38-45,
     58, 74, 75, 81, 86, 128, 135, 151,
     154, 165, 171, 173, 208, 239, 261
- activities 58, 259, 264
- dialogue 36
- medical 38
- strategies 154, 165, 171, 173, 259
- together working of small groups 36
problem-based learning (PBL) xiii, 29,
     30, 35-40, 229
- fundamental approach 36
- in Medical school 36
- real-world case studies 36
professional development 91, 98, 113,
     206, 211
project space 114, 122, 156
- definition 110
project-based learning 36, 92, 93, 132
project-based science (PBS) 38, 39
psychology of learning 262

QUADS grid 192

reflection 3, 35, 42, 45, 53, 60, 62, 64,
     65, 69, 80, 102, 103, 130, 134, 153,
     157, 164, 166, 171-173, 182, 183,
     189, 227, 268
- in action 69, 80

reflective observation (RO) 230
reflector 230
- evidence 181
research-based practice 268
revised curriculum activities 33

schemas 11, 17, 112, 183-185, 191
school cultural change 203
school-based curriculum 211, 212
school-based investigation 196
science education 127
science knowledge 135, 138, 139, 143
Scientific and Mathematical Arenas for
     Refining Thinking (SMART) 35
scientific knowledge 33
- building 132, 134, 136, 137
scientific processes in the classroom 34
Sci-Fi perspective 155
Second International Information
     Technology in Education Study 214
self-assessment 257
- of project work 259
self-competence 232
self-confidence 226, 232, 233
self-efficacy 219, 232
- beliefs 34, 35, 39
self-regulated learning 29, 40, 225, 227,
     238, 253
- literature of 35
self-regulation 29, 34, 153, 166, 172
- social dimension of 34
self-regulatory actions 29
self-regulatory behaviors 34
self-regulatory learning 29, 30
self-regulatory processes 42
semantic memory 82
semantic modeling tools 1, 9, 23
situated annotation authoring 80
situated e-learning xiv, 69, 70
- methods 69
situated learning viii, 69, 71, 79, 83,
     177, 186, 187
Smartcard 162, 163, 173
social constructivism 44, 52, 55, 185,
     234
social constructivist 185
- learning activities 38

- philosophy 104
- tools 45
social context 34, 39, 76, 83, 236
- individuals acting in 34
social discourse 34
social factors 226, 231, 235, 247
social interaction 34, 70, 83, 185, 208, 236, 245
social sciences 13, 209, 255, 257
social software 240, 245, 246
- usage 245
spider web 192
staging activities 39
Stanford Research Institute (SRI) 92
Stella 13-15, 20, 21
student
- engagement 33
- knowledge 34
- participation 129-132, 135, 139, 140, 144
- perceptions 127, 131, 132, 134, 135, 138, 139, 142, 144, 253
- - change 142
- with cultural background 246
- with linguistic background 246
student-centred learning xiii, 203, 209, 213, 217, 219, 255-257, 260, 267
supportive tools 39
sustained voluntary attention 263, 270
systems
- modeling 1
- tools 9, 13, 21, 23

teaching science 128, 136
- basis xiv, 127, 135, 143

teaching strategies 203, 212, 258, 263
techniques xiv, 34, 39, 42, 116, 121, 151, 160, 171, 247, 256-260
technology
- in education 149, 157, 158, 160, 173, 208, 259
- need to design x
- roles of 55, 56, 61, 155, 160
theorist 6, 152, 187, 198, 230
tools x, xvi, 1-3, 8, 10-15, 17, 18, 20, 21, 23-25, 32, 34, 35, 38, 40-45, 49, 50, 57, 62, 63, 65, 70, 71, 75, 79, 80, 83, 85, 86, 108, 109, 123, 128, 144, 156-159, 173, 182, 204, 213, 215, 218, 219, 232, 237, 239-241, 245, 246, 267
training on the job 71
transformation 37, 39, 182, 183, 227
transformative assessment 97

understanding vii, viii, 3, 177

venn diagram 192
VenSim 15, 21
visibility 114, 243
visual conventions 116
Vygotsky, L.S. vii, viii, 152, 177, 185, 186, 234
Vygotksy's socio-cultural psychology vii
Vygotsky's zone of proximal development viii

web environments 50, 56, 59,, 61, 62
- learning resources 49